Writing the Screenplay

TV AND FILM

SECOND EDITION

Writing the Screenplay

TV AND FILM

ALAN A. ARMER

California State University, Northridge

Wadsworth Publishing Company
Belmont, California
A Division of Wadsworth, Inc.

PUBLISHER: Rebecca Hayden

EDITORIAL ASSISTANT: Katherine Hartlove

PRODUCTION EDITOR: Angela Mann

DESIGNER: Kaelin Chappell

PRINT BUYER: Diana Spence

PERMISSIONS EDITOR: Robert Kauser

COPY EDITOR: Pat Tompkins

TECHNICAL ILLUSTRATORS: Kaelin Chappell, Kathryn Werhane

COVER: Studio Silicon

SIGNING REPRESENTATIVE: Cynthia Berg

COMPOSITOR: Thompson Type

PRINTER: Malloy Lithography

This book is printed on acid-free paper.

1 2 3 4 5 6 7 8 9 10 — 97 96 95 94 93

Library of Congress Cataloging in Publication Data

Armer, Alan A.
     Writing the screenplay : TV and film / Alan A. Armer. — 2nd ed.
          p.   cm.
     Includes bibliographical references and index.
          ISBN 0-534-16668-7
          1. Motion picture authorship.   2. Television authorship.
     I. Title.
     PN1996.A74   1993
     808.2'3 — dc20   92-12141

FOR ELLEN, MICHAEL, DAVID, AND AIMEE—
FAVORITE CHARACTERS IN MY PERSONAL SCREENPLAY

CONTENTS

CHAPTER 7

More About Dialog

TECHNIQUES AND TABOOS

131

CHAPTER 8

Revealing the Subtext

WHAT SCENES ARE ALL ABOUT

165

PREFACE

Because of literary tradition, this section of *Writing the Screenplay* is labeled "Preface." A more appropriate title would be "Pep Talk" because it is primarily designed to stimulate. To encourage. To build excitement. Much like the football coach's halftime words inciting his team to action.

Nobody needs encouragement more than would-be screenwriters. I know. I've taught screenwriting courses for over a dozen years and before that worked with hundreds of professional writers and would-bes in that Grand Guignol known as television.

Alarming stories abound. Agents won't read your material. Producers slam the door in your face. Most screenwriters are out of work. It may be years before you sell something. The marketplace is glutted with scripts. It's not what you know, it's who you know. And if, finally, the Red Sea parts and you're lucky enough to sell a story or screenplay, somebody totally lacking in sensitivity and skill rewrites you—and screws it up.

I must be honest. There is an element of truth to those stories. But in that truth lie the seeds of promise.

Most screenwriters *are* out of work. Why? Because (and this is the bottom line, my friends) most of them simply aren't good enough. At present the Writers Guild of America, West, numbers about 6,500 members. Out of those 6,500, about 650 are competent or better. Turning that around: *90 percent of Hollywood's writers are less than competent.* Shocking words, perhaps, but true. Almost every producer I know complains constantly about the scarcity of good writers. Does that 90 percent make a living? No, not at writing. Many work at other jobs, full or part time. Some are retired.

"Competent" writers know their craft. They can put a screenplay together in a reasonably professional fashion, but they bring little freshness or creativity to their work. Producers hire such writers with reluctance, only if they cannot acquire the services of a "good" writer.

Of the 650 writers who are competent or better, approximately half are good. That's 5 percent of the total Writers Guild West membership. Those 325 writers (and even this figure may be high) devise the screenplays of most of the movies and television shows we watch.

You may find these percentages difficult to believe. When writers make the transition from free-lance writing to a staff position such as story editor, most are shocked when they discover the shoddy work that their peers are submitting. One reason why so many TV producers, associate producers, and story editors are experienced writers is that their creative skills are needed to breathe life into the second-rate material they receive. Yes, they often rewrite material. Not because of ego or money or the chance to get their names on the screen. They rewrite screenplays because most simply aren't funny enough or clever enough or suspenseful enough as the original writer submitted them.

Addressing one of my screenwriting classes, a reader for United Artists said that in the four years he had been reading submitted screenplays — and he had critiqued literally hundreds — he had found only two or three that were original enough to pass on to his bosses. Most were derivative. That is, they were rehashes of recent successful feature films. Words were often misspelled. Pages were sloppy. And the vast majority of submitted material demonstrated little or no awareness of structure. Of the few he recommended, only one screenplay was ever actually produced.

I've called this preface a pep talk. How can such dismal facts possibly be encouraging to would-be screenwriters? Because they demonstrate that both the motion picture and television markets are wide open. Creative writers are needed. If you have talent, the entertainment industry needs you.

At a recent conference of women writers, one experienced pro declared that original material is so rare in Hollywood, in such consistent demand by producers, that a fresh screenplay almost glows in the dark. A writer with such a screenplay could drive down a freeway at four in the morning, speeding along at eighty miles an hour, and if he or she recklessly tossed the screenplay out a window, some entrepreneur inevitably would find it and produce it. (Please don't attempt this!) The experienced pro was joking, of course, but beneath her humor lay a bedrock of truth.

Realistically, launching a professional writing career is seldom quick or easy. Because of inflated pay scales and the supposed glamour attached to screenwriting, competition is fierce. Achieving success requires both talent and perseverance. Yes, and a modicum of luck. Nevertheless, every year, every month, every week, new writers break into the business. That bears repeating. Every year, every month, every week new writers break into the business. Someone reads your material, likes it, and pays either to option or to purchase it. At the magic moment that such a discerning person writes a check or even authorizes you to put words on paper (which constitutes a verbal, legally binding contract), you have become a professional.

Case in point: One of my more talented students had two screenplays optioned by motion picture production companies in the first six months after she graduated from college. And for her the Red Sea did part; she sold a third screenplay, "The Cheese Stands Alone," for a cool one million dollars, becoming the first woman in the history of the film industry ever to receive such a hefty sum. She describes her happy odyssey at the end of Chapter 13. But she is the exception. Most talented new writers need considerably more time to write the powerhouse screenplay and connect with the appropriate agent or the receptive producer.

The pages that follow mix time-honored theory with down-to-earth, practical advice about writing for the screen — the large motion picture screen as well as the smaller television screen. The material is based on my twenty-two years of experience in the entertainment industry, first as a director and then as a writer-producer, developing approximately 350 screenplays. That professional experience was then refined and tested in a university classroom, giving me a singular opportunity to balance professional screenwriting methods with techniques that would explain and clarify those methods for students.

This second edition of *Writing the Screenplay* has been updated throughout. A new feature is the step-by-step development in the early chapters of a brief newspaper item, demonstrating the principles contained in those chapters as the item gradually expands into a full-fledged screenplay story. I have added a new chapter specifically dealing with comedy based on personal interviews with talented comedy writers. And another new chapter mines the gold beneath a scene's surface, externalizing characters' thoughts and emotions. In addition, there are new scriptwriting projects and dozens of additions or tightenings that make the text more effective in conveying its message.

Writing the Screenplay is designed for both beginning and advanced students — indeed, for anyone interested in writing screenplays. The book's early chapters cover such basic information as the nature of screenplay drama, plotting, structure, and conflict. Chapter 5 discusses techniques for building dimensional characters. Chapters 6 and 7 provide one of the most comprehensive discussions of dialog I have seen anywhere, with a wide variety of examples from movies and television. Chapter 8 explores a scene's subtext and examines what its content is really about. Chapter 9 discusses the entertainment elements that please or move audiences, on both conscious and subconscious levels. Chapter 10 provides the specifications of screenplay format. A new chapter, 11, examines the serious business of writing comedy. Chapter 12 discusses the art of adaptation, comparing literary with screenplay structures and providing a challenging adaptation project. And Chapter 13 discusses the practical realities of marketing a script.

In addition to the text, three established professionals and one brand new professional present their personal writing techniques, theories, and advice in a series of informative "Writer Revelations." These include Oscar-winner Paddy Chayefsky on *structure*, writer/executive producer George Eckstein on *dialog*, Oscar-winning writer-director Frank Pierson on *character*; and my former student, Kathy McWhorter, on *breaking into the business*. The book thus presents a unique double perspective: the professional and the academic.

A number of challenging "Scriptwriting Projects" appear at the end of each chapter, designed to enhance your narrative skills.

I use the terms *narrative* and *drama(tic)* almost interchangeably throughout the text. They represent fictional motion pictures or television, stories told on film or videotape with drama's traditional elements of identification, character conflict, and rising action, all of which are discussed at length.

This book shatters no precedents in its position that a well-written screenplay is the single most important ingredient in the making of a successful motion picture or television show. Such a screenplay attracts stars, directors, and financing. It is the base of the entire production pyramid. Without a well-conceived, well-structured screenplay, a first-rate film is almost impossible to achieve. (Bad films, however, can derive from good scripts.)

Film and television students often become impressed by hardware. Cameras, lighting panels, electronic switchers, character generators, and computerized editing all dazzle the eye and spark the imagination. The script — mere words on paper — is less glamorous. Some years ago, Howard Suber of UCLA wrote about the significance of those "words" in the *AFI Education Newsletter* (Summer 1982), remarking on film failures by directors Michael Cimino and Francis Ford Coppola.

> Perhaps the fundamental importance of the script is so easily overlooked because it sometimes appears to be "just words," when film is clearly so much more than that. But the words are not merely dialogue, something for the actors' mouths to do while the camera is moving. The words provide a structure. And it is structure more than any other single element of the filmmaking process that will ultimately determine whether a film is an empty succession of costly sounds and images or an integrated work that fulfills the vision of its creators.
>
> Our students often seem to believe that if they can only learn to master the machinery, they can become master filmmakers. Cimino and Coppola in their recent works have proved how wrong-headed this is. While the right camera and its operation are important, the right concept is infinitely more important. Until you've got the one, the other is nothing more than an expensive toy.*

I wish you well. And I hope that this book will help you join the ranks of the competent and, ultimately, the elite ranks of the "good."

I will look for your name on the TV or movie screen, immediately following those gratifying words: WRITTEN BY.

---

*The films to which Suber refers are Cimino's *Heaven's Gate* and Coppola's *One from the Heart*.

Acknowledgments

I would like to express my deep appreciation to George Eckstein, Kathy McWhorter, and Frank Pierson, distinguished and talented professionals whose Writer Revelations enrich the text enormously. Thanks to Susan Chayefsky for allowing me to reprint Paddy Chayefsky's sage words on script construction. I'm also grateful to Bernard Slade and Richard Baer, for helping me to discover some valuable truths about comedy writing.

Thanks also to my Wadsworth family. Their good-humored professionalism and continuing support made the writing chores almost pleasant. In particular, I'm grateful to Publisher Becky Hayden whose sensitivity and understanding warmed me and whose suggestions challenged me; to Production Editor Angela Mann for her good ideas and patience; and to Designer Kaelin Chappell for her originality and style.

My appreciation also to those generous academicians who took the time to review this second edition manuscript, contributing more than criticisms or assessments; their questions made me dig for answers. Their proffered nuggets of knowledge added significantly to the text. My thanks to Mara Alper of SUNY at New Paltz; Richard Blumenberg, Southern Illinois University at Carbondale; John Smead, Central Missouri State University; Cynthia Walker, Jersey City State College; and Edd Whetmore of Green Light Entertainment and California State University, Fullerton. Also thanks to Edd for his excellent ideas on marketing a screenplay (included in Chapter 13).

To the radio-television-film students at Cal State, Northridge, I send my gratitude and love. They stimulate me and brighten my life. Special thanks to Judith Breen, Donna Gonzalez, and Professor Fred Kuretski for allowing me to include their photographs.

ABOUT THE AUTHOR

At the age of fifteen, Alan A. Armer won the title of "World's Fastest Talker" in an NBC radio contest, reciting Lewis Carroll's "The Walrus and the Carpenter" (613 words) in 57 seconds. He's slowed down considerably since then.

After graduating from Stanford University with a degree in speech and drama, Alan Armer tried his hand first in radio as a disc jockey for San Jose's KEEN and then in advertising, writing, staging, editing, narrating, even acting in early TV commercials. Because of what he had learned about television, Armer was able to write and produce a weekly showcase for young professional actors, *Lights, Camera, Action*, for Los Angeles station KNBH.

When the show expired three years later, Armer became a stage manager for the station. Six months later he started directing; he was a staff director there for over four years. When the days of live programming were fading, 20th Century-Fox hired Armer to produce some of their early TV films.

During the next twenty years, Armer wrote, produced, or directed over 350 television programs for Fox, Desilu, Quinn Martin Productions, Paramount, and Universal. Many of his series were in the Top Ten. They included "The Fugitive," "The Untouchables," "Cannon," "The Invaders," "Broken Arrow," "Lancer," and "The Name of the Game," plus a number of TV movies.

During his years in television, Armer won almost every major industry award, including the TV Academy's distinguished Emmy Award, Mystery Writers Award, TV Guide Award, Western Writers Award, and Sound Editors Award. He also served twice as president of the Hollywood Chapter of the Television Academy, was a trustee to the National Academy, and served repeatedly as a member of the Board of Directors for the Producers Guild.

After twenty-five years in television, Armer moved into academia. To enrich his teaching career, he attended graduate school at UCLA and earned his M.A. degree. Now, after a dozen years, Armer continues as head of screenwriting at California State University, Northridge, where he teaches classes in screenwriting and directing.

He is listed in *Who's Who in Entertainment* and has published two books with Wadsworth: *Directing Television and Film* and *Writing the Screenplay*.

xviii

Writing the Screenplay

TV AND FILM

CHAPTER 1

The Blank Page

WHERE STORIES COME FROM

*I*t is easy and it is difficult.

If you follow certain rules and have a logical mind, you can construct a reasonably entertaining screenplay. That's the easy part. Writing a truly original screenplay, on the other hand, one that elicits deep emotional response and exalts the spirit, is far more difficult.

Effective stories emerge from opposite poles of our creative imagination. Scientists tell us that the brain's left hemisphere provides mathematical logic, enabling us to put together the pieces of our story puzzle. The right hemisphere gives us the ability to dream, to conjure up characters we have never met, who live in a world we have never seen, who fight battles with dragons from the fiery caves of our imagination.

Whether that scientific theory is simplistic or accurate, there can be no question that story elements emerge from two widely divergent elements: logic and fantasy. Accordingly, there can be no single "correct" method of combining them into a narrative structure. Every writer has his or her highly individualized system. Some stare at a blank wall for hours at a time. Others take long walks or make notes on matchbook covers. Still others write exploratory pages of a first-draft screenplay, tear them up and start over, write new pages, tear them up and start over, write new pages, tear them up and start over. . . .

That there's no single "correct" way to build a screenplay does not mean that the process is impossible — or even difficult — to learn. On the contrary, a few relatively simple principles provide convenient guidelines. In this respect, screenplay narrative resembles other art forms (classical music, painting, architecture) that also emerge from established principles of construction. Learning those principles is relatively easy, like learning the rules for playing chess. But, as in chess, the simple mechanics of the game are only a beginning point. It's what you *do* with those rules that determines your skill.

The process of scriptwriting begins with an understanding of certain fundamental principles. In this chapter we will examine:

➤ **SCREENPLAY NARRATIVE**: its emphasis on strong or painful emotions

➤ **A PERSON WITH A PROBLEM**: the need for an emotionally involving character and a problem that will worry audiences

➤ **DRAMA AND REAL LIFE**: the two major differences between them

➤ **STORY CONCEPTS**: where they originate

➤ **BEGINNING A STORY**: the first steps in developing a newspaper item into a screenplay story

SCREENPLAY NARRATIVE

What kinds of stories usually appear on the front pages of newspapers or among the lead items on the Six O'Clock News? Happy, upbeat stories filled with smiling faces? Or stories dealing with murder, rape, kidnapping, floods, fires, bombings, and terrorist attacks? If you've read one newspaper or watched ten minutes of a newscast recently, you'll know that stories of violence dominate — violence created either by humans or by nature, leaving pain in its aftermath.

Such stories dominate because newspaper editors and newscast producers understand their audiences. They know that generally we are more interested in problems than solutions, in the dark side of the human animal rather than the bright. To be sure, an occasional story of joy and fulfillment can be heartwarming. The tattered orphan who finds her real parents on Christmas Day provides an upbeat closing story for newscasts. But such a story is the exception, not the rule. And note: It is the closing item rather than the lead story.

For the most part, screenplay narrative deals in pain. Not necessarily physical pain; the pain usually is purely *emotional*. A lost child, for example, will become frightened, perhaps panicky, perhaps hysterical, before finding the way home. When a wife betrays an adoring husband, she leaves anguish behind her. When a father coldly destroys his son's career, he creates despair and then hatred in his son. No physical violence here. No gunfights or car crashes. But there's emotional blood all over the floor.

It seems paradoxical that in a world that sickens from daily news of murder, molestation, and mayhem, audiences should actually seek trauma in their entertainment. Attempting to explain such a need, Aristotle theorized that involvement with heroes facing disaster provides a kind of **emotional catharsis*** for audiences, a purging of inner poisons.† The greater the threat posed by such a disaster, the more audiences will worry. The stronger their **identification** with hero figures, the more audiences will immerse themselves in the hero's problems and participate in his or her struggles.

> When we find ourselves deeply moved by a story, with an intensity we can hardly understand, it is because we have secretly accepted it as our own, *identifying* ourselves with the people in it. Identification — this is the mechanism that taps imprisoned emotions. If [audiences] weep, it is not for the heroine but for themselves. If they laugh, it is not because the hero's tensions are being relieved, but their own.‡

*Boldface terms are defined in the Glossary at the end of the book.
†Aristotle, *Poetics*, trans. James Hutton (New York: Norton, 1982).
‡Erik Barnouw, *Mass Communications* (New York: Rinehart, 1956), p. 56.

Out of an audience's continuing need to (1) identify with a hero figure and (2) worry over his or her fate, we may derive a beginning definition of screenplay **drama**: *a person with a problem.* You will find this simple five-word phrase appearing again and again throughout this book; if a screenplay **narrative** doesn't focus upon a person with a problem, chances are it will never be produced.

A PERSON WITH A PROBLEM

Meet two contrasting characters. Both will give you a better understanding of what screenplays are all about.

Johnny Holcomb leaves his small Montana town to enter college. Johnny's a lanky, shy, warm-hearted young man with clothes that look like hand-me-downs. He has promised his parents (who sacrificed to send him to college) that he will work diligently to repay their love and confidence.

Johnny discovers that college is considerably easier than he had expected. By the end of the first year he is averaging A— in most of his subjects and has become captain of the soccer team. Just before final examinations, Johnny spots a paper on the floor of the administration building. It is the final exam of his most difficult course. He faces a moral dilemma: Should he read the questions or throw the exam away? Johnny does not hesitate. He tosses the exam into a trash can and is rewarded for his strength of character by passing the course with a grade of A+ . Johnny learns later that the exam he discovered was from a previous year; if he had read its questions, he would certainly have gone astray.

At the end of his third year, Johnny is elected president of his class. His parents beam with pride. A decade later, he discovers a way to stop the nuclear arms race and is awarded the Nobel Peace Prize.

Before commenting on the strengths or weaknesses of Johnny's story, let us meet a second, equally fascinating character, Sadie Guttweiler. People shy away from Sadie, not because of her loud, belligerent manner, her stained and wrinkled clothing, or her excessive facial hair. Not because she reeks of cheap wine and garlic. Not because she ran out on her husband and three small children after gambling away their money. No, people avoid Sadie because she's dishonest; she'd cheat a starving man out of his last crust of bread.

Sadie has managed to save a few dollars and one morning takes the money to her favorite gambling palace. On her way to the poker table she notices that the door to the cashier's cage, usually locked securely, has been carelessly left a few inches ajar. Sadie stops and lights a cigarette by the door and through the crack sees stacks of money piled on a table just inside. The cashier is busy cashing a check for a customer at a window on the far side of the cage, so Sadie looks around quickly and then slips her hand through the doorway crack and deftly removes a wad of fifty-dollar bills. She slides the money casually into her coat pocket, exhales a puff of cigarette smoke, and then heads toward the restroom to count her haul, brushing aside a frail old woman as she enters. In one of the stalls she counts the money. Almost $4,000! When she emerges from the restroom a few minutes later, she discovers two security officers waiting for her, their guns leveled. Someone had obviously witnessed her theft. The officers remove the money from her pocket, handcuff her, and take a loudly protesting Sadie to jail.

Although these two stories won't win awards at the Cannes Film Festival, they do demonstrate some of the essential characteristics of screenplay drama. Their contrasting inadequacies provide insights into why some stories work and why others don't.

Let's imagine that we are watching these two stories in a motion picture theater. With Johnny Holcomb, we become interested immediately. He's a nice kid, worthy of our involvement, and so we root for him to succeed in college. But as he succeeds again and again, our interest fades. It revives momentarily when Johnny discovers the final exam and wrestles briefly with his conscience — and disappears when he throws away the exam. The remainder of his odyssey is downhill, a succession of victories that whittle away at our interest.

The problem with Johnny's story, of course, is that there *isn't* any problem. His college career goes from good to better. Remember, audiences love to worry. Unless writers give them the opportunity, making life miserable for the characters they care about, audiences quickly become bored. Without problems, screenplays cannot succeed.

If a problem is the key to a story's success, then why isn't the Sadie Guttweiler story more effective? Someone witnessed her theft. She's handcuffed, on her way to jail. That certainly sounds like a serious problem.

As the quotation from Erik Barnouw illustrates, identification is a key to audience response. The more strongly audiences identify with a character, the deeper their emotional involvement. Few people can identify with Sadie; she's a generally repulsive character, morally and physically. It's difficult to care what happens to her. Note that we don't hate her; we just can't identify strongly. And so, when she's faced with a jail sentence, our concern is relatively mild. Were Johnny Holcomb somehow to face imprisonment — especially for a crime he did not commit — we would take a far stronger rooting position.*

An involving character without a problem creates little interest. A problem without an emotionally involving character fares little better. Put the two together and magic can happen.

The Person.   Rule number one for creating effective screenplays: Audiences must be able to identify with a **protagonist** (the **person**); the stronger their

---

*In this book's first edition, Sadie confronted knife-wielding hoods from the gambling palace and our involvement was far greater. She suddenly became acutely vulnerable, a victim, an underdog, so we rooted for her in spite of ourselves.

emotional involvement, the better. A protagonist is usually the central character in a screenplay, the character your audience roots for most strongly, the person who moves your story forward. In an essay at the end of Chapter 5, Frank Pierson states, "A story doesn't exist, except as a series of unrelated incidents, unless there is . . . a will driving the action that makes all of the incidents inevitable." That will is the determination of your protagonist to reach a goal.

When identification is strong, the audience actually shares the protagonist's feelings. "Whatever affects one similarly affects the other."* His worries become the audience's worries; his joys or fears become theirs. When a screenplay really works, members of the audience forget they are sitting in a theater. They enter the protagonist's world and get so involved in his or her struggles that they *become* the protagonist.

Emotional involvement arises most often from *sympathy* and to a lesser extent from *empathy* or *antipathy*. Certain characteristics tend to make audiences sympathize. For example, audiences usually sympathize with an underdog. That's why writers so often pit their heroes against formidable adversaries and make them battle against incredible odds. In the original *Rocky*, Sylvester Stallone plays a gentle, good-hearted slob capable of loving even goldfish. Out of shape physically and possessing only limited boxing skills, he faces a powerful antagonist, the heavyweight champion of the world. We sympathize with Rocky because he's an underdog.

Vulnerability is sometimes a part of the underdog role, a characteristic that seems inevitably to evoke audience sympathy. A television series I produced called "The Fugitive" concerned a decent, caring man who had been convicted unjustly of killing his wife. On the way to the death house, his train derailed and he escaped. Episodes dealt with his life on the run as he frequently stopped to help others, usually at considerable risk to himself. The TV audience cared about the protagonist to an astonishing degree, pleading in letters and phone calls for the producers to give the poor devil another court trial. Such deep emotional involvement was achieved — at least in part — because of the protagonist's acute vulnerability.

Director Alfred Hitchcock built no less than a dozen films around a protagonist accused of a crime he did not commit (including *Spellbound*, *Suspicion*, *The Wrong Man*, *The Thirty-Nine Steps*, and *North by Northwest*). Hitchcock knew the tremendous audience sympathy that such circumstances create.

Dozens of personal characteristics enable audiences to care about a protagonist, ranging from physical appearance to personality to the nature of his or her character or morality. We tend to sympathize, for example, if a protagonist has a physical handicap. If he or she possesses a well-developed sense of humor, we warm to it. If heroes are kind, gentle, loving, honest, self-sacrificing,

---

*The definition of *sympathy* in *Webster's Ninth New Collegiate Dictionary*.

patient, generous, or any of a dozen other admirable qualities, we will usually root for them to succeed.

But this advice does not mean that your characters must all be Boy Scouts: clean, reverent, obedient, and honest. Characters must appear human and, let's face it, most humans have flaws. Some of us are lazy. Others are quick tempered. Even the most angelic get cranky and irritable when they're pressured. Such flaws, even more serious ones, won't detract from your characters. On the contrary, they will make them seem dimensional, more believable, and ultimately more involving. A good rule of thumb for creating multidimensional characters: give your "good guys" some flaws; give your "bad guys" some redeeming characteristics (more about creating characters in Chapter 5).

In an interview in *Playboy* several years ago, playwright and screenwriter Neil Simon describes why his script for *The Goodbye Girl* worked as well as it did.*

> PLAYBOY: Why do you think the film did so well?
>
> SIMON: I feel it had to do with the purity and healthiness of the relationship between the two characters. I also saw *The Goodbye Girl* in a movie theater and more and more I see how important it is for an audience to root for your characters, to care very much about what happens to them. When people care, even the slightest joke will get a big laugh, for they'll be so caught up in what's going on. If they *don't* care and are *not* caught up, you need blockbusters every two minutes and even that won't fulfill an audience.

Closely related to sympathy is **empathy**, an understanding or experiencing of a protagonist's thoughts or feelings. Let's say that a daughter turns against her mother, forcing her to leave the daughter's house and live elsewhere. With no insight into her character, audiences might be repelled by the daughter's act, unable to involve themselves emotionally. But if they know that the mother purposely drove the daughter's husband away so that the mother could have the daughter to herself, then audiences will understand the anger that led the daughter to her action and they will empathize.

In *Amadeus*, an understanding of the anguish beneath Salieri's jealousy of Mozart and beneath his despicable actions against the young composer enables us to care about the character, even if we cannot root for him. In gangster films, the protagonists frequently commit acts of chilling violence and yet we become emotionally involved with them because we understand their human needs. In *GoodFellas*, for example, the protagonist allies himself with cruel and savage characters and yet we can relate to him, even root for him, because we also know him on a family level — in a memorable scene, preparing marinara sauce for a family party while the gangster world outside his kitchen crumbles.

In *Ghost*, an underworld character coldbloodedly slaughters the protagonist. The killer has been paid to commit this murder by the protagonist's close

---

*"Playboy Interview: Neil Simon," *Playboy Magazine*, Feb. 1979, pp. 57–78.

"friend." Naturally, we hate these two antagonists, and throughout the film we wait for the satisfying moment when they will be punished. Hatred is a primal emotion, as strong as or stronger than sympathy. The desire to see a villain punished constitutes real audience involvement. As with sympathy and empathy, antipathy creates involvement in a story. Throughout drama's long history, audiences' emotions have churned at villainous characters. Shakespeare's tragedies are filled with them. Lady Macbeth, Richard III, and Iago are celebrated examples.

Thus, the "person" in our definition of screenplay drama must create some kind of emotional involvement in audiences, usually through *sympathy, empathy,* or *antipathy.* The deeper the emotional involvement, the more audiences will submerge themselves in (and enjoy) your story. The more strongly they identify with your protagonist, the more likely they will be to overlook script or production shortcomings. We have all seen films with slender, almost nonexistent plots. *When Harry Met Sally* falls into this category. The only plot question raised is "Will these two friends discover that they love each other?" And yet, because we care so much about them, we laugh, worry, suffer, and rejoice at their experiences.

The Problem.   In almost all screenplays, protagonists strive to attain something they desperately want or need. Such clear-cut goals give screenplays a sense of direction. The problem arises when some person, force, or thing opposes their attaining these goals. This relatively simple pattern is what most screenplays are all about. Your hero strives to achieve a goal, to find the mythic pot of gold at the top of a mountain. And the **antagonist** — a mad scientist, the mafia, a snowstorm, the hero's own conscience — fights to keep him or her from getting there. Now the plot becomes a series of struggles, battles, or tugs of war, building from scene to scene, act to act, crisis to crisis, until, finally, the protagonist either reaches the goal or fails — or the goal changes.

We can usually phrase a screenplay's central struggle in the form of a question: Will the protagonist achieve his or her goal? For example, will Sadie succeed in stealing the casino's money? Will the gunfighter avenge the death of his brother? Will the mother hold her family together? Will Luke Skywalker save the princess from the forces of evil?

Because audiences need to worry, screenwriters devise harrowing obstacles that make it appear that their protagonists will not reach their worthwhile goals, that the bad guys will defeat them. As the screenplay builds from act to act, so do the tensions; your protagonist encounters setbacks and the **adversarial forces** appear more and more invincible. "Get your hero up a tree and then throw rocks at him," is how one writer describes the process.

In those few screenplays where the goal is not specifically stated, the writer usually provides a **foreshadowing** of the direction the story will take. Foreshadowings imply a kind of inevitability and are common in tragedy. Many of Ingmar Bergman's films hint in their early scenes at the story's resolution.

Protagonists must feel strongly about attaining their goals. They must have dedication, a sense of commitment. If story goals are unimportant to them, they will seem unimportant to us. If a student wants to join a sorority, for example, the goal will seem trivial unless there is a compelling reason why she must join. If she is black, for instance, and her joining the sorority would break down racial barriers on campuses all over the country, then such a simple goal becomes truly dramatic. In such a story, racists in the sorority would fight to keep her from joining and that fight would become the screenplay's central conflict. Antagonists require the same sense of commitment that protagonists have. They, too, have goals and their goals are in direct opposition to the goals of your protagonist. Audiences should feel they are witnessing a battle between irresistible forces. If one is weak and the other strong, there can be no contest. If both are weak, the contest won't be worth watching.

Although problems emerge in a variety of ways, there is a surprising consistency to their pattern. Usually something calamitous happens about 30 percent into most screenplays that makes the protagonists realize (a) that they have a problem, an antagonist that may keep them from reaching their goals, or (b) that the problem is very different — and probably far more serious — than the one they first envisioned.

In *The Wizard of Oz*, Dorothy's goal is to return to her home in Kansas. She seeks the wizard, hoping he will help her achieve her goal. Each of Dorothy's friends also has a goal. The tin woodsman wants a heart; the scarecrow, brains; the cowardly lion, courage. Who is their antagonist? The Wicked Witch of the East is certainly the most formidable.

In *Misery*, the protagonist's goal is to get his new novel to the publisher. Because of a blinding snowstorm, his car goes over an embankment and crashes. But he is rescued by an apparently kind woman, a devoted fan of his novels, who will nurse him back to health. About a quarter of the way into the screenplay he (and we) realize that he is actually a prisoner in her home and that his benefactor is really a merciless and psychotic jailor.

In *Ghost*, the protagonist dies about 25 percent into the screenplay; his primary goal now becomes making contact with his beloved fiancée. The problem is that they're living in two different worlds and it's apparently impossible to break through the barrier between them. The words *apparently impossible* apply to attaining almost every screenplay goal.

In *Dances with Wolves*, the protagonist discovers at approximately 25 percent of the way into the screenplay that the outpost he will command has been deserted, that he must face a hostile environment completely alone. We will discover in Chapter 3 that most screenplays break into a three-act pattern. The 25 percent mark, roughly thirty pages into the screenplay, thus signals a crisis or turning point at the end of the first act.

Sometimes the nature of the goal shifts at the end of act one. In *Witness*, for example, the protagonist's initial goal is to find the killer of a fellow policeman. At the end of act one, he discovers in shock that his superiors are responsible and that he is now in mortal danger. His new goal is to stay alive (and ultimately to expose them).

Similarly, in *Kramer vs. Kramer*, the protagonist's initial goal is to become a successful advertising executive. Act one ends with a bitter quarrel between father and five-year-old son, a low point in their developing relationship, and the father's discovery that his son's love means more to him now than his job. In *Kramer*, a totally new goal emerges in the second act: to keep his son, whose mother threatens to take him away.

In *Thelma and Louise*, Louise kills a rapist at the end of act one (roughly 25 percent of the way into the film), radically changing the story's direction. What the two women had planned as a carefree escape from domestic or work chores becomes instead a flight from the law.

Sometimes the antagonist sets your story in motion; sometimes the protagonist. When the antagonist starts the fireworks, your hero usually wants only to be left alone to pursue his or her normal day-to-day activities.

The daughter of a wealthy corporate executive is accosted and kidnapped while crossing her college campus. An elderly woman discovers that her son will put her in a hated retirement home. Engine failures force the pilot and crew of a commercial airliner to ditch their plane at sea. In each of these examples, the protagonists are minding their own business, attending to the chores of everyday life when an adversarial force suddenly appears and creates emotional havoc. In these examples, the protagonists' goal is to escape the painful burden that has been thrust upon them.

When the daughter of a wealthy executive is kidnapped, her goal is self-evident: to escape from her captors. If she is bright and her captors are stupid, there will be no contest. But if even a single member of the kidnapping team is brilliant—as brilliant as she and maybe more so—then audiences will have real cause to worry. If her captors are also vicious, with no respect for human life, then the struggle will be suspenseful.

When the elderly woman discovers that her son intends to send her to a retirement home, her goal is to prevent it. Her adversaries will be her son and perhaps her son's wife. If the son is weak, then our story might become a tug of war, with the mother pulling her son in one direction and his wife pulling in another. (See Figure 1.1.) This classic tug-of-war pattern occurs again and again in motion picture and TV screenplays.

The pilot's goal will be to save the lives of his passengers and crew. His antagonist is the forces of nature, dramatized through the turbulent sea, high winds, freezing temperatures, and sharks. Because screenplay stories are primarily about people, we will probably search for human adversaries, too. Perhaps a cowardly copilot disagrees with the pilot's plan to ditch the plane. (We've all seen this one, haven't we?)

Disaster movies also fall into the pattern of an antagonist setting the story in motion. *Towering Inferno* and *Earthquake* are examples in which nature is the antagonist. Other examples include *Die Hard I* and *II*, in which terrorists threaten airports, airplanes, or office buildings with their brutal schemes.

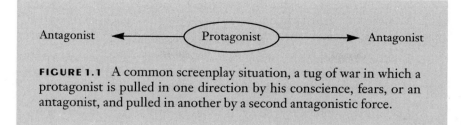

FIGURE 1.1 A common screenplay situation, a tug of war in which a protagonist is pulled in one direction by his conscience, fears, or an antagonist, and pulled in another by a second antagonistic force.

Frequently the protagonist sets the wheels in motion. For example, he defects to America in his high-tech submarine (*The Hunt for Red October*). She devises a clever investment scheme (*Working Girl*). He picks up a pretty prostitute and takes her home (*Pretty Woman*). He wishes to be an adult and his wish is granted (*Big*).

Writing a screenplay is not an exact science. You cannot construct one with a slide rule. We are dealing here in patterns rather than formulas. *Generally*, screenplays divide into three acts. *Generally*, the problem locks in at about the 25 percent mark. *Generally*, it erupts from actions of either the antagonist or protagonist. You will find exceptions to all of these patterns. Artists sometimes break rules. But beginning screenwriters would be wise to observe the time-honored patterns described in this text. Once they have sold a couple of motion picture or TV screenplays, they are welcome to define their own rules.

The concept of a person with a problem may seem obvious and elementary. But professional writers sometimes get lost in building intricate plots, multi-dimensional characters, fascinating relationships, and clever dialog. When they read their completed screenplays, they discover in shock that somehow, somewhere, something is wrong. When this happens to you, apply the person/problem yardstick: Can an audience become emotionally involved with your protagonist? Does a formidable adversary fight to prevent your protagonist from reaching a worthwhile goal? If these two fundamental building blocks are solid, your screenplay structure can emerge as strong and compelling.

DEPARTURES FROM THE PERSON/PROBLEM PATTERN

Although most motion pictures and television movies use the person/problem yardstick, other perfectly respectable entertainment forms — such as mysteries, certain **art films**, quiz and game shows, and documentaries — deviate from it. Such entertainment is often intensely dramatic, but it is not drama. Comedy sometimes follows the pattern closely. And sometimes it veers wildly away from it. The more bizarre the comedy (for example, farce), the more it deviates from our person/problem pattern (see Chapter 11).

Nondrama entertainment forms sometimes cater to our rational, cerebral sides. Mysteries (so-called whodunits) are usually intellectual in nature, a battle of wits between spectator and sleuth.

> I don't really approve of whodunits because they're rather like a jigsaw or a crossword puzzle. No emotion. You simply want to find out who committed the murder.*

Successful whodunits, however, often seek to involve their audiences emotionally. For example, an innocent woman has been accused of murder; she will certainly be convicted unless her attorney can locate the real killer. Incensed at the injustice, we root for her to reach her goal: acquittal. Many whodunits also use entertainment elements, such as spectacle, to dazzle and intrigue us.†

Film and television documentaries also cater primarily to our intellectual side. So do magazine-format TV programs, newscasts, educational shows, and quiz programs. The quiz program/game show exploits conflict, drama's key element, yet it lacks the formal features of screenplay structure described in these chapters. Magazine-format programs such as "60 Minutes" or "20–20" frequently involve us emotionally with characters, yet they lack drama's scene/act structure, goal orientation, and antagonist.

DRAMA AND REAL LIFE

Since the birth of motion pictures, some critics have used snapshot reality as a criterion with which to judge a film's success or failure.‡ Given a fine script, cast, and director, a motion picture need only come close to everyday life, the closer the better, to be aesthetically satisfying. However, students of screenplay structure have come to realize that this is not the case. Drama and real life are significantly different.

In 1971 producer-director Craig Gilbert conceived the idea of filming the everyday life of a normal American family. It was a kind of sociological experiment in which Gilbert "became convinced that there was something special and unique called The American Culture. And that that culture contained within it certain accepted attitudes about what it means to be a man, woman, or child in this time."§

He obtained funding from the Corporation for Public Broadcasting and on May 31, 1971, began a **cinema verité** (literally, truth cinema, or the art of

---

*François Truffaut, *Hitchcock/Truffaut* (New York: Simon & Schuster, 1967), p. 52.

†For more on the elements of entertainment, see Chapter 9.

‡The most outspoken of these critics is André Bazin in *What Is Cinema?* Vol. I (Berkeley: University of California Press, 1967).

§Craig Gilbert as quoted in *Television Quarterly, The Journal of the National Academy of Television Arts and Sciences*, Fall 1973, p. 12.

conveying candid realism) study of the William Loud family of Santa Barbara, California. Gilbert took his 16mm camera and small crew into the Loud home daily for seven months. There he filmed the family's most significant moments, remaining sometimes until 9 or 10 o'clock at night. On occasion, Gilbert's camera followed the Louds to restaurants or to William Loud's office.

At first, Pat and William Loud and their four children (the fifth was in New York) were self-conscious. They found it difficult to behave normally with a camera scrutinizing their actions. After a while, they grew accustomed to the equipment and ignored it.

During the filming, two extraordinary events occurred. Pat and William Loud decided to get a divorce, and their son Lance returned home from New York and shocked his family by announcing that he was gay.

In all, Gilbert filmed 300 hours. He edited this footage down to twelve hours, which aired on PBS in 1972 under the title "An American Family." Consider this: (1) each day Gilbert filmed what he regarded as the most significant moments, ignoring the trivial, the dull, the unimportant; (2) two major events occurred during his filming; (3) in editing, he selected only the best of his material, twelve hours out of 300.

With three such positive factors, the series should have been fascinating. To most viewers, however, it wasn't. Why? Because real life simply isn't narrative in form. Occasionally, in real life, events occur that are intensely dramatic. But being dramatic does not make them drama. Conversations in "An American Family" were often long, rambling, unfocused. There was movement—but it wasn't action. Audiences could not endure the formlessness. Many critics flayed the series, perhaps unfairly, for it was never intended as entertainment. Real life seldom is.*

Director Alfred Hitchcock once remarked that drama is "life from which we have wiped the stains of boredom." You may remove those stains by observing the two primary characteristics that separate screenplay drama from real life: *economy* and *logic*.

Economy. Experienced writers get rid of the "fat" in their screenplays before they submit them to producers. They practice dramatic economy in three areas: **dialog, characters**, and **scenes**.

In "An American Family," people repeated themselves endlessly, wandered all around a subject, and brought meaningless and unnecessary details into conversations, even when their stories were potentially exciting. Listen to conversations on the bus or in your home. You will discover that speech patterns in real life seldom are economical.

---

*Some hailed the series as a sociological milestone. Anthropologist Margaret Mead called it "extraordinary."

Unnecessary words destroy the effectiveness of dialog because they dissipate its energy and muddy its ideas. The screenwriter therefore pares away unnecessary words, boiling speeches down to their essence. Because writers strive to create the appearance of reality, speeches retain the *sound* of everyday life but the excesses have been carefully deleted.

The screenwriter economizes also with characters. Examine almost any book that has been adapted into a motion picture. The film usually uses only a fraction of the book's characters; the screenwriter selects only those that contribute significantly. Unnecessary characters clutter a show, taking attention away from central characters. In the interest of economy, screenwriters sometimes combine two or three characters into one. By using fewer characters, the writer may explore each in greater depth.

Screenwriters also economize on the number of scenes in a screenplay. If a scene does not contribute a new plot development or reveal something new about a principal character, it probably should be deleted.

Logic.   The second characteristic that separates screenplay drama from real life is logic. Screenplays are structured logically; real life is usually not.

Greg Mitchell urgently needs $20,000. Two weeks ago his daughter was injured in a hit-and-run accident that jeopardized her eyesight. The $20,000 will fly her to Boston for needed surgery. Greg doesn't even have $1,000. The medical bills have depleted the family savings, and Greg has been out of work for months.

On his way home from the unemployment office, Greg sighs, thinking of the total impossibility of getting so much money. As he walks, he spots a bulging manila envelope on the pavement. He stoops and picks it up, opens the clasp, and glances inside. What do you suppose the envelope contains? How did you ever guess? Almost $22,000!

Because Greg's an honest man, he reports his find to the police and advertises for the owner in the newspaper. No one claims the money, and so Greg is allowed to keep it. His daughter has the operation and regains her eyesight. What an incredible stroke of good fortune!

Such a human interest story might appear in a newspaper but never in a carefully crafted screenplay, because the solution to Greg's problem did not emerge logically from the fabric of his story. The writer conveniently handed it to him.

In ancient Greek tragedy, problems sometimes were solved in the last act of a play, when a golden chariot descended from above. Out stepped a god who produced a miracle, instantly solving everyone's problems. Modern audiences generally reject such convenient solutions (**deus ex machina** — literally, god from a machine). We regard them as cheating — the writer apparently could find no legitimate way of ending the story.

Because screenplays are logical, events that occur in the third act grow out of material established in the first two acts. Events in the second act grow out of material established in the first. The solution to a problem cannot descend conveniently from the heavens, as did Greg's discovery of the manila envelope; such easy solutions smack of coincidence. Because it defies the laws of logic and therefore appears unrealistic, coincidence plays a limited role in screenplays.

Is it ever appropriate to defy the laws of logic? Yes, on two occasions. First, **coincidence** may occur at the beginning of a story. Many of Alfred Hitchcock's most successful films began with such coincidences. In *North by Northwest*, for example, an advertising executive (played by Cary Grant) called for a telephone in the bar of New York's Plaza Hotel at the exact moment that foreign spies were paging a CIA agent. This outrageous coincidence plunged him into a bizarre series of misadventures. Audiences accept initial coincidences with the apparent rationale that if they hadn't occurred, the stories would never have taken place.

Second, coincidence is accepted by audiences when it worsens the protagonist's problem. When a small boy, fleeing through crowded New York streets, accidentally bumps into one of his pursuers, the accident (coincidence) is not only acceptable but also savored by audiences. In this case, the writer isn't taking shortcuts to solve problems. On the contrary, the boy is now in deeper trouble than before, and the writer must work harder to free him. Remember, audiences love to worry. They gratefully accept coincidences that give them more to worry about.

One way to eliminate an illogical coincidence is to *make it logical*. You can do this simply by laying the groundwork for it earlier in your screenplay, **setting up** the situation.

Let's look at the example of Greg Mitchell's convenient discovery of an envelope full of money. How can we make that discovery appear logical, an outgrowth of what has gone before? Perhaps by revealing how the money came to be there. If, for example, an earlier incident showed bank robbers who had lost a portion of their booty, then the audience would be more prepared for Greg's finding it on a city street. In this circumstance, the robbers might read Greg's newspaper advertisement but would be afraid to come forward, fearing a police trap. Once a coincidence grows logically out of earlier plot circumstances, it can no longer be labeled a coincidence. Now it is simple cause and effect.

Because screenplay drama and real life have significant differences, we must conclude that writers do not create literal reality in their scripts. They try to make audiences *believe* they are watching reality — dimensional people facing understandable problems in a believable world. But what screenwriters create is only the appearance of everyday life.

The word *reality* is deceptive. Because screenplays are more logical and economical than real life, they do not present literal reality as their subject matter. And yet, paradoxically, screenwriters strive to present the *essence* of life.

In historical movies, for example, writers frequently distort textbook reality, inventing some characters, altering the nature of others, omitting births, deaths, or entire wars. What writers seek in such screenplays is not literal, historical accuracy but the deeper, more significant emotional truth that underlies the event, perhaps as revealed through character relationships or human motivations. Such films create their own reality.

STORY CONCEPTS: WHERE THEY ORIGINATE

Screenplay stories seldom emerge full blown. When they do, beware. When an entire story pops into your head — beginning, middle, and end — it probably resembles a movie or TV show you saw recently. The "story that writes itself" usually falls into this category. It's not that you're consciously appropriating someone else's characters or plot but rather that stories (especially those that strike responsive chords) sink into our subconscious minds. They pop to the surface when we search our imaginations. If you think about your "instant story" for a few minutes, you will probably find its source.

Stories usually emerge from fragmentary ideas: a colorful character, a poignant or offbeat relationship, a childhood incident, a physical object, or a problem in your own family. Dozens of successful motion pictures originated in the pages of the daily newspaper. Remember that newspaper items (or other sources) seldom contain all — or even *most* — of a screenplay's elements. You will have to find some ingredient in the news item that excites you, that stimulates your imagination, and then build your story on that. It's a game that professionals call "what if."

From a newspaper story detailing the break-in at a defense plant you might conjecture: What if the robber in the newspaper story weren't a bad person at all? What if he committed the robbery for some truly commendable reason? Then you'd try to figure out what that reason might be. What kind of person is the robber? What are his goals? Who is fighting to keep him from reaching those goals? It's a trial-and-error process of searching until you find elements that feel honest and logical and that light a fire in your imagination.

The two magic words "what if" start the wheels of creation turning. You see a young woman crying and you wonder: What if she lost her job? Or her lover? Or her parents? What if she knows she has only a few months to live? You see a dark stain on the sidewalk and you wonder: What if it were blood? What if some crime took place here, perhaps a kidnapping? What if? What if?

Here's an idea you can have for free. Read again some of the myths and fairy tales that you enjoyed as a child and then ask "What if?" What if they took place in today's world? This is a way of charging your creative batteries, transforming myths into up-to-the-minute dramatic stories, placing fairy-tale characters in modern jobs or locales. Or simply place fairy-tale *ideas* into contemporary story patterns. You'll be surprised at the delightful stories that emerge, so long as you let your imagination run free. Take Cinderella, for instance. She's certainly a person with a problem. Her goal? To get to the palace ball and, perhaps, to meet the prince himself. Her antagonist? Her wicked stepmother, who tries to keep her from reaching that goal. Cinderella gets to the ball, of course, with the help of a kindly fairy godmother. Think: How would you update Cindy's story? Again, play the game called "what if."

We should note here that Cinderella is an archetypal story. That's a word that's come into some prominence lately in the entertainment world. Psychiatrist Carl Jung coined the word **archetype** to describe primordial images or "archaic remnants" (his words) that constitute the essence of myths, legends, and fairy tales. Archetypes (AHR-kih-types) deal with such elemental stuff as birth and rebirth, death, sex, the mother-son relationship, the father-daughter relationship, rites of passage (such as adolescence), and with characters or symbols that are common to the mythic patterns of almost all races, cultures, and civilizations. Significantly, the dreams of Australian aborigines and American corporate executives contain almost identical archetypes.

Archetypes had a rebirth with George Lucas's *Star Wars*. A student of myths, legends, and fairy tales, Lucas created archetypal characters in his screenplay, knowing that they would reach audiences everywhere on a primitive level. Luke Skywalker is the universal/archetypal hero who sets out on a quest, leaving his comfortable home, traveling to a frightening, alien world to face a supreme ordeal. In the third film of the trilogy we learn that his archenemy is his own father. (Have you ever read *Oedipus Rex* or studied Sigmund Freud?) Obi-Wan Kenobi is the archetypal wise old man who helps the hero. Note that Cinderella's fairy godmother is the identical character, the wise old helper who gives our hero the materials that she needs (gown, coach, horses, coachman) to reach her goal.

The mother figure is archetypal. In Cinderella the kindly mother is displaced by an evil one. (In *David Copperfield*, his mother is displaced by an unfeeling stepfather.) Think about it: As a child, wasn't one of your most basic fears, "What if she abandoned me, this woman who loves me, cares for me, feeds me?" Feelings as deep as this are common to everyone. When you tap into them in your screenplays, you're affecting the audience on both a conscious and subconscious level. The material that makes up legends, myths, and fairy tales is powerful stuff; it strikes chords that are deep and universal, that you and I can recognize in our own lives. When we use such elements in our screenplays, they take on richness.

Joseph Campbell has explored the content of myths. Read his work. Find the books of myths and fairy tales that you stored in the attic years ago. Dust them off and read them again. Look for characters and themes that strike deep, responsive chords. Look for ways of using those themes and characters in your screenplays.

Whether they originate in a myth, a fairy tale, or in your aunt Sarah's living room, the people who stride through your screenplays will eventually take on familiar characteristics. We all tend to write about people we know, whether we realize it or not. Whether we write about King Henry VIII, a lovesick Samoan princess, or aliens infiltrating a western town, we still give characters feelings and traits that are familiar to us. We build characters and relationships from our imaginations, but their thoughts, words, and actions derive from our own practical experience.

Neil Simon recognizes this tendency in his own writing:

> If you read the biographies of all the great writers, they were always writing about themselves, about their families. Tolstoy was writing about everyone he knew, always worrying about what society, what the public, was going to think. Sometimes I'm very specific about my characterizations; sometimes I disguise them; and sometimes my subconscious disguises them and they become other people. . . .
>
> I write about myself, my brother, my parents, my wife, my children, my friends, my coworkers, the people I meet all the time. I always try to write about them with some affection, but mostly with some honesty. And I have never once had anybody come up to me and say, "How dare you put me down that way." Never.*

The cliché telling writers to write about familiar subjects is true — but also misleading, because it severely limits our imaginations. Were the story material to originate solely from personal experience, our scripts would have a stultifying sameness. Specific and factual subject matter for scripts (vocations, background locales, historical data) should be carefully researched. Once writers have studied their subject matter, they will, indeed, be writing about subjects they know.

Although the subject matter of scripts does not have to derive from personal experience, it certainly *can*. Personal worries or dilemmas can result in legitimate, recognizable story values for a screenplay, values with which audiences can identify. In scriptwriting classes, certain story patterns emerge again and again because they represent family or career dilemmas with which students are deeply concerned. The story in which a protagonist wants to become an actor or a rock musician despite parental protests is a prime example.

Writing about subjects that have deep personal meaning has another advantage. Despite the so-called glamour associated with scriptwriting, the process involves a lot of plain, old-fashioned hard work: trying ideas; rejecting them and trying others; building a cohesive structure; writing scenes, rewriting them, then rewriting them again. Along the way, you may run out of steam —

---

*John Brady, ed., *The Craft of the Screenwriter* (New York: Simon & Schuster, 1981), pp. 317–18.

unless you begin with a subject that truly excites you, that will provide enough stimulation and psychic energy to take you down the long road ahead.

Writing about subjects that have personal meaning—that you feel passionately about—brings strength to a screenplay. It creates electricity. When writers feel deeply about an injustice in society or grieve for a lost friend or grow angry at some flaw in the judicial system, their intense emotions are communicated through their words to the actors—and through the actors to their audience.

BEGINNING A STORY: A NEWSPAPER ITEM

The guidelines in these chapters are practical. You can use them to build your own screenplays. To make that point, we're going to construct a screenplay story during the next few chapters, applying concepts from those chapters to help put the pieces together. Whether our story becomes an Academy Award winner or a total disaster is unimportant. What counts is the *process*, which illustrates that the chapter guidelines aren't gobbledegook or impractical mumbo jumbo. They work.

Where do we begin the process? Let's look to the pages of our daily newspaper. The following item appeared in the Metro section of the *Los Angeles Times*, January 12, 1991.

Murder Charge Against Boy, 11, Is Thrown Out

By LORI GRANGE

TIMES STAFF WRITER

A judge Friday threw out charges against an 11-year-old Anaheim boy accused of helping his mother kill his grandmother, despite a prosecutor's argument that the youth was a clever assassin's apprentice acting out of hatred.

After two days of testimony, Pasadena Juvenile Court Judge Sandy Kriegler dismissed the claim that the youth had aided his mother, Victoria Elizabeth Jacobs Madeira, in the Oct. 14 stabbing and shooting of Roma Jaul Jacobs at her La Canada Flintridge home.

The youth was believed to be the state's youngest murder defendant since 1981.

Let's use this item as a beginning point in developing a screenplay story. To start, we'll need to determine who our person (protagonist) is. Because the boy is the focus of the newspaper item, let's temporarily make him our protagonist. Later we may decide that the mother (or someone else) will make a better protagonist. We can always change any element in our story if we find another that builds it more effectively.

To start, let's give our protagonist a name. It's always easier to discuss characters when they have names. How about Marty? We can change it later if the name doesn't suit him.

Marty is accused of a heinous crime, the killing of his grandmother, Mildred. He swears almost in tears that he is innocent. He loved Grandma Millie dearly. What is Marty's goal in this story? To clear his name and avoid years of incarceration in a boys' home. Who is his antagonist? Who is fighting to keep him from reaching his goal? Initially, it would probably be the Los Angeles police department and the district attorney's office. Later we may find more specific antagonists.

What place will his mother have in our story? Initially, she would probably be shocked at the charges against Marty or any implication that he may have committed the act at her behest. Perhaps, as the evidence against him mounts, she will be torn, her love for her son in conflict with her fear that he might have actually committed such a despicable act. Let's call her Lynn. Does she have a husband? Let's leave that open for now. Later, if we feel we need him, we can bring him to life.

Is Marty actually guilty? That's the core of our story, isn't it? If he is, we're going to have a devil of a time maintaining audience sympathy. Can you think of any way to keep an audience caring about a character who has killed a loved one, especially a helpless old woman? Let's turn this problem over to our subconscious and come back to it in the next chapter. It may be too early to make such a critical decision.

Even if Marty's guilty, at the beginning of our story we probably should believe him innocent. He's open-faced, likable, apparently a decent kid. Belief in his innocence gives us an immediate rooting interest and will raise the intriguing question: If not Marty, then who else?

Since we're just beginning our exploration, let's leave Marty's and Lynn's characters undefined. We can explore them later, after we know the kinds of characters we need to make our story work.

So what have we got? Eleven-year-old Marty is horrified to find himself accused of shooting his own grandmother. You will notice that as we develop our story, it will move further and further away from the news item that triggered our thinking. As the story builds, Marty and his mother will strive to clear him of these (apparently) unfair charges.

Not a bad start. We're using Chapter 1 elements: a person we can care about and a problem consisting of a goal and something standing in the way of reaching that goal. We can pick up the threads of our developing story at the end of Chapter 2. Stay tuned.

CHAPTER HIGHLIGHTS

➤ Screenplay stories emerge from diametrically opposite poles: logic and fantasy. Mathematical logic helps us build a logical structure. Fantasy helps us create imaginative incidents, characters, and plot directions.

➤ There is no single correct pattern for conceiving stories, since they arise from such contradictory sources. Each writer develops a personal, individualized system, applying certain principles.

➤ Dramatic stories usually concern emotional pain. Audiences identify with a protagonist and worry as he or she encounters problems. By suffering with a protagonist facing disaster, audiences achieve a release of tension or a sense of fulfillment.

➤ An effective definition of screenplay drama: a person with a problem. The person is a character with whom audiences can become emotionally involved, either through sympathy, empathy, or antipathy. The deeper the involvement, the more complete their emotional experience will be.

➤ Problems manifest themselves in two ways. Either the antagonist starts the fireworks (*Die Hard I* and *II*) or the protagonist (*Big, The Hunt for Red October*). When the antagonist sparks the story, the protagonist usually wants only to continue his normal, daily activities.

➤ Screenplays do not slavishly imitate life; instead, they create an appearance or illusion of life. When directors photograph life situations, the results often are dull and tedious. Screenplays usually are logical and structured; real life is not. Screenplays are economical in dialog, characters, and scenes; real life is not. Yet screenplays strive to present the essence of life.

➤ Story concepts that emerge complete usually derive from shows recently seen. Original stories derive most frequently from fragments: a character, a problem, or an idea. The best stories emerge from archetypes and concern subject matter that has deep personal meaning for the writer.

➤ Most of the characters we create emerge from personal experience. We may consciously pattern characters after family members or friends, or characters may emerge from subconscious recollection.

$\mathcal{S}$CRIPTWRITING PROJECTS

EXERCISES DESIGNED TO
SHARPEN YOUR NARRATIVE SKILLS

THE PERSON

Find an appropriate *character* for each of the following problems. Don't settle for the first character that occurs to you; first thoughts are usually trite. Search for freshness, even if the idea seems bizarre at first.

Consider this question: Will the relationship between your character and the problem allow room for exciting development?

1. The person must overcome deep-seated, nearly paralyzing fears to reach an important personal goal. (It may help to define your goal first — for example, to make peace with a hated father.)

2. The person must hurt someone he or she loves deeply to reach an important personal goal. (Again, determining the nature of the goal may prove helpful — for example, winning an athletic contest.)

3. Earlier in life, the person committed a serious indiscretion, perhaps a crime. Now the past incident suddenly emerges, threatening to destroy the person who has become respected and successful.

THE PROBLEM

Find an appropriate *problem* for each of the following characters. Remember that the problem emerges because someone or something (your antagonist) is fighting to keep your hero from reaching an important personal goal. Select a problem that will provide a series of struggles between each of the following characters and his or her antagonist.

1. A policeman nearing retirement

2. An intensely moral and religious foreign student

3. An escaped convict hiding in the basement of a school

THE PREMISE

Write a sentence or two summarizing the story for each of the above persons and each of the above problems. (For example, a college student struggles with his conscience over whether to expose to the press the illegal experiments conducted in the college's science department.)

NEWSPAPERS AS A STORY SOURCE

Select an item from the daily newspaper and develop it, using the "what if" technique. Write a paragraph or two specifying the protagonist, antagonist, and the protagonist's goal. Suggest a possible ending for your story.

SCREENPLAYS VERSUS REAL LIFE

Tape conversations at the dinner table or at a party or family gathering. Write a page or two of the recorded conversation (1) as it actually occurred and (2) as you would reshape it for a screenplay, practicing dramatic economy.

CHAPTER 2

Structure, Structure, Structure!

Many aspiring writers believe that fine scripts come from inspiration. All they have to do is sit down at their typewriters, communicate with their muse, and then—shazam!—something magic happens. Brilliant ideas suddenly flood their minds and scenes of incredible poignancy and beauty emerge on paper.

Nothing could be less true. Fine screenplays, like other creative works, emerge from careful crafting. They are built on the foundation of rock-solid story outlines or treatments. Treatments emerge from thought and more thought, from expertise, from trial and error, from writing and rewriting—and from inspiration. If you're alarmed by such a truth, don't be. If there's hard work to plotting, it's worth it.

Building an exciting and structurally solid treatment can be fulfilling. And writing a script can be exhilarating. Seeing characters come to life on paper, speak lines of dialog, laugh, cry, suffer, and triumph can be an exciting experience. And seeing your name on a screen after the words "written by" is unquestionably one of life's better moments.

In this chapter we will examine how professional writers organize and structure their material. The chapter consists of four major discussions:

➤ **THE PREMISE**: crystallizing the concept in your mind

➤ **STORY CONSTRUCTION**: two methods of building a story — the logical and the imaginative

➤ **THE TREATMENT**: describing the story on paper — beginning, middle, and end — before writing the screenplay

➤ **NEWSPAPER ITEM DEVELOPMENT**: continuing to flesh out the story started in Chapter 1

Richard Walter, chairman of the screenwriting faculty at UCLA, says, "The three most important facets of story craft are: (1) structure; (2) structure; (3) structure."*

In the preface to this book, Howard Suber, also of UCLA's film faculty, says, "It is structure more than any other single element of the filmmaking process that will ultimately determine whether a film is an empty succession of costly sounds and images or an integrated work that fulfills the vision of its creators."

William Goldman, one of the entertainment industry's most successful screenwriters (*Misery, Butch Cassidy and the Sundance Kid*) says, ". . . the single most important lesson to be learned about writing for films:

Screenplays Are Structure.

Yes, nifty dialog helps a hell of a lot; sure, it's nice if you can bring your characters to life. But you can have terrific characters spouting just swell talk to each other, and if the structure is unsound, forget it."†

Even our old friend Aristotle over two thousand years ago said, "Most important of all is the structure of the incidents."

If the structure is unsound, forget it. Screenplays are structure. Most important of all is the structure. Structure, structure, structure. Are you beginning to get the message?

There are several key steps to developing your screenplay's structure. The first is to crystallize your premise.

THE PREMISE

Once screenwriters know who their person is and the nature of his or her problem, they next need to determine what events or circumstances might resolve their story. Remember, the problem is always goal oriented, so writers must know in advance where they are going, what they are working toward, as they assemble the pieces of their story puzzle.

Once they have found the most significant elements of their story, and this may take considerable time, they now may write a **premise**, which is simply the basic idea of the story, sometimes described in a sentence, sometimes in a paragraph or two. Some writers structure their premises in terse three-act patterns: beginning, middle, and end, with a sentence or two about each.

---

*Screenwriting (New York: NAL Penguin, 1988), p. 37.
†*Adventures in the Screen Trade* (New York: Warner Books, 1983), p. 195.

A premise contains the essence of a story. It defines the major ingredients. For example, the premise for *Casablanca* might read: When Ilsa Lund shows up at his café in Nazi-controlled Casablanca, Rick Blaine, bitter because of an earlier betrayal, refuses to give her documents that would permit her escape to America. Once their love is rekindled, Rick selflessly sends her off with her husband who will continue the fight for freedom.

The premise for *Sleeping with the Enemy* might read: A young woman escapes from her brutal, abusive husband and finds love in another community. But the obsessive husband tracks her down and she is forced to kill him.

A premise is more than a vague idea; it is a crystallization of basic plot elements, the first step in the writing of a screenplay. The second step is the treatment; the third step is the first draft of the screenplay itself. In the early stages of story development, a dozen disparate elements compete in the writer's mind. Ideas are hazy, unfocused. The very act of putting a premise on paper forces writers to sort out and define their ideas and to examine their plot elements critically. Then begins the work of story construction: putting the pieces together.

*S*TORY CONSTRUCTION

Because the construction of stories is an imprecise art, each writer usually develops a personal technique that works for him or her, but probably for no one else. Because construction deals with many disparate elements, because it derives from the cool mathematical logic of the brain's left hemisphere and the dream fantasy of the right, because construction is often a hit-or-miss, trial-and-error process, no single rule or principle can be appropriate for all writers.

There are two general ways to construct a screenplay story, each diametrically opposed to the other. Somehow, eventually, these opposite poles must meet and integrate. The only "rule" that binds them together is that the writer must know in advance how the story will end.

If, on a vacation, you get in your car and drive without knowing your destination, you probably will meander aimlessly and never arrive at any worthwhile vacation spot. On the other hand, if you know your destination in advance, you can take a dozen colorful side trips, knowing that the highlight of your trip lies ahead. When you plan either a vacation or a screenplay, you must have some general sense of direction; it doesn't always have to be specific. If you don't plan, your vacation will be wasted and your script will founder. The two approaches to developing a story are the logical and the imaginative.

THE LOGICAL APPROACH

Aware that screenplays build through a series of crises to a final climax, writers who use the logical approach begin story construction by searching for three major story crises or turning points. In hour-long TV shows, writers must search for four such landmarks. Because writers often face multiple options and must select from story paths leading in a dozen disparate directions, the plotting process can be frustrating. However, once they determine their three (or four) major crises, a certain sense of security takes over. Often such story-path selections are tentative, subject to change. Now writers will fill in the blanks, determining which scenes will advance the story from fade-in to the first-act crisis/turning point.

Once they have plotted the first act, writers must develop scenes that will take them logically, honestly, and colorfully to their second landmark. Determining these landmarks in advance makes the plotting easier; it's not too difficult to envision a single act, whereas trying to plot a script from fade-in to fade-out can be mind boggling. After you have constructed two acts, it's relatively easy to figure out the steps necessary for the third, because you know exactly where you're going.

Some years ago I worked with a distinguished historical novelist, Elliott Arnold, on a TV series called "Broken Arrow." He wrote the novel *Blood Brother* from which the original 20th Century-Fox feature had been adapted, a true life story of the friendship, respect, and love that grew between Tom Jeffords, an Indian agent, and Cochise, the Apache chief. (The two men were on opposite sides during the bloody wars between whites and Apaches in the middle of the nineteenth century.) At lunch one day, Arnold told me how he had put together the novel. His procedure directly parallels the steps many writers take in constructing their screenplays.

After settling on the concept, he read volumes of historical data, searching for characters and events that would provide an exciting novel. Next, he visited Tucson, Arizona, the town that served as a home base for Jeffords. He spent months researching the historical background, digging into yellowing newspaper files, talking to old-timers who had been alive during the 1870s and 1880s, and reading letters written during the period. He visited the actual site in the Chiricahua Mountains where the Apaches had lived and where Cochise and Jeffords had become blood brothers. He hired a secretary to copy or transcribe all pertinent information.

Arnold's first step parallels the first step taken by all serious writers: They research their scripts. They do their homework. Such writers find the honesty of their characters, their dialog, and the world they live in by reading about that world, interviewing its inhabitants, or visiting — and experiencing — that world themselves.

Once he returned to Los Angeles, Arnold began to construct the major events of his novel. He started by tacking pieces of paper to the four walls of his office. On these papers, spaced some distance apart, he described actual historical milestones in chronological progression. Now, standing in the center of his office, he could look around and trace major events in the Arizona Territory between (roughly) 1850 and 1880. His procedure approximates the concept of determining a story's three major crises, as noted earlier.

Finally, as he invented the threads of his fictitious story, he wrote each incident on a sheet of paper and tacked it to the wall between historical events at a place where it seemed most appropriate, integrating fiction with historical fact. As his story gained detail, he added more and more sheets of paper until his entire wall was filled. Now he could examine the progression of events, fictitious and real, evaluating, changing the sequence, adding incidents, refining again and again until he felt secure. After nearly a year's preparation, he was ready to begin his novel.

Many professional scriptwriters use a system similar to Arnold's when constructing stories. They describe each scene on a 3″ x 5″ card — just a few words for each scene, to give them a handle on it. Perhaps at first they describe only their major story crises or any other big moments they have preconceived. Then, as they invent ideas for scenes that will advance their stories from fade-in to the first crisis, they describe those scenes on other 3″ x 5″ cards. By placing those cards on a table or on the floor, they can determine how the various story elements fit together and where additional scenes will be needed, moving the cards about to find the most logical, honest, and dramatically effective sequence.

After following this procedure for all three acts, writers may then sit down and write their treatments with the comfortable knowledge that their plots are structurally sound. They may add final refinements at the treatment stage to flesh out the scenes and add dimension to characters.

THE IMAGINATIVE APPROACH

At the opposite pole from the procedure just described is the imaginative approach in which (at first) logic is thrown out the window.

Using this approach, writers lie on the grass, stare up at the blue sky, and ask themselves such questions as: Given my premise, what wonderful things conceivably could happen to my characters to give my story distinction? What incredible scenes might occur? What marvelous twists and turns in my plot might shock or delight an audience?

Allowing their minds to drift into a dreamlike state, writers let their imaginations wander freely, not censoring or inhibiting any story directions, no matter how bizarre. Sometimes new and unexpected characters emerge. Sometimes, surprisingly, snatches of dialog evolve. Sometimes, by using this imaginative technique, writers discover plot directions that are astounding but totally at odds with their original concept. If the new direction is sufficiently exciting, the original concept must be changed, discarded, or adapted to fit.

Sometimes as you drift into this dreamlike world you may discover characters or images that seem to have unusual emotional power (you almost cry as you think about them), that seem somehow to connect with memories of another time or another world. These are archetypal images residing deep in your subconscious mind, half-forgotten images that you share with other races and other cultures. They manifest themselves most often in the content of myths, fairy tales, legends, and folk ballads, expressions from the deepest heart of humankind. Because audiences everywhere recognize and react to these primal images consciously or subconsciously, they will be moved by them, perhaps not even understanding the cause of their sudden deep rush of emotion.

When you happen upon such powerful material, respect it. Use it. Work it into your story. If necessary, reshape your story to accommodate it.

Ultimately, after hours, days, or weeks of dreaming, logic must return and the story must be pounded into a traditional three-act structure. And now the plotting principles discussed in "The Logical Approach" may be used to advantage.

Each writer has his or her own way of constructing stories. One of the entertainment industry's top writers describes his method at the end of Chapter 3. His essay may help to illuminate this difficult process.

After putting the elements of your story together in your mind or on paper, the next step is to consolidate them in the form of a treatment.

*T*HE TREATMENT

The **treatment** (sometimes called a story **outline**) is nothing more complicated than a screenplay told in story form. Treatments usually avoid the scene-by-scene, action-by-action, line-by-line minutiae of a screenplay, concentrating instead on major moves. They allow the writer to review story elements early and determine who the characters are, their relationships and goals, and (in general terms) how all of the major pieces of the puzzle fit together.

Some writers include bits of dialog in their treatments or prepare detailed character backgrounds; other writers don't. Some write extensive sixty- or seventy-page treatments, working out structural problems early; others prefer to sketch their stories in more general terms, saving such detail for their screenplays. The point is: There is no single correct form or style for a treatment. Each writer has an individual, personal preference, often modified by the needs of a particular producer.

As with screenplays, treatments are written in the present tense. The action is happening *now*. Some beginning writers, accustomed to essays, short stories, and novels, occasionally lapse into the past tense and then drift back again into the present. Such lapses are annoying to the reader and are a sign of carelessness and lack of professionalism.

The purpose of the treatment is to evaluate a story and its characters early and find the weaknesses so they can be corrected or avoided before beginning the more detailed labors of writing the screenplay. It is important to discover areas of strength so that they can be expanded or enriched in the screenplay. If you have to make mistakes (and mistakes are almost inevitable), make them in the treatment, fix them, and move on.

Some writers try to avoid writing treatments. They look for shortcuts, figuring that maybe they will get lucky and the script will "write itself." (As we discussed in Chapter 1, scripts that write themselves often derive from a movie or TV show that the writer saw recently.) Surprisingly, even some professionals (who should know better) try to convince producers that they can skip the treatment and work out the structure while writing the screenplay. When inexperienced producers allow such an omission, they inevitably regret it later.

Writing a screenplay without a treatment is like erecting a skyscraper without a blueprint. Imagine a contractor showing up at a construction site. With him are a truckload of workers, a cement mixer, and assorted tools and equipment. The contractor walks up and down and surveys the building site thoughtfully. Then he instructs the workers, "All right, gang, we'll pour some cement along here. No, better pour it over there! And while we're doing that, you carpenters get some boards and nails and let's put up some walls. What's that? Sure, put in a door if you want to. Hell, as long as we're at it, let's put in a couple of doors. Anybody else got any ideas?"

A skyscraper built by a contractor who makes up the rules as he goes will be pathetic; it will probably collapse from lack of a solid foundation. Screenplays written without carefully crafted treatments also collapse for much the same reason.

Once the producer (and, in television, the network) has approved the treatment, writers sometimes construct a **step sheet** (or step outline), which defines more specifically the story's progression. Step sheets usually are written on a scene-by-scene basis and explain where each scene takes place, who its participants are, and (very briefly) what happens.

Even when step sheets are not required by a producer, professionals often write them for themselves, knowing that the time spent constructing such blueprints will save countless hours when writing their screenplays. They won't have to stop at the end of each scene to ponder what happens next. They won't discover that they have written unnecessary scenes that must be discarded. They will be able to give their full creative attention to the actions and dialog in each scene, with the comfortable security of knowing exactly where they're going. (The Appendix has an example of a treatment. Be sure to read it.)

DEVELOPING THE NEWSPAPER ITEM

In Chapter 1 we began to build a screenplay story from the following newspaper item.

Murder Charge Against Boy, 11, Is Thrown Out

By LORI GRANGE

TIMES STAFF WRITER

A judge Friday threw out charges against an 11-year-old Anaheim boy accused of helping his mother kill his grandmother, despite a prosecutor's argument that the youth was a clever assassin's apprentice acting out of hatred.

After two days of testimony, Pasadena Juvenile Court Judge Sandy Kriegler dismissed the claim that the youth had aided his mother, Victoria Elizabeth Jacobs Madeira, in the Oct. 14 stabbing and shooting of Roma Jaul Jacobs at her La Canada Flintridge home.

The youth was believed to be the state's youngest murder defendant since 1981.

We decided (temporarily) that our protagonist should be the boy (we're calling him Marty) and that his logical goal would be to clear himself of the charges against him.

Now we must dig deeper to create the kind of structure, structure, structure that Chapter 2 talks about and to determine whether Marty actually committed murder. Let's start with a few questions. Why do the police believe that Marty committed the crime, perhaps at the behest of his mother? Well, maybe the boy has a blemished record. He once took his mother's pistol to school and threatened another student with it. (Living alone, Lynn kept the gun in her nightstand for self-defense.) Perhaps he was suspended from elementary school because of this and other disciplinary problems. What else might make him suspect? Well, maybe he was seen by a neighbor in his grandmother's house an hour before the old woman was killed. Is there a motive? No, apparently not. Why then would he be there? Well, one answer, of course, is that he did kill the old woman but such an act would almost certainly destroy our rooting interest in the boy. We're going to have to stare at the sky and think about this.

To start, we will need to see where our story is headed. What if—what if we gradually come to believe that the *mother* committed the killing? What if she and the police lieutenant investigating the murder (we'll call him Brent) are physically attracted to each other so that we can put him in the difficult position of having to arrest the woman he loves? What if she confesses to the killing to protect her son? But did she really commit the act? And why would she? Does *she* have any motive?

This jumble of confused thinking is typical of story development. It's an often frustrating process of trying ideas, throwing them away, trying others, throwing them away, trying others. . . .

For the moment, let's settle on a simple pattern. We can refine it later. Let's start with the boy being accused. We root for him because we feel he's innocent. Our suspicions slowly grow that the mother committed the crime — and perhaps along the way we'll suspect someone else — but, ultimately, in the final moments, we'll be shocked to discover that Marty actually *did* commit the murder. Such an ending won't be predictable. Maybe the boy killed his grandmother for a "good" reason. For example, maybe his father died some months ago and Marty has proudly assumed the role of Man of the House. He believes his grandmother has been unjustifiably cruel to his mother whom he adores. And he killed the old woman to protect his mother from some new act of cruelty. (Will this be enough to keep us caring about him? Probably not. We'll have to come up with a more compelling motivation. Let's keep working on it.)

We'll probably need another character or two to keep our story from being too simple, too obvious. Another suspect, a "red herring," would help. Perhaps Lynn's brother Phil has had a number of fights with Mildred, his mother. Perhaps he's weak, irresponsible, unable to hold a job, always leaning on the old woman for money. This is a character we can certainly suspect of the murder. He's something of a cliché at this stage, but we can add dimension later.

Lynn's relationships with Brent, the police lieutenant, and with her brother Phil can provide subplots to add texture to our story. We have a rough sense now of how our story might develop, but let's stop for a moment. We learned in Chapter 1 that a good protagonist is an active one. Will Marty be able to act if he's being held by the police? Doubtful. I wonder if his mother might not be better able to push our story forward. Let's see how the pattern works with her as our person with a problem. Lynn's goal will be to clear her son of charges against him (and herself of any suspicions of complicity). Does she achieve her goal? If he's guilty, probably not, but she will certainly gain greater understanding of her son and greater love for him. And once the background story is known (if we can come up with an effective one!), the boy will receive a minimal or suspended sentence.

We still have plenty of rough spots, of course, but now we've provided the kind of rudimentary skeletal structure that Chapter 2 calls for. We'll add flesh to our skeleton in Chapter 3.

CHAPTER HIGHLIGHTS

➤ Successful writers plan their screenplays carefully. They write *premises*, which are crystallizations of basic plot elements.

➤ Writers use *logic* in structuring their stories, often planning their three major crises (landmarks) and then inventing the scenes that will take them honestly and colorfully to those crisis points. Creating three moments of crisis simplifies the plotting chores.

➤ Writers also use *fantasy* in planning their stories, letting their imaginations roam freely in the search for fresh story directions. Eventually, the two extremes, logic and fantasy, must be combined.

➤ Before beginning the screenplay, writers construct *treatments*, which set forth the plot development in story, rather than screenplay, format. Sometimes, especially in longer scripts, they also write *step sheets*, defining the screenplay story in a scene-by-scene construction.

SCRIPTWRITING PROJECTS

EXERCISES DESIGNED TO SHARPEN YOUR NARRATIVE SKILLS

BUILDING A STRUCTURE

Step one: Select one of the problems or characters from the Scriptwriting Projects at the end of Chapter 1 and think about it. That's all, just think. Let your mind wander. Stare at the sky. Dream a little. (Brush aside your first ideas. Chances are, someone else wrote them first.) Search for offbeat scenes or exciting, deeply emotional moments that might fit into your story. Look for twists, unexpected endings. If you discover such exciting developments and they don't exactly jibe with your original concept—and they are sufficiently wonderful—perhaps it would make sense to change your original concept to accommodate them.

Remember, the most important creative moments happen before a screenwriter puts one word on paper!

Step two: Find a series of three *crises* that arise logically from your developing concept, three setbacks or turning points that jeopardize the chances of your protagonist reaching a worthwhile goal, making it appear that the antagonist will certainly win the war. The crises should build in importance.

Congratulations! You have just completed the most difficult part of constructing a screenplay.

WRITING A TREATMENT — THE FIRST STEP

Take three sheets of blank paper. At the bottom of each sheet, write one of the landmark crises you created for your protagonist. Each sheet of paper represents an act of your screenplay.

Now, see if you can find a series of events that will take your protagonist honestly and colorfully from the beginning of your story to the first crisis point. This is part of the puzzle that every professional screenwriter must solve. It's called "How do you get from here to there?" As you explore the almost endless possibilities, you will need to ask some questions. What kind of person is your protagonist? Who are the people who inhabit his or her world? Does your protagonist have a profession? Will friends and family members be a part of the developing story? How will they interact with your protagonist? Will they be allies or obstacles? What about the antagonist? Is he or she a dimensional character or a stereotype?

Write down your ideas. They can be scribbled notes at first. Try to arrange the events in a sequence that builds in tension. Now transfer these events to the sheet of paper that represents act one. And follow the same thought pattern in developing acts two and three, building a series of events from the beginning of each act to the crisis point. When finished, you will have completed the first rough step in constructing a screenplay treatment.

The following chapters will provide additional insights, especially the Writer Revelations by Paddy Chayefsky at the end of Chapter 3.

Anatomy of a Screenplay

Screenplay stories are broken into smaller units called acts, each of which moves the story forward through a series of crises to the climax. Each act, in turn, is broken up into smaller units called scenes. Each scene contains physical actions or dialog (or both) that reveal the nature of the characters and their relationships — and that dramatize the protagonist's struggles to reach a personal goal against the opposition of an antagonist who fights to keep the protagonist from achieving that goal.

In this chapter we will discuss:

➤ **PROGRESSION:** an element intrinsic to screenplay narrative

➤ **WHAT IS AN ACT?** an examination of the essential ingredients in each of the three acts, including exposition, introduction of characters, establishment of major story problem, subplots, the creation of dramatic crises, and denouement

> **WHAT IS A SCENE?** the specific requirements and functions of scenes and of sequences, which make up a group of scenes

> **THE NATURE OF ACTION:** the telling of a story through incidents, changes in plot direction, or character revelations

> **THEME:** the underlying meaning of a screenplay; an expression of the writer's point of view

> **THE NEWSPAPER ITEM REVISITED:** continuing the development of a newspaper item into a screenplay story

> **WRITER REVELATIONS:** personal techniques for plotting and structuring screenplays as described by award-winning writer Paddy Chayefsky

*P*ROGRESSION

In Chapter 1 we described "a person with a problem" as the basis for screenplay drama. We determined that the person, usually called a protagonist, involves an audience emotionally. The problem arises when a formidable adversary fights to keep the protagonist from reaching his or her goal.

Screenplays traditionally build and grow, increasing in tension, raising the stakes from **fade-in** (the beginning) to **fade-out** (the end). We will call this building action **progression**, which is often represented graphically as a jagged fork of lightning (see Figure 3.1). Progression is so intrinsic to screenplay drama that it is an essential ingredient of each act, each scene, and even the construction of major speeches within a scene.

Here is an example of progression: A sympathetic young businesswoman tries to prove that she is not guilty of stealing from her employer. The first act might end with the discovery of stolen merchandise in her bedroom closet, planted there without her knowledge. Act two might end with witnesses coming forward and "reluctantly" admitting that they saw her stealing, positively identifying her as the thief. The act-three climax might dramatize her imminent conviction in court. In this sample plot line, each **crisis** is more damning than the one before, creating growth, an overall progression in tension.

After the third-act crisis, the climax of the show, a **denouement** (French for "untying"), or "falling action," occurs, allowing story elements to settle and thus providing the viewer with a sense of fulfillment: Equilibrium has been restored. In television, these denouements are sometimes called "**tag scenes.**"

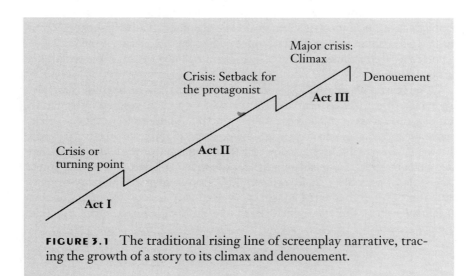

FIGURE 3.1 The traditional rising line of screenplay narrative, tracing the growth of a story to its climax and denouement.

Screenplay progression implies forward movement, that is, new events, new complications, or new revelations that heighten audience interest. Because children are more impatient than adults, their movies or TV programs usually accelerate rapidly. (Think of Saturday morning kids' cartoons; they are filled with exciting incidents, continually climbing to higher and higher peaks of suspense.) When action becomes static — that is, when a screenplay's rising line flattens out or when writers stray far from the main plot line — even the most indulgent adults tend to become restless.

Sometimes writers rearrange the linear progression of their stories. They may begin their screenplay at a crucial point (perhaps the first- or second-act curtain) and then "flash back" to the beginning. Such a construction is usually for the purpose of "hooking" an audience, compelling their attention through some threat to the protagonist. Once hooked, the audience will now stay around to watch developments as they build to the crucial point. In this pattern, a story has a traditional beginning, middle, and end, but their order has been rearranged.

Flashback patterns were once extremely popular in Hollywood films. *Citizen Kane*, for example, unfolds its story through the reminiscences of four people who have been close to Kane. As each relates his or her story to a newsreel interviewer, the picture dissolves to some point in Kane's life and then dramatizes a series of significant events. Together, the four interviews form a composite portrait of the celebrated newspaper publisher. When created by sensitive writers, flashbacks can occasionally be effective, as demonstrated in such motion pictures as *Citizen Kane*, *Midnight Cowboy*, and *Annie Hall*. Most flashbacks are subjective; that is, they are colored by memory. If Joe Carter had a miserable childhood, for example, that misery will alter the nature of his memories. Audiences cannot accept his recollections of childhood as factual, therefore, because emotion has reshaped them.

Beginning writers too frequently believe that flashbacks give their scripts sophistication, a kind of instant professionalism. In truth, flashbacks often make a screenplay appear old fashioned. They seem contrived; the audience becomes aware of the writer's presence, bending and twisting time to suit his or her whims.

One reason why flashbacks undercut screenplays is that beginning writers frequently use them as crutches, as ways of getting necessary information (exposition) across to an audience. When a writer, for example, needs to explain that a character grew up with frightened, clutching, overprotective parents, the writer drops a flashback scene or two into the script to demonstrate that fact. Such usage makes flashbacks little more than explanatory program notes. Unless flashbacks carry their own weight — that is, advance the story or generate their own excitement — most experienced writers avoid them, preferring to tell their stories in a straightforward, chronological progression, building from act to act.

The term *progression* also applies to character change or character growth, sometimes called a character **arc**. When you create pressures for your protagonist — as well-written screenplays inevitably do — he or she will undergo some degree of character change. Thelma in *Thelma and Louise* changes significantly during the course of that film. In the beginning she is submissive, dependent, a timid field mouse frightened of her husband and acutely lacking in confidence. After near rape, a harrowing police chase, and a brief sexual encounter, she becomes an independent, assertive adult, capable of robbing to survive and doing battle with the entire male sex.

The protagonists in most films mature. When writers place them in emotional vises, they change for the better or worse. If characters do *not* change after experiencing major story pressures, it is likely that the writer hasn't taken the time to understand them sufficiently.*

$\mathcal{W}$HAT IS AN ACT?

Most hour-long television shows are divided into four parts called **acts**, each separated from the others by commercials or a station break. Such a division is frequently arbitrary rather than organic; the breaks are determined primarily by financial needs. Modern stageplays divide into two or three acts separated by a curtain or intermission. Motion pictures also (perhaps surprisingly) usually divide structurally into three acts although, of course, no commercials or station breaks separate the acts.

Each act contains an indeterminate number of scenes and builds to its own dramatic climax. In a three-act pattern, the climax of the second act reaches a higher tension level than the first; the third act reaches a higher tension level than the second, thus becoming the climax of the entire screenplay. Each act helps the story progress. Each act differs in function and components from each of the others.

ACT ONE

Sometimes I ask my writing classes which act they think is the most difficult to construct. They usually guess the third. In fact, the first act is the most difficult, if only because it must perform the greatest number of functions. These include establishing the primary story problem, introducing all major characters, and presenting most of the story's exposition.

*Character progression is explored in greater detail in Chapter 5.

The Primary Problem.   A television executive for whom I once worked describes a strange little man, bearded and dressed in black, who walks onstage in the first act of every screenplay. He carries a round black bomb with a fuse on top, the kind you have seen in political cartoons. He gently places the bomb on the floor, lights a match, sets the fuse sputtering, and then hurries offstage. The bomb, of course, represents your major story problem. Before the little man appears, the audience is free to change channels or leave the theater. But once the fuse has been lit, the audience will sit glued to its seat, awaiting the explosion it knows will come.

Audiences will give you only so much time to light the fuse. Motion picture audiences have parked their cars, paid their admissions, and bought popcorn; they are, therefore, more patient than television viewers. Most movies establish their problems within the first ten minutes (approximately ten script pages). Most television viewers hold in their hands a device that instantly changes channels, thereby sending your show to oblivion. Accordingly, most TV dramas establish the problem earlier, usually in the first three or four minutes.

Sometimes it may be difficult to establish a major story problem early in the act. Sometimes an understanding of the problem depends on knowledge of character relationships or plot circumstances that require time to establish. Frequently, the major story problem cannot be established until the very end of act one.

When this is the case, writers dare not risk losing their audiences. If story problems cannot be established early, writers use other devices to seduce audiences into staying around. Because audiences need to worry, writers may provide another, smaller problem that will hold their attention until the major problem can be launched. Once the major problem has been introduced, writers are then free to resolve the smaller one, usually early in the second act.

Sometimes just the knowledge that a problem exists is enough to hold an audience, without its knowing the exact nature of the problem. For instance, the protagonist's best friend begins to act strangely, does odd, inexplicable things. When your protagonist asks what's wrong, his best friend, obviously lying, stammers that everything is fine. We don't know the nature of the problem, but we know that one exists and will, therefore, stay around to await developments.

A bizarre action by your protagonist's friend might be labeled an **inciting incident**, usually a dramatic event that triggers the story to come, that promises problems, that sets in motion the forces that will involve your protagonist in a gathering storm. An inciting incident usually occurs within a screenplay's first ten pages. In *Witness*, a young Amish boy witnesses a killing in a men's room. In *Casablanca*, Ilsa shows up at Rick's Café Americain. In *North by Northwest*, Cary Grant is seized by an international spy ring.

Certain highly entertaining elements will also attract audiences, almost compelling them to watch. Audiences love to laugh. If you sprinkle your early screenplay moments with humor, the audience will be entertained and stick around. Audiences love the male-female relationship. They will watch courtship or mating rituals for a surprisingly long time, until you can establish a more durable story "hook" to hold them. And they enjoy spectacle. Inclusion of these intriguing elements will make it difficult for audiences to leave you. (For a discussion of these and other entertainment elements, see Chapter 9.)

The Major Characters.   Traditionally, all major characters are established in the first act. As we discussed in Chapter 2, screenplay drama builds on itself; act three derives from elements established in the first two acts. Act two builds on elements established in act one. Since act one becomes the base of the pyramid, providing a foundation for the rest of the narrative structure, it is essential to establish all major story elements early.

To avoid confusing audiences, introduce characters slowly, a few at a time. We have all read mystery stories in which we meet a dozen colorful characters in the first few pages, all of whom had reason to commit the crime. Our heads swim as we try to remember who is related to whom, what their motives are, their alibis, and their activities at the time of the murder.

Meet Lord Chalmley Biddiscombe, who had been in love with the murdered man's mother and who some people suspect is actually his *father*. Meet attractive Agatha Threadneedle, apparently a cleaning woman but actually the murdered man's fiancée, who was in the mansion at the time of the murder and was caught concealing the murder weapon. Meet Fenwick Strothers, a geology professor who's secretly in love with Agatha and therefore bitterly jealous of the murdered man. Meet Elaine Fensterwald, the murdered man's sister, a lesbian who's in love with Agatha Threadneedle and angry at her brother for inheriting her share of their parents' estate. Meet Barnaby Greco, who announces he's from Scotland Yard but who turns out to be an imposter, a mild little man who's actually the brother of Lord Chalmley Biddiscombe. Meet white-haired Lorene Greystoke, composer, musician, owner of the mansion in which the killing took place and secretly in love with. . . .

But that's enough. By now you understand the dangers of introducing too many characters too quickly. Without rereading the paragraph, can you remember who Fenwick Strothers is?

A good rule of thumb is, when introducing characters, go from the known to the unknown. In scene one, we meet Mike and Ellen. In scene two, Ellen leads us to new characters, perhaps Mike's parents. In scene three, Mike plays a scene with two fellow musicians. After three scenes, we have met six characters, yet there is little likelihood of confusion because we have met them slowly. Were we to introduce all six characters in the first scene, we would put a strain on our audience. In **ensemble films** featuring multiple protagonists, such as *The Big Chill* or *The Breakfast Club*, the writer always is careful to introduce characters one or two at a time.

Exposition.   When audiences watch a movie or TV program, they suddenly encounter new faces, new relationships, new problems, new locales. Inevitably, they try to find out who these characters are and what the show is all about.

One of a writer's continuing problems is to provide the audience with information, to tell them unobtrusively all the facts they need to know. Such information is labeled **exposition**. Although some information is revealed throughout a play, most of it is usually presented in the first act. Mystery stories (whodunits) provide an exception to this pattern. In whodunits, great chunks of background information are presented in every act, with a massive description of who, why, when, and where at the ending.

By the time writers are ready to begin a screenplay, they have thought long and hard about their characters' physical world, their relationships, backgrounds, goals, and problems. Some writers compose dozens of pages of backstory just for themselves, to provide a comfortable familiarity with their primary characters. Most of this material will never appear in the screenplay. Writers provide audiences only with information they *need* to know to understand the story. (Note that I emphasize the word *need*.)

Sometimes writers reveal their exposition visually. When a sequence begins with a shot of a large, modern building and the camera zooms in to a sign that reads "County Hospital," the writer is presenting necessary information. When a man walks into a room wearing a police uniform, we don't have to explain to anyone what his profession is. When an executive displays framed pictures on his desk, the objects tell us more than the fact that he has a wife and kids. Their prominent display tells us either that he is genuinely proud of them — or that he's trying to present a solid family-man image to his colleagues.

Writers often present essential story information in dialog. When someone introduces a character by saying "I want you to meet my sister," the writer has defined a relationship. When a wife asks her husband why he hasn't eaten his dinner and he tells her of work problems, he's also informing the audience. Skilled writers manage to convey essential information by slipping it gracefully into the dialog, a word or two at a time, without audiences realizing that they are being spoon-fed.

Inexperienced writers sometimes allow characters to explain things to each other, presenting information that both already know. Audiences quickly realize that such blatant exposition sounds false or dishonest, often without knowing why.

Stories that require a lot of background information force writers to dig deep into their bag of tricks. Oscar-winning screenwriter Ernest Lehman describes a couple of useful techniques.

> One of the tricks is to have the exposition conveyed in a scene of conflict, so that a character is forced to say things you want the audience to know — as, for example, if he is defending himself against somebody's attack, his words of defense seem justified even though his

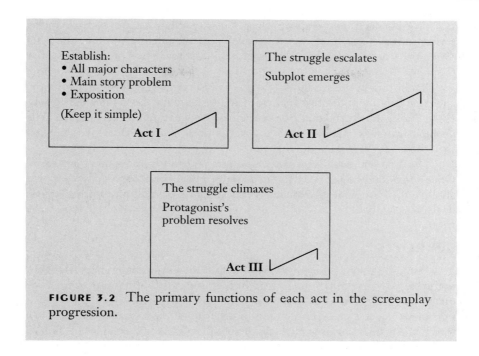

FIGURE 3.2 The primary functions of each act in the screenplay progression.

words are actually *expository* words. Something appears to be happening, so the audience believes it is witnessing a *scene* (which it is), not listening to expository speeches. . . . Conflict is an excellent device for conveying exposition. Humor is another way of getting it across.*

A final note about the first act: Keep it simple. When audiences watch a movie or TV show, they must absorb a lot of information relating to characters, relationships, goals, and problems. Make it easy for them. Don't make your structure too complicated or introduce too many elements too quickly. Audiences will be grateful. And they'll stick around. (See Figure 3.2.)

ACT TWO

Writer Syd Field calls the second act of a screenplay "confrontation."† Here the protagonist and antagonist square off, clashing with each other in action, intention, or reaction.

---

*John Brady, ed., *The Craft of the Screenwriter* (New York: Simon & Schuster, 1981), pp. 182–83.

†Syd Field, *Screenplay* (New York: Dell, 1979), pp. 9–10.

The first act usually ends on a crucial note, perhaps a major setback for the protagonist as he or she strives to achieve a goal or a turning point in the story's direction. Occasionally the act ends with the first revelation of the major story problem.

Traditionally, the second act begins at a lower level of tension, giving the audience a moment to catch its breath and prepare for the greater tensions to come. Now, slowly, the **conflict** intensifies. New complications develop. The problem worsens. Action builds to a crisis point higher in dramatic tension than the crisis that ended the first act.

The first act establishes the characters and the primary story problem. Once the audience has been hooked (we've given them something to worry about!), we have time to embark on subplots or parallel plots, which often develop in act two.

SUBPLOTS

The "sub" here stands for *subordinate*. A **subplot** is a secondary story tangent that interweaves with the main story line. It is usually built around one of the major characters. As you know, the main story line concerns a protagonist fighting to reach a goal. The subplot is often a new story that develops out of that pattern, that surfaces after the main story has been established. Sometimes, especially in half-hour TV shows, there's time for only a single subplot. But in feature films, which run approximately four times as long, there usually are several.

Example: Two women flee from the police (main plot). Along the way, one of them has an affair with a drifter who robs her of her money (subplot).

Example: A famous author is held captive by a psychotic woman (main plot). A rural police chief tries to find him (subplot).

Example: A young man, slain by an assassin, tries to make contact with his beloved fiancée (main plot). A close business associate threatens his fiancée to find secret computer codes (subplot).

You will recognize the first example as *Thelma and Louise*, the second as *Misery*, and the third as *Ghost*.

In most cases, subplot characters are introduced in act one and their story ripens in act two. (See Figure 3.3.) In *Witness*, for example, the love story between a peace-loving Amish woman and a violence-prone police lieutenant grows out of an initial plot development in which her son witnesses a killing. During the film's "second act," the love story moves center stage and the melodrama recedes to the background. In the third act, the melodrama again boils up and becomes the film's climactic action. The love story resolves in the denouement.

A rare exception to the usual pattern of a subplot arising from first act elements is *The Graduate*. Here the film *begins* with the subplot. Ben has an affair with Mrs. Robinson (first act) and later falls in love with her daughter

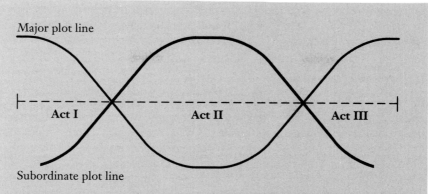

Major plot line

Act I   Act II   Act III

Subordinate plot line

FIGURE 3.3 A typical screenplay structure that establishes the major plot line in the first act. The subordinate story (and there may be several) emerges in the second act. The major story is kept alive during the second act but maintains a background position. It moves to the foreground and resolves in the third act.

(second and third acts). The primary plot (Ben's) doesn't begin until a third of the way into the screenplay!

How can you tell which is the subplot and which is the main one? The main plot almost always involves a protagonist struggling to reach a goal (where have you heard this before?) with an antagonist fighting to keep him or her from getting there. In *The Graduate*, Ben's struggle to win Elaine's love clearly follows this basic pattern with her mother fighting to keep the two apart. In the first act subplot, a directionless Ben is manipulated by Mrs. Robinson. It isn't until he meets Elaine that he acquires a real sense of direction. Now, for the first time, he has a goal. Now, for the first time, he becomes a proper protagonist. As a matter of fact, it is difficult for audiences to identify strongly with Ben in the first act simply because he drifts aimlessly; it is the humor of his relationship with Mrs. Robinson that compels audience attention.

Because a plot gambit is labeled "sub" does not necessarily mean that it is inferior in quality to the main story line. Often it contains more emotion or originality than the primary plot. For example, it is Ben Braddock's affair with Mrs. Robinson that most people remember from *The Graduate*. And the love affair in *Witness* is remembered long after the melodramatic police story has been forgotten.

Many writers believe that a subplot should maintain a thematic relationship with the primary plot. For example, if the primary plot concerns man's fight against new technologies, the subplot might deal with woman's emerging role in the business community. Both plot and subplot relate to the theme "The old gives way to the new." Subplots sometimes conclude before the resolution of the primary story line, sometimes simultaneously, and sometimes (as in *Witness*) immediately after.

PARALLEL PLOTS

As television has developed, its storytelling has become more complex. An audience watching a half-hour show that contains two or three simultaneous story lines feels it's getting more for its money than with a show containing only a single plot. The complexity adds texture and seems to be a more sophisticated way of developing a script. More importantly, with two or three story lines the audience cannot become bored; every time events get dull, the producer can revive interest by cutting to a parallel plot. It's a little like a three-ring circus. When you get tired of activities in one ring, you can always watch another.

These **parallel plots** are sometimes referred to as story line "A" or story line "B." The "A" line is usually the major plot involving the TV series star. The "B" line may involve one or more of the subordinate characters. The series "Cheers" almost always has two story lines. So does the Cosby show. When "The Love Boat" was on television, several writers created story lines involving totally different sets of characters (other than continuing members of the ship's company) and their stories were then edited together into a single show to indicate that the stories were developing simultaneously.

Writers of TV police shows often structure their programs with parallel plots. The criminals escape from (or plan) a caper; the police seek them out or try to prevent their committing a crime. The writer now becomes a juggler, trying to keep both stories in constant motion. Imagine the plot lines as locomotive engines chugging forward on two parallel railroad tracks. The writer cuts back and forth between them, a process that is highly dynamic because the energy of such a structure seems to propel the story forward. Parallel cutting sometimes implies that both plots are taking place simultaneously, or it can allow audiences to assume a passage of time as, for example, when cutting from a day sequence in plot line "A" to a night scene in plot line "B." In *Thelma and Louise*, the film cuts back and forth between Thelma having an affair with a drifter in one motel room and Louise having a serious conversation with her lover in another, a perfect example of cutting between parallel plots to suggest simultaneity. Parallel cutting gained prominence in pioneer director David Wark Griffith's *The Lonely Villa*, *Birth of a Nation*, and other silent films.

A parallel plot is really just another name for a subplot except that it is usually structured to develop simultaneously, side by side with the main story line.

ACT THREE

The third act, like the second, usually begins at a lower level of tension than that generated by the preceding crisis. The audience has a moment to collect its wits and shake off accumulated nervous energy, a moment similar to the pause on a roller coaster ride before the downhill plunge. In many of Hitchcock's films, the writers used humor after crisis points to provide audiences with just such an escape valve.

Also like the second act, the third builds through a series of struggles to a major crisis, which constitutes the show's climax, the moment of greatest audience suspense in which the protagonist either achieves his or her goal — or doesn't.

After the climax, most writers create a denouement, a final resolution of story elements. Often upbeat in nature, this final action provides audiences with a feeling of completion, of satisfaction. For example, after the police lieutenant (the protagonist) has apprehended the murderer, he finally tells off his overbearing superior and quits the police force. Even when protagonists fail to achieve their goals, denouement scenes often imply that something positive has been accomplished, that the trip has been worth taking.

Acts are made up of smaller dramatic units, called *scenes*, and of *sequences*. No specific number of scenes or sequences constitutes an act.

$\mathcal{W}$HAT IS A SCENE?

A robber breaks into a Beverly Hills mansion. A young man tells a woman that he wants to end their relationship. A Jewish surgeon operates on a former Nazi. A murderer confesses his crime.

Each of these is a dramatic *scene*, defined here as a single event or interchange between characters, having a unity of time or place. When a robber sneaks up to the mansion, snips the wires of the alarm system, and climbs over the wall, such action constitutes an *event*. When police officers relentlessly question a murderer and force his confession, such dialog constitutes an *interchange between characters*. Note that both scenes happen in a single location and within a single time frame.

Let's assume that when the police officers question the murderer, he remains stubbornly silent. The picture dissolves to the same location hours later, and the weary murderer finally confesses. Even though the same characters are continuing the same conversation in the same locale, the second interchange becomes a new scene because time has passed.

Let's assume that the officers fail to get a confession. They walk their prisoner to the captain's office. The moment the officers and murderer leave the interrogation room and enter the corridor, a new scene begins because the locale has changed.

DEVELOPING A SCENE

Writers often skip tedious story mechanics. Watching the officers and murderer walk down a long corridor to the captain's office, for example, would bore audiences; it would consume thirty seconds and would contribute nothing dramatically (unless, of course, the prisoner tried to escape!). Therefore, most writers would simply cut ahead to the captain's office as the group enters. Audiences would never miss the tedious walk down the corridor. Writers don't always have to show how characters get from here to there. Cutting ahead to the next significant action constitutes streamlined storytelling and propels a story forward.

Writers can eliminate tedious material in other ways. Many begin a scene at the latest possible moment, eliminating dull introductory material by beginning with subject matter that is most relevant to the plot. Sometimes writers conclude a scene in the middle, cutting to new material (another scene) once they have dramatized significant story points.

Scenes can run as long or as short as the story requires. It would take a page or less to describe a burglar snipping alarm wires and climbing over a wall. Police officers grilling a murder suspect, on the other hand, might consume three or four pages. A scene can play in just one-eighth of a page; for instance, a flash cut of a stabbing in a dark alley. Or it can run nine pages, if the tension sustains. Because audiences have been conditioned (probably by television) to stories that develop quickly, most scenes today seldom run longer than two or three pages (two or three minutes).

Remember: Every scene in a script should advance the story in some way. Each scene should either add some new plot development, reveal significant new information, or, where essential or relevant, contribute to the story's mood or atmosphere. If the scene does none of these, get rid of it.

ADDING TENSION TO SCENES

If scenes play placidly and resolve easily, they usually lack conflict and audiences lose interest. Once writers create obstacles that make it difficult for characters to reach their goals, audience attention picks up.

I once watched a circus performer precariously balance two chairs, a table, an umbrella stand, a vase, a silver tray, and a small stepladder, one atop the other. Then he attempted to climb the teetering structure. When halfway to the top, it collapsed and he tumbled to the ground. Painstakingly, he balanced the elements and again attempted to climb. This time he almost reached the top. Just as he started up the small ladder, the structure wobbled and crashed to the ground. Everyone groaned. The performer looked at the crowd. Should he try again? They applauded loudly.

Now, very slowly and carefully, he rebuilt his strange structure and began his ascent. Once the structure started to teeter. The crowd held its breath. But the structure steadied, and the performer moved on to the very top, where he stood on his hands, high in the air. The crowd screamed its approval.

It occurred to me on the way home that the performer probably could have climbed successfully to the top on his first try. If he had, the feat would not have appeared nearly as difficult, and the audience would not have experienced such suspense or excitement. If he had achieved his goal quickly and easily, the act would have been routine, mediocre at best. Instead, he used showmanship.

The big lesson here for all aspiring scriptwriters is that audiences need to worry. When protagonists reach their goals easily, scenes become dull, flabby, lacking in suspense. Suppose a young woman, Sharon, confronts her boyfriend after work and tells him she is pregnant. He smiles, delighted. Such a scene is neither exciting nor suspenseful.

If Sharon is nervous to begin with and then is repeatedly *prevented* from reciting her news, the scene will create suspense. If we as writers invent *obstacles* that make it *difficult* for her to tell her story, then we will involve our audience. Remember: To create obstacles, we can play scenes anywhere we want, add characters, or change circumstances. We have total control.

Suppose we stage the scene at a playground with dozens of dirty kids hollering loudly as they play. Sharon starts to tell her boyfriend the news, but the youngsters make so much noise that it's difficult to talk. Now an obnoxious little boy spills ice cream all over the boyfriend's trousers. And the boyfriend (who has just lost his job) goes into an angry tirade about how much he hates kids. Now we've made it difficult, almost impossible for our protagonist to reach her goal. Aware of her need, the audience will agonize at the obstacles she encounters. The fear that she may not succeed will compel them to watch. Making the audience worry — that's what screenplays are all about.

REFINING SCENE CONTENT

Don't be in a hurry. Before you write any scene, take a few minutes to think about it, to examine its subject matter. Where will you play the scene? Will the locale add dramatic value or will it detract? What additional values (such as other characters, special circumstances, atmosphere, conflicts) can you bring to the scene that will increase its color or interest?

Try to visualize the action as you write your scene. What does the locale look like? How will your characters relate to that locale? What specific actions will they take during the scene? In real life, people seldom stand in the center of a room addressing each other. Usually, they busy themselves with such routine day-to-day activities as eating or drinking, leafing through a newspaper, polishing their fingernails, or cooking dinner. Such activities bring an appearance of reality to your scene. And physical actions help prevent a scene from becoming static.

Ask yourself what your characters were doing immediately prior to the scene. Those earlier activities will affect their wardrobes — and perhaps their attitudes. For example, if a woman just had a fight with her boss, she would probably begin the next scene in a foul mood.

What was the relationship between your characters the last time we saw them? Has anything happened since that would change their relationship? Do emotional values lie beneath the surface, values that never appear in dialog? If so, how will you reveal them?

Good writers are also good actors. As they put words on paper, they immerse themselves in their scenes, imagining that they are one of the characters, experiencing that character's emotions, and determining what they would say or do in that specific situation. Such involvement sometimes includes pacing angrily, pounding on tables, laughing, shouting, or crying, actions that occasionally cause roommates to seek other quarters.

Good writers also search for the small, specific details that bring a scene to life — details of action, physical appearance, costume, and scenery. Surprisingly, such details often can be more effective in achieving believability than actions or speeches. This is especially true when stories (such as westerns or fantasy and science fiction) stray far from today's reality. In these cases, accuracy of detail helps viewers accept the setting and believe the story. Research on the topic can be invaluable in providing such detail.

Many beginning writers include a lot of telephone conversations in their scripts, partly because telephones are significant in our lives and partly because it's a convenient way to initiate conversations. Directors tend to photograph such scenes in individual **close-ups** or in a split screen. As a result, phone conversations are usually static, lacking movement, and sterile because the characters cannot physically interact. They cannot hug, touch, kiss, or strike each other. There are no movements that can provide viewers with clues to relationships (as, for example, when a husband turns his back on his wife and moves away from her). A caution: When you *must* use telephone conversations, keep them short. If the conversation has real significance, find a way to play it in person, not with your characters separated by miles of telephone wire.

Remember that every scene has a purpose, a direction, a destination, a goal. Something must be accomplished by the scene, otherwise you wouldn't have included it in your script. If that goal is accomplished easily, your scene will be unsatisfying. But if you use showmanship — if, like the circus performer, you can rig circumstances to make it appear *difficult* for a character to achieve a goal — your scene will involve audiences and build genuine **suspense**.

SEQUENCING SCENES

When screenwriters create stories, they sometimes think in terms of blocks of action rather than individual scenes. Such units, called **sequences**, consist of a group of scenes tied together by a single story purpose or direction. Sequences accomplish a larger sweep of action than may be achieved in a specific scene. For example, in *Robin Hood*, when the remainder of Kevin Costner's brave little band starts to infiltrate the Sheriff of Nottingham's castle, the action is dramatized in a series of cuts to individual members assuming new identities, moving past guards, taking positions on castle walls, placing a barrel of gunpowder in position, and so on. The total action takes several minutes. The sequence could be labeled "infiltrating the castle." When you can label a series of actions, you can be confident that all of the bits and pieces (short scenes) have a single, unifying purpose and constitute a true sequence.

$\mathcal{D}$RAMATIC ACTION

We saw earlier that each act consists of a series of narrative actions. The term **action** does not refer only to physical movement. It isn't always depicted in terms of car chases, fistfights, and gun battles. **Narrative action** often is internal, consisting of emotional or intellectual change within a character or personal decisions that alter the direction of a story. For example, when a young white man from a bigoted southern family falls in love with a college classmate, a young black woman, the emotional development simultaneously advances the plot and promises major problems. The simple act of falling in love thus represents powerful narrative action. When his family threatens to disown him if he marries the young woman — and he swallows hard and promises never to see her again — his decision also qualifies as action. Something has happened. The plot has advanced. Its direction has changed.

New revelations also qualify as narrative action. If, for example, we learn at the end of the second act that the young man's grandfather was half black, a fact that the young man's parents have concealed, that discovery (in reality, exposition) constitutes strong narrative action.

One of the most significant functions of action is that it defines characters. What characters *do* tells us what they *are*. Some authors go so far as to state that character *is* action; action *is* character. When a woman tells her fiancé that she wants to call off their marriage, his response — his *actions* — tell us more about him than a dozen lines of dialog. Does he strike her? Does he threaten? Does he whimper and plead? Does he turn silently and walk out the door? Since characters sometimes say what suits their purpose, stretching truth when necessary, dialog cannot always be trusted. The actions taken by characters provide a far more accurate indication of their true nature. (See Chapter 5.)

Remember that every action creates a corresponding reaction. The reaction, in turn, becomes a new initiating action, evoking a further reaction. For example, when Sigourney Weaver in *Aliens* destroys eggs laid by the monstrous alien queen, she evokes the queen's anger. The queen's reaction is to attack, pursuing Weaver into the space vehicle. Weaver reacts by climbing into a metallic loading device from which she attacks the queen.

Similarly, in *Robin Hood* each thrust by the outlaw's band against the Sheriff of Nottingham prompts a counterthrust by the sheriff. In turn, each counterthrust by the sheriff prompts a new response by Robin Hood, and so on, creating a pattern of action/reaction/action, which forms the structural basis of most screenplays.

*T*HEME

Some writers ignore theme. Others dwell on it. Some call it by its rightful name. Others call it a message, a moral, a root idea, a personal statement, or a question about life.

What is a **theme**? All of the above. It is the underlying *meaning* of a play, the message communicated to audiences not through the speeches of its characters but by its action and content. It is the play's **subtext** realized by the audience in retrospect, perhaps consciously, perhaps subconsciously.

Most TV police or private eye shows convey the theme "Crime does not pay." The movie *Star Wars* tells us that "Good destroys evil." Some parents and PTA groups worry that motion picture and TV programming instill in children the theme "Violence solves all problems." For example, the resolutions to many police or private eye shows often depend on who fights the hardest or shoots the straightest, the protagonist or the bad guy.

Writers seldom if ever begin a project with a theme. Few sit down at a typewriter in creative excitement, thinking, "I've got it! I'll do a story that states 'Pride goeth before a fall!'" Writers usually begin a project with an idea, not a theme. They find a fascinating character relationship or colorful incident with which to begin their plotting. Themes emerge later, sometimes not until a screenplay has been completed. Stories totally lacking in themes, however, usually are shallow or formless.

Some writers never become aware of their themes. If screenplays can be written without the writer's awareness of their themes, what is their value? Why do authors waste pages discussing them? Because awareness of themes can be helpful to writers and can improve screenplay quality enormously.

This is the way it happens: You are developing your story, perhaps in the treatment stage, perhaps in the screenplay. You probably haven't given a thought to your story's theme. Somewhere along the line, you gradually become aware of the statement that your story is making. Because you feel strongly about your subject matter (and it's important that you do!), you're expressing a point of view — an attitude, a vision, a moral position — in your script. Because you're emotionally involved, because you care, it's inevitable that you will make a personal statement in your characters, in their scenes, and in their dialog.

Once you become aware of this statement (your theme), you will reexamine your screenplay to make certain that all its elements conform logically and honestly. If a character acts in ways that violate your theme, change the action — or eliminate the character. If a scene contradicts your point of view, junk it. Such a procedure ensures that your screenplay has unity, consistency, and strength.

Finally, remember that your statement emerges from the actions of your characters, not their dialog. Your characters don't know or care what your theme is. All they want is to reach their goals and wage their battles. So they're not going to discuss your story's theme for you. That would be dishonest. Your theme must emerge from the subtext — for the audience to think about as they turn off their TV sets or leave the movie theater.

Continuing our
Story construction

In Chapters 1 and 2, we started to develop a screenplay story from the following newspaper item:

Murder Charge Against Boy, 11, Is Thrown Out
By LORI GRANGE
TIMES STAFF WRITER

A judge Friday threw out charges against an 11-year-old Anaheim boy accused of helping his mother kill his grandmother, despite a prosecutor's argument that the youth was a clever assassin's apprentice acting out of hatred.

After two days of testimony, Pasadena Juvenile Court Judge Sandy Kriegler dismissed the claim that the youth had aided his mother, Victoria Elizabeth Jacobs Madeira, in the Oct. 14 stabbing and shooting of Roma Jaul Jacobs at her La Canada Flintridge home.

The youth was believed to be the state's youngest murder defendant since 1981.

In Chapter 2 we created a rough structure for our story. We dreamed a little (right brain) and studied its structure (left brain), and now we can try to fill in a few blanks so as to visualize an overall pattern.

First in importance is determining why Marty would shoot his grandmother and still somehow retain our sympathy. It's time to face this knotty problem. In Chapter 2, we felt that he might shoot his grandmother because of her cruelty to his mother. Let's examine that. In what ways would the old woman be cruel? Well, money seems the most likely. Many older people become insecure about money as the years advance.

Grandmother's withholding money from Lynn would be more logical, wouldn't it, if the old woman were not Lynn's mother but rather the mother of Lynn's deceased husband? Perhaps Grandma Millie felt that her son should never have married Lynn, which also explains her reluctance to solve Lynn's financial needs.

But we need an inciting incident, don't we, something that would motivate the shooting. It would be ideal if we could make Marty feel responsible for this inciting incident so that he would bear the responsibility as Man of the House of solving his mother's money problems — or at least of trying to.

Scanning the newspapers again we read of senseless drive-by shootings, always apparently gang related. What if — what if someone in our story is wounded in a drive-by shooting and urgently needs expensive medical care? Could it be Marty? No, we need him to shoot the old woman. Lynn? If she's disabled in a hospital bed, she won't be an active protagonist. Maybe we need to invent another character. Perhaps Marty has a younger brother. Let's call the little guy Rick. He's critically injured in a drive-by shooting. But how could Marty feel any kind of responsibility for such an incident? Responsibility and guilt would help to redeem him and might explain his willingness to take a gun to Grandma Millie's house, an almost inexcusable action.

What if Marty started to join a gang or actually joined? His mother angrily protested. Marty respected her wishes and withdrew. The drive-by shooting may or may not be a result of Marty's defection from the gang, but the important thing is that he *feels* it's his fault. We may need to change Marty's age now. Let's make him thirteen. Rick would be nine or ten.

The gun is Lynn's. Marty takes it from her nightstand. His goal: to threaten the old woman, to get her to write the check that will pay for Rick's mounting hospital bills. Perhaps Grandma Millie keeps a stash of cash in the safe in her home. Marty has seen the bundles of bills once or twice. He wants $5,000 but Grandmother won't give it to him. She starts to call the police, Marty rushes to stop her, and the gun goes off. We'll have to stage that action carefully.

Lying on the grass and staring up at the blue sky has paid off. We now have a more substantial background for the killing. In any mystery story, the backstory must be rock solid since it provides the foundation for the entire plot structure.

But wait. Let's stop and consider. Should we tell this as a mystery story, keeping the audience guessing until the third act? Or should we open it up, letting the audience in on the story's development? My hunch is that we can build more emotional involvement if we open it up. We lose the puzzle element but we gain far more in emotional involvement. In addition, by telling the story more or less in sequence, we avoid the awkwardness and difficulty of having to reveal reams of backstory. Huge blocks of exposition are always a problem. Are you with me? We'll tell our story starting from the beginning . . . from just before the drive-by shooting.

How does that affect our structure? Well, our first act could end now with the killing of Grandma Millie. We'll play the shooting onstage rather than off. (We have to really hate this miserable old woman; otherwise we'll end up hating Marty!)

Marty would be apprehended by police in act two, and maybe we could end act two with Lynn's "confession." I wonder if we will need her brother Phil, whom we added earlier as a red herring, to create another murder suspect. Let's put Phil on the back burner. We can always call him into action if we need him.

In the third act, Marty will come forward to clear his mother, and a jury will find that Grandma Millie's death was accidental but will give Marty a nominal sentence for carrying a gun with intent to do bodily harm. (We must research the legalities with a lawyer.) Brother Rick recovers during act three, and the relationship between Lynn and police detective Brent seems to be flowering as our story concludes.

Enough. The overall pattern seems clear. With this material, we could now sit down and write a treatment. We'll add some finishing touches in Chapters 4 and 5.

CHAPTER HIGHLIGHTS

➤ Most screenplays divide into three acts. In each, tension grows, and each crisis is more threatening to the protagonist than the one before. Such growth, called progression, is intrinsic to screenplays and manifests itself in scenes, acts, and even in individual speeches.

➤ Writers construct most motion pictures and some TV plays in a traditional three-act pattern. The first two acts end in crises; the third resolves the story.

➤ The first act performs three necessary functions: (1) It establishes the basic story problem; (2) it introduces all major characters; (3) it presents most of a story's exposition (information an audience needs to understand the story). Because audiences have much to assimilate, first acts should be simple.

➤ The second act develops a series of struggles or confrontations between protagonist and antagonist, building to a crisis greater than the crisis that ended act one. Subplots or parallel plots often begin in the second act.

➤ The third act builds to the story's highest point of tension and then resolves, with the protagonist either achieving his or her goal or failing. The falling action after the climax is called the denouement. Acts are made up of smaller units called scenes.

➤ A scene is a single event or interchange between characters with a unity of time and/or place. A scene is a screenplay's basic building block and must contribute some new character or plot development. It may be as short as one-eighth of a page or as long as tension will sustain.

➤ Each scene has a goal or purpose. When characters reach a goal quickly or easily, audience interest fades. Because audiences need to worry, writers invent obstacles to make the achievement of goals problematic.

➤ Some writers devise their screenplays through the building of sequences, defined as a series of scenes that dramatizes a larger sweep of action than is possible in a single scene.

➤ Narrative action refers not just to physical happenings but also to character changes or decisions that affect the story flow. An emotional event, such as falling in love, thus advances a story and qualifies as narrative action.

➤ A screenplay's theme is its underlying message or meaning, expressed not through dialog but through narrative action and story content. Once writers understand their themes, they may then reexamine their screenplays to make certain that all elements are consistent, ensuring coherence and unity.

$\mathcal{S}$CRIPTWRITING PROJECTS

EXERCISES DESIGNED TO
SHARPEN YOUR NARRATIVE SKILLS

THE SCENE

Select one of the following premises and develop it into a scene, two to three pages in length. Before writing the scene, think carefully about (1) the nature of your characters and their relationship, (2) obstacles that will prevent the scenes from resolving too easily, (3) what has transpired immediately preceding your scene, and (4) details of the physical setting.

Try to visualize the action as you write. Imagine that you are one of the characters. What would you say? How would you act?

Don't worry about proper script format. We'll get to that in Chapter 10. Select any comfortable format, but write your scene line by line, action by action, with as much specific detail as you feel necessary. Finally, avoid stating what your characters are thinking. For the most part, screenplays describe only what characters say and do.

1. While robbing the safe in a high-security building, the thief is discovered by an armed guard — who happens to be his brother.

2. A lawyer running for election to the U.S. Senate confronts his eighteen-year-old daughter who has been arrested on a narcotics charge.

3. A successful young architect tries to explain to her highly neurotic live-in boyfriend why she cannot accompany him to his new job in another state.

EXPOSITION

In whatever scene you select to write, include at least three items of background information concerning the characters and their relationship. Work the information into the dialog as unobtrusively as you can. If possible convey some exposition visually — through what audiences can see rather than through dialog (for example, a sign or a uniform).

*W*RITER REVELATIONS

CONSTRUCTING A STORY

*During what was called the Golden Era of television, Academy Award–winning writer Paddy Chayefsky (*Network, Hospital, Marty*) wrote a half-hour play, "Printer's Measure," that depicted the efforts of an aging print-shop compositor to fight new technologies. When the script was later published as part of an anthology (now out of print),* Chayefsky included a short essay describing the creative steps by which a writer constructs a teleplay and his own thoughts while writing "Printer's Measure." His description is by far the most insightful examination of that difficult process that I have read.*

*W*hen a writer tries to convey the sort of thinking that goes into the construction of a story, he runs into trouble. Dramatic writing is really nothing more than telling a story, and nobody ever tells a story quite like anyone else. In fact, no two writers will literally agree on what constitutes a story. There are some arbitrary rules of construction, but even these can occasionally be violated without losing your audience. I have only one rule that I consider absolute and arbitrary, and that is: A drama can have only one story. It can have only one leading character. All other stories and all other characters are used in the script only as they facilitate the main story line. . . .

Dramatic construction, as far as I am concerned, is essentially a search for reasons. That is to say, given the second-act curtain incident, construction consists of finding the reasons why the characters involved in the incident act as they do. Each reason must be dramatized by at least one scene, and the scenes must be laid out so that they inevitably grow into a crisis. Of course, this is about as elementary as you can get.

---

*Television Plays (New York: Simon & Schuster, 1955), pp. 81–88. Copyright 1955 by Paddy Chayefsky. Renewed 1983 by Susan Chayefsky. Reprinted with permission of Susan Chayefsky.

The construction of a drama, like every other aspect of writing, never follows any precise line of logic. The writer frequently starts off on a drama with no idea of the crisis; he may have a character he wants to write about or a setting that has impressed him. Then he has to sit down and slowly work out the dramatic significance of his character or setting. Then he has to invent a basic situation that will best dramatize this significance. Eventually, however, he has to conceive his moment of crisis; and from this point he works back, motivating his characters so that they fit honestly into this moment of crisis. Sometimes, in fact usually, the moment of crisis is lurched at rather than sensibly worked to, and much of the difficult laying-out of scenes that went before its discovery must be thrown out and a new order of scenes invented. The point is that no matter how the writer approaches the construction of his script, it always comes down to justifying his moment of crisis, and this is what I call the search for reasons.

Perhaps the best way I can indicate the fumbling logic of construction is actually to reconstruct the first act of "Printer's Measure" as if I were approaching it for the first time. Needless to say, this will be a highly distilled picture of what my thinking was. An accurate version of a writer's thoughts in the course of construction would be far too jumbled to put down in words. I only intend to suggest the few half-steps of architecture that went into the relatively simple outline.

"Printer's Measure" was based on a short story I wrote in college. It was about a boy who comes to work in a print shop. He is befriended by a rancorous old compositor. The old compositor has an immense pride in his craft, but he knocks it down continually in the eyes of the boy. When the boy leaves for a better-paying if less-rewarding job in a furrier's shop, the old compositor suddenly slaps the boy, revealing how deeply he is hurt by the boy's defection.

Well, it's not a bad story, really, even if it was written in college. It has a good character, a good emotional relationship, and even a good crisis in that relationship. That's all you need for a good drama. It even has a social significance, for the old compositor stands for the dying handicraftsman in this world of machinery. The character of the crusty old printer has charm and color, and the set is an interesting one: a little, dank print shop, stained black from years of spilled ink, musty, dense with the smell of kerosene, overcrowded, littered with piles of ems and ens — in short, my uncle's print shop.

Well, what have we got to start with? We've got the crisis, the slapping incident. It is always good to start a dramatization with a crisis if you can get one. For one thing, it promptly tells you what your basic story is and keeps you from getting confused with other story elements. The crisis is where the old man slaps the boy and the strange, rather tender friendship is ruptured. So the basic story line is the friendship between the old man and the boy. The basic story is always the emotional line of the script. Don't ever make the basic line the social comment of the script. Drama is concerned only with emotion. If your characters also carry a social value, that's fine. It gives your play added dimension, but that's all it is, a dimension.

So we've got the basic story line, and we've got the crisis. The problem now is to justify the depth of friendship between the old man and the boy. The old man must really love the boy if the boy's defection is going to pain him enough to merit a second-act curtain. Why does he love the boy? Because the boy shares his love for printing. The boy is, of course, a nice kid — well mannered in a tradition that the old man understands, respectful. But the old man represents the old handicraftsman, and the basic attraction between the two must be on that level.

Well, what have we got so far? A crotchety old printer and a nice kid who are attracted to each other by a common love for the handicraft of printing. That gives the kid a pleasant quality — a sensitivity for other people and for his trade. He's about seventeen, out of a lower-bourgeois or working-class family. He goes to a manual-training high school — is probably in his last semester — and he got into printing because it was one of the courses at high school that interested him. That is the case with most printers' apprentices. (I happen to know this because I worked a number of years in a print shop. If you don't know anything about the printing business, you shouldn't be writing this story.) At any rate, the kid is pleasant, seventeen, sensitive to the old man. He recognizes the warmth beneath the crusty exterior. A deep fondness grows between them. What breaks them up? What leads to the incident of the face slapping?

This is really a love story; we need the third angle of the triangle. The basic communication between these two is a common love for the craft of printing. The interloper would have to be someone who represents mechanized printing or the inexorable advance of the mechanized world. We need a symbol of the mechanization of printing. The mechanization of the compositor's function is the linotype machine. A linotype machine is installed in this shop. That gives us our basic situation. A linotype machine is installed and the old man declares a personal war on it. That's a charming concept — a crotchety old man's personal war against a machine. He vies with the machine for the boy's love. This is the basic line. But if the boy loves the handicraft aspect of printing, why would the linotype machine have any attraction for him?

Linotypists get more money, have a better future. But money is a shallow motivation; it makes the boy callous and unsympathetic. We must contrive a situation in which he needs money immediately and for sympathetic reasons. His father dies and he has to support his family. We'll worry about that later. Let's stick with the old man and the linotype machine.

The old man declares war on the machine. He despises what the machine represents in our way of life. The machine is taking the boy away from him. There is not enough urgency. There is nothing immediate about these motivations to make our story move along quickly.

The linotype machine is a threat to his job. This means he is working in this shop at a job and is not his own boss. That makes sense because if he were his own boss he wouldn't install the machine in the first place. That means we have to have another character, the boss.

All right, we have three characters in this shop now—the old compositor, the boy apprentice, and the boss. The boss decides to install a linotype machine. Why? Well, why not? It's not too usual for a small shop like this to have a linotype machine, but there must be a certain level of production where it would be advantageous to the boss to have one. Check with some printers to find out at what level a linotype machine is profitable.

All right, the boss decides to install a machine. We must already have planted the love story between the old man and the boy and also the fact that they share a common love for printing. So we need two scenes showing (1) the old man's almost medieval love for his craft and (2) the growing affection between the old man and the boy. Then the linotype machine enters their lives. But the actual installation of the machine sounds like a first-act curtain, so we need to plant the coming of the linotype machine before. And we also have to establish that the linotype machine is a threat to the old man's job. Let's block it out and see what we've got.

1. *Old man and the boy.* Establish the old man's skill and love for his craft. Establish sweet friendship between old man and the boy.

2. *The boss, the old man, and the boy.* The boss decides to install a machine. Show old man's violent distaste for machine and what it stands for.

3. *Need to establish threat to the old man's job.* The boss can't threaten the old man with firing him, or we don't have a story. Our concept now is to keep the old man through two acts of personal war against the machine, so the boss can't fire him. How to establish threat to the old man's job? Well, another old compositor who was fired when a linotype machine was installed in his shop would drive the point home to the old man. Make a sweet scene. Two old compositors bleakly regarding the inexorable advance of

mechanized civilization. We've had the first two scenes in the shop. Set this scene in neighborhood cafeteria — gives us a change of scenery. Keep the boy in this scene. We don't want to lose our basic emotional line.

4. *The actual installation of the linotype machine.* We have established what the machine means to the old man's story. Cut to the old man's grim face and fade out. Curtain.

This is all you need for an outline. Actually, when you sit down to write these scenes, you will find that one scene with one old colleague of the compositor is not enough to give proper weight to the first-act curtain. The threat to the old man's job is vital, and somehow one such scene is thin and far outweighed by the preceding scenes. So you will invent a second old colleague, who will aggravate the old compositor's fears, and even a home scene for the old compositor, which will give you a proper graduation of urgency. Then, when you show the linotype machine being installed and cut to a close-up of the old compositor's bleak face, the full dramatic meaning of the moment is clear and balanced.

This is more or less the way I hacked out the first act of "Printer's Measure." The logic of the thinking, such as it was, implies a few subrules, which I think are rudimentary. The first of these is: There shouldn't be a character in the script who doesn't have to be there to answer the demands of the main character's story. The boss is there because somebody has to install the machine and because the old man's job must be threatened. The old compositor's friends are there to establish the threat to the old man's job.

No matter how delightfully a character is written, he is a bore if he serves no definite plot purpose. George Bernard Shaw will drag in any number of peripheral characters just to indulge a dissertation, but he is guilty of this only in his inferior plays; and then, how many of us can entertain an audience simply by our wit and charm?

There is a second implication, which is that character traits that go into the various characterizations are likewise contrived solely to satisfy the demands of the main character's story. It is a common illusion that dramatists sit down and preconceive a detailed biography and character study of each character in a script. To a professional writer, this would be a palpable waste of time. A writer usually starts off his thinking with a rough feel of the character absorbed from some experience in his own life. It is inevitable that the preconception of the character will change a thousand times during the course of construction in order to satisfy the demands of the story line.

Drama unfortunately will not allow for the complex, contradictory impulses that constitute real-life people. The best you can hope to achieve in dramatic characterizations is an essence or basic truth of the character you had in mind when you started. Holding on to a preconception of a character is one of the worst stumbling blocks in the construction of a story. It keeps you from openly accepting or even looking for the correct incidents to tell your story, because these incidents are not suited to the preconception of the character. In the end, you will have to change your preconception, but only after you have gone through hours of despair and excessive smoking. Generally, the characterizations are devolved from the incidents of the main story and not preconceived.

It is, of course, not as simple as all that. That is the difficulty with theorizing about such things as writing. Obviously, the characters are not deduced merely from the incidents — because the incidents are derived from the characters. Writing is such a confused business of backing and filling, of suddenly plunging into the third act while you are still pondering the first act.

Writing is unfortunately an emotional as well as a mental trade, and the simplest steps in logic are obscured by the writer's own fears and anxieties, most of which he is unaware of. The writer's mind may flood with images or run raspingly dry so that he cannot pull himself out of a fruitless line of thought for hours, even days, sometimes never, and the script has to be abandoned in the middle. Nevertheless, the overall logic of characterizing the people in the drama is one of devolution rather than preconception. "Printer's Measure" is not a good script for demonstrating this devolution, because the characters are simple and not particularly explored. The characters are symbols of social currents rather than psychological studies. . . .

Each story demands its own kind of construction, and each writer must construct his stories as best suits his ways. I wouldn't recommend that people just starting out as writers take this extravagant attitude, at least not at first. It is best to study the worn techniques of Ibsen or the wonderful preciseness of Lillian Hellman, after whom I carefully modeled my first dramas. *The Front Page* by Hecht and MacArthur is another fine piece of orthodox structure. And the television drama is really not too different in structure from the stage play. They differ in weight and approach and substance, but they are both in the three-act form and follow the lines imposed by that form. Eventually, the writer attains a security in his ability, and he breaks out here and there from the techniques of other writers and tells his own stories in his own way.

CHAPTER 4

Characters at War

A few writers learn their craft from books. A few learn from teachers. A few from studying motion pictures. Some — a minuscule minority — are born with an innate gift for narrative expression. Most writers, however, learn their craft from the physical act of putting words on paper, studying those words critically, and then writing them again. Most writers teach themselves, which is not to say that books or instructors cannot be helpful. On the contrary, they can help enormously in providing stimulation, encouragement, objectivity, and instruction in dramatic principles. But instructors cannot transform you into a writer. Only you can do that. Books and teachers merely help you to help yourself.

Putting words on paper is not in itself instructive. Developing screenplays and spewing forth pages of dialog will do little to further your writing career unless you apply two magic words to the process, words so significant that you should paint them in glowing letters on the wall of your workplace: *Be dissatisfied!* When you apply these two words to your writing, growth is almost inevitable. When you're dissatisfied with scenes, you will work to improve them. You will determine what is old fashioned or clichéd or badly conceived. You will find a more scenic road to travel. And in the process, you will expand your creative capabilities and become a better writer.

The process of putting words on paper has a second, equally significant benefit: If done with regularity, it oils the creative wheels. When we first start writing, most of us are less than fluent, grinding out words awkwardly, painfully, one at a time. But as we embrace a routine of daily or near-daily writing workouts, words begin to flow more freely. So do ideas.

Mental workouts are much like physical workouts. When we begin to jog, for instance, we proceed slowly and painfully. The first day we attempt half a mile. After three or four blocks, we are winded, dizzy, ready to collapse. But as the days pass, the running becomes easier. Our leg muscles develop. Our wind improves. Weeks later, we're running a mile. After a month or two, we're running three miles and feeling proud of ourselves, exhilarated! Exhilaration feels just as good when you're seated at a type-writer or word processor.

As you gain experience, you will discover techniques that give your writing greater quality: unique patterns of building characterization, plot, or dialog or of constructing a scene. Given sufficient time, you will also discover certain fundamental principles or dramatic elements. Foremost among these and indigenous to screenplays (in fact, the glue that holds most scenes together) is conflict. In the following pages, we will examine:

➢ **SCREENPLAY CONFLICT:** its origins and its significance

➤ **VARIETIES OF CONFLICT**: the four traditional forms in which conflict usually appears, plus ways of revealing internal conflicts

➤ **PRACTICAL USES FOR CONFLICT**: an examination of conflict's role in specific scenes, focusing on the detective form

➤ **CONTRASTING CHARACTERS**: another way in which conflict charges narrative action

➤ **TESTING THE NEED FOR CONFLICT**: challenging some of the chapter's assertions

➤ **ADDING TO THE NEWSPAPER STORY**: adjusting relationships to maximize conflict

SCREENPLAY CONFLICT

Conflict has primal power. It compels our attention. It draws us magnetically, even when we're unaware of the identities of the combatants. Note the crowds that gather when a fight erupts at a ball game. Note the commercials that we watch because two jocks argue over the attributes of a light beer. Note the lukewarm movies we attend because Superstud singlehandedly battles armies of blood-thirsty savages.

Watch puppies at play. They fight with each other endlessly, growling, biting, attacking, lunging for the throat, retreating, and attacking again — but seldom hurting each other. For them, as for humans and other animals, conflict is play; play is conflict. Watch the teasing that goes on between young men and young women, part of the courting ritual but still conflict, stimulating each and creating an exhilarating tension.

Perhaps conflict achieves its raw power from race memory, dim recollections of an earlier time when we battled primordial monsters to stay alive. Scientists claim that memories of those battles appear in our dreams, still vivid and terrifying after millions of years.* Those battles rage on in our subconscious. But we have replaced tooth and claw with more acceptable forms of conflict. We still participate in the life-and-death struggle but vicariously now, by extension, sublimating it in athletic contests, quiz or game shows, and drama.

In Chapter 1 we saw that the essence of screenplay drama is contained in a simple phrase, "a person with a problem." The problem usually arises because a protagonist tries to attain a goal and someone or some force tries to prevent it. A series of battles ensues. These battles, struggles, or tugs of war make up the content of almost all screenplay stories. Thus, conflict lies at the very heart of screenplay drama.

Beginning writers sometimes wonder why their scenes turn out unexpectedly short or why they seem bland. The answer, almost always, is that such scenes lack conflict. When characters demonstrate conflicting points of view or must struggle to achieve some short-term goal, a scene cannot resolve quickly. Conversely, when a scene resolves quickly and easily, it is seldom exciting.

Every scene improves with the addition of conflict. Such a broad generalization may be challenged: What about a love scene, for instance! Isn't it ludicrous to think that two people in love would generate conflict?

Consider the most famous of all love scenes: the balcony scene in *Romeo and Juliet*. Does it contain conflict? No, not in its dialog. Yes, the physical space separating the lovers might be construed as an obstacle. More significantly,

*Carl Sagan, *The Dragons of Eden* (New York: Ballantine Books, 1977), p. 158.

since the families of the two lovers are enemies committed to deadly conflict, Romeo's declaration of love for Juliet plays against a backdrop of major dramatic tension. Their falling in love moves the story closer to an eruption of familial warfare. Conflict remains vivid in the audience's consciousness and floats like a dark cloud above the young couple's love scene.

Admittedly, some scenes without conflict play reasonably well. Usually, such scenes contain other elements of entertainment that delight and distract audiences: spectacle, humor, curiosity, or sex. (Elements of sex, of course, are also present in *Romeo and Juliet*, especially as presented in the Zeffirelli film.) But in most cases, even scenes containing colorful elements of entertainment would improve significantly with the addition of conflict.

A scene between characters with identical attitudes, who agree on all plot aspects, generates little or no tension. The characters have little to say to each other. In truth, they are the same character.

Some writers fear that introducing the element of conflict into every scene would create a uniformity, a predictable pattern of sameness that would reduce audience attention. This would certainly be true if characters shouted angrily at each other in every scene. But conflict is so varied in its expression that it defies uniformity. It may be overt, expressing itself in violent physical actions. It may lie buried beneath the surface, simmering, steaming, adding pressure, coloring the characters' words. It may be revealed only through body language such as fingers twisting paper or fists clenching — indicators of inner tension. It may emerge as gentle teasing, as banter between a teenage boy and girl — mocking words that still express the language of love.

VARIETIES OF CONFLICT

Traditionally, screenplay conflict has divided into three convenient categories: conflict with others, conflict with the environment, and conflict with self. Fantasy films provide a fourth category that doesn't precisely fit the other three: conflict with the supernatural.

CONFLICT WITH OTHERS

A desperado escapes from a western jail and tries to outwit the sheriff who trails him. A husband tries to reclaim the love of his wife, aware that she has a younger, more glamorous lover. A high school girl runs from the street gang she has informed against. Luke Skywalker battles Darth Vader. Robin Hood fights the Sheriff of Nottingham.

Each of these examples demonstrates the pattern of conflict with others, a protagonist fighting against one or more human antagonists. This is the form of conflict found most often in movies and television shows, probably because it is found most frequently in everyday life. Most successful scripts contain more than one of the four conflict categories, and some contain all.

Conflict with others most commonly is expressed through dialog or dramatic action. It may even manifest itself through business (specific character actions). For example, in *Citizen Kane*, when young Kane's father closes a window, shutting out the sound of the boy at play, his mother a moment later deliberately opens the window, needing to hear the boy, in direct conflict with her husband's needs.

Conflict with others sometimes manifests itself subliminally. For example, two students are roommates. Roommate A dominates roommate B in every way, taking the best bed and desk for herself, forcing B to run errands, belittling B as a student, as a lover, and as a person, grinding him into submissiveness. B never complains; there are no scenes of overt conflict. Yet such a relationship nevertheless generates uneasiness within the audience, an awareness that these two are psychologically at war, perhaps an anticipation that B will eventually erupt in anger or rebel. Hidden warfare is often richer than warfare expressed overtly because it encourages the audience to probe beneath the surface and to guess at the nature of a future eruption.

Put two characters together in a room. If they disagree, you have a scene. If they disagree superficially, you have a superficial scene. If they disagree fundamentally — holding diametrically opposed views with unalterable commitment — you have a powerful scene.

CONFLICT WITH THE ENVIRONMENT

The most common form of conflict with the environment uses nature as an antagonist. In the example of the sheriff pursuing the escaped desperado, the story incorporates environmental conflict at the moment the sheriff starts across the vast expanse of southwestern desert. Now he will have to face merciless heat, sunburn, lack of water, and poisonous snakes as he trails his quarry.

Other examples in this category include such films as *Backdraft* (fighting fire) and *Jaws* (fighting the great white shark). In *City Slickers*, Billy Crystal must fight the turbulent rapids to save a baby calf.

Writers often overlook conflict with nature. It can serve as a catalyst, fanning personal or other conflicts. When the weather is scorchingly hot for an extended time, characters tend to become testy. Tempers flare. Scenes that otherwise would generate only mild disagreement now suddenly erupt into violent displays of anger. Perspiration, electric fans, or soggy clothing all remind the audience of environmental pressures. In *Body Heat*, the steamy atmosphere contributes significantly to the film's sensuous qualities and to the conflicts that ultimately erupt. Conflict with nature creates a visual friction and the expectancy of conflict between characters.

Conflict with the environment also includes the category of conflict with society. A prominent example is *1984* in which a man fights for love and identity against a bizarre, all-powerful Big Brother society.

For writers, conflict with society is often difficult to dramatize. Society is impersonal and amorphous. How does a protagonist fight against such a faceless entity? Most writers solve the problem by creating a few key characters who symbolize the larger environment. In *Jaws*, for example, the writer capsulized Roy Scheider's secondary antagonist (the town of Amity) in the characters of the mayor and one or two others.

CONFLICT WITH THE SUPERNATURAL

This category includes stories in which a protagonist battles God or the devil (including their representatives, angels or demons) and all of the undead, including ghosts, spirits, zombies, poltergeists, vampires, and werewolves. Categories of conflict necessarily overlap. For example, the shark in *Jaws* is a manifestation of nature. And yet Quint, the character played by Robert Shaw, regards the shark as almost a supernatural force, to be feared and respected. Science fiction aliens often fall between categories. The benign creatures who appear in the final scenes of *Close Encounters of the Third Kind*, for example, are more than natural and less than supernatural. The monstrous creatures in *Aliens* are natural, but only within an alien planet's grotesque definition of nature. Whether natural or supernatural, such creatures become formidable adversaries for a protagonist.

CONFLICT WITH SELF

Perhaps the richest of these categories, conflict with self, is found in most well-written movies and TV shows, stories in which protagonists fight an internal battle, usually with their fears or their conscience.

Returning to our western sheriff, let us assume that he pursues the escaped killer across the desert and finally captures him. On their way back to town, sheriff and prisoner are attacked by hostile Apaches. In the encounter, the killer reveals his humanity by saving the sheriff's life. Now the sheriff faces a torturing dilemma. Can he turn his prisoner over to a town that will certainly lynch him? Or must he betray the town's trust by giving the prisoner his freedom?

How to externalize internal conflicts is a problem that faces most writers. Novelists have a number of answers for this; most commonly, they simply tell their readers how a character feels. But screenwriters have no such convenient way of revealing what's happening inside a character's heart or mind. The screenwriter's most direct solution usually is to use dialog, allowing a character to verbalize inner feelings to another character. In *City Slickers*, Billy Crystal discusses his depression with his wife and with his pals. A more visual, less simplistic method is to do what Robert Louis Stevenson did in *Dr. Jekyll and Mr. Hyde*: externalize the conflict by creating characters (or symbols) that represent the two sides of the internal struggle.

JoBeth is acutely afraid of the water. She almost drowned eight years ago in a boating accident. Her beloved father did drown. JoBeth has fallen in love with (wouldn't you know it?) the owner of an ocean salvage operation. When her story creates terrifying internal conflicts, the writer may externalize those conflicts in two ways: (1) by creating a character who will express JoBeth's fears or (2) by using a symbol of the dead father or of the boating accident. JoBeth's mother, a woman haunted by death, might well symbolize and voice her daughter's fears, expressing JoBeth's anxieties as her own, desperately pulling the young woman away from her lover's terror-filled world. When JoBeth argues with her mother, stating her love for the salvage operator, her mother's answering protests are really the internal protests JoBeth is herself experiencing. Scenes between the two thus represent the battle raging within JoBeth.

A photograph of JoBeth's father or the life jacket he wore during the boating accident might serve as a physical symbol of JoBeth's fears. Through her interplay with the photograph or life jacket, we can infer her state of mind. For example, suppose JoBeth returns home after a date with her lover. As she hums happily, she sees the shadow of the life jacket across her bed. Her smile disappears. She goes to the jacket, stares at it for a long moment, frowning, then takes it down from its position on the wall, almost angrily throws it into the closet, and closes the door. Such actions, called business, are extremely useful to writers as ways of revealing a character's inner feelings.

A gift from JoBeth's lover might also become a useful symbol: a bracelet personally fashioned by him from salvaged gold coins. When JoBeth ultimately throws away the bracelet, she is, in a sense, throwing away her lover.* Symbols usually evoke more emotion in audiences than photographs since they are less literal and more universal, forcing audiences to supply missing material from their imaginations.

*P*RACTICAL USES FOR CONFLICT

A detective format often creates problems that may be resolved by adding a judicious bit of conflict. In the early stages of most investigative shows, the protagonist gathers clues. The process usually involves confronting a number of people who may shed light on circumstances surrounding the crime. If the

---

*More on the use of symbols to reveal character in Chapter 8.

investigator secures answers quickly or easily, each scene becomes dull and painfully short. A succession of such scenes becomes a visual treadmill.

The investigator visits the murder victim's landlady. "Good afternoon, ma'am. I'm investigating the killing of Agatha Apple. Was she living here on February 26th?"

"Yes, she was."

"Did you see her after that date?"

"No."

"Did she receive any visitors?"

"No. Never."

"Any suspicious happenings?"

"None."

"Thank you very much."

The investigator gets into his Italian sports car and drives off. An exciting scene? Suspenseful? Only if treadmills are your idea of fun.

If we make the investigator's job more difficult, the scene instantly gains interest. Let's assume that the youthful landlady is attracted to the investigator and wants him to come inside and have a beer with her. But he's in a hurry. He doesn't have time for a beer. When he tries to obtain information, the landlady has trouble remembering. She again invites him to have a beer with her. The businesslike investigator refuses, hammering away with his questions. When the landlady continues to hem and haw, he finally realizes (he's a little slow!) that the only way he will get straight answers is to indulge this woman. Inside, over a beer and popcorn, he secures the information he needs; the landlady gets the companionship she needs, and they make a date to see each other again.

Seeking more information, the detective then goes to a grumpy, seventy-year-old inventor. But the inventor can't waste time with foolish questions. He must finish his invention today. He tries to shoo the investigator away. Our hero keeps pressing, humoring the eccentric old man, asking him to demonstrate his invention. The investigator watches in admiration as wheels turn, lights flash, sirens moan, and smoke billows out of the strange contraption. And now, mollified, the inventor gives our detective the information he needs.

The investigator goes to a child of four who might have witnessed the crime. But the boy has a vivid imagination; he cannot separate fact from fantasy. Now the detective must labor to determine the truth, perhaps playing a game with the youngster to help him reveal the facts.

Each of these scenes could be played in a dull question-answer pattern. Instead, each sparks our interest through the addition of entertainment elements (sex, spectacle, mystery) and colorful characters — and something more. In each of the preceding situations, we have devised a way for *conflict* to enter the scene. When our protagonist found his answers easily, the scenes were dull. When the going became difficult, his encounters became entertaining. Such a pattern does not pertain only to detective shows; it is relevant for almost all screenplays.

There's a major lesson here about screenplays and about life. Things easily obtained seem to have little value. Goals that we must struggle to achieve, clawing our way past formidable obstacles, take on increased value. In screenplay scenes, make life difficult for your protagonists by keeping their goals elusive. Make them work, struggle, agonize to achieve those goals. Allow your audience the luxury of worrying. They'll love you for it!

Contrasting Characters

Conflict almost inevitably emerges in scenes in which characters have different goals or different points of view. Scenes between a story's protagonist and antagonist, for example, will necessarily strike sparks because their goals are diametrically opposed. The conflict may not be overt. The two may smile at each other and pretend friendship or affection. But audiences will quickly sense the conflict that simmers beneath the words.

Characters with similar or identical points of view rarely argue. Their scenes together usually are dull because they agree on almost every issue. Professional writers search for **contrasting characters** whenever possible because they create texture in scenes by presenting different points of view. They create tension by making a scene's outcome problematic. And they create entertainment through the sparks of conflict.

Contrast between leading characters so strengthens a concept that it has formed the basis of countless feature films and stage plays as well as entire television series. Recall *48 Hours* in which two members of a police investigative team (cop and criminal, one black, one white) were constantly at war. Recall bigoted Archie Bunker in "All in the Family," fighting with his liberal son-in-law and daughter and most of his neighbors. Recall the movies of Neil Simon; almost every one of them contains major central conflicts between characters: *The Odd Couple* is the prototype.

In *The Odd Couple* play, movie, and TV series, the effete, meticulous, sensitive Felix Unger shares an apartment with heavy-drinking, cigar-smoking Oscar Madison, a man of sloppy personal habits and animal appetites. In the television series, no matter what situation the writers devised, the odd couple faced it with conflicting attitudes. No matter what the plot progression, their opposing points of view placed them on a collision course, and the stories inevitably erupted into open warfare.

When characters share the same attitudes toward life and toward story issues, they are, in effect, the same character. Wise writers have two alternatives: either eliminate one character from the script or change his or her attitude. When mother and father both agree that their daughter should forget her career aspirations and marry the young man next door, a wise writer either kills off the mother or changes her point of view. Perhaps she becomes weak, changing positions depending on the person to whom she last talked. Perhaps she has secret knowledge about the young man next door that she has sworn to conceal. Perhaps she's the family peacemaker, taking the father's position with the daughter and the daughter's position with the father. In any case, the mother becomes an individual capable of creating sparks in scenes rather than just a mirror image of the father.

Remember, conflict is the essence of screenplay drama. And contrasting characters are the essence of conflict.

Testing the Need for Conflict

Test Number 1: We turn on our television sets. On the screen, two fighter planes engage in combat. The larger plane pursues the smaller one, intermittently firing machine-gun blasts. Now the smaller plane climbs steeply. The larger plane, less agile, tries to follow, but cannot. The small plane swoops down, trying to get into position behind its adversary. The larger plane attempts to maneuver away, but now the smaller plane is behind the larger! The tables have been turned. The small plane fires blast after blast, scoring direct hits into the larger plane's fuselage. Smoke billows from the larger plane. It plummets down, apparently out of control. But, no! The dive was just a maneuver, and the large plane swings around, climbing, now bearing down on the small plane, firing its guns savagely. The small plane turns to the left, starts to climb, and. . . .

Ho hum. We reach for the controls on our TV and change channels. Why? The scene represents conflict, deadly conflict. And Chapter 4 of *Writing the Screenplay* claims that conflict is the magic ingredient that makes scenes work, that grabs audiences' attention. Can Chapter 4 be wrong?

No, conflict works. It's as dependable as the sunrise. But conflict must be dramatized in terms of *people*! Remember that scriptwriting is about a person with a problem. The moment we cut to the pilots of the two combat planes, we begin to become involved. If the pilot of the small plane is a skinny Nebraska farm boy, frightened, inexperienced, knuckles white on the controls, we will sympathize. If the pilot of the large plane is older, vastly tougher, with a scar on one cheek and a sneer on his lips, we will probably form a clear-cut rooting position. The more our story familiarizes us with these characters, building involvement, the stronger our identification. Now the conflict may be dramatized in terms of *people*.

Test Number 2: A number of motion pictures seem to contradict the idea that conflict must be dramatized through people. In *Star Wars*, we root for the robot R2D2. When he is injured in the final battle sequence and will be disassembled, perhaps permanently, audiences brush aside tears, worrying over the little guy. But he is just a robot. How can audiences become emotionally involved?

In a number of Walt Disney films, audiences root for deer, baby elephants, dogs, mice, cows, and even toys. They aren't people. How is it possible that audiences become so emotionally involved?

The answer, of course, is that R2D2 isn't really a robot. He just looks like one. Dumbo isn't really an elephant. He just looks like one. In each of their stories, these characters demonstrate such distinctly human emotions and characteristics that we relate to them as people. We recognize the person within. In Disney's *Lady and the Tramp*, the little dog exhibits traits of jealousy, loyalty, anger, and timidity; he falls in love, eats spaghetti with his lady on a checkered tablecloth behind an Italian restaurant. Is he a dog? Not for a moment! He is an adorable child whom the Disney artists disguised to look like a dog.

*A*DDING CONFLICT TO OUR STORY CONSTRUCTION

We have been building a story from chapter to chapter, using the following newspaper item as a beginning point.

Murder Charge Against Boy, 11, Is Thrown Out

By LORI GRANGE
TIMES STAFF WRITER

A judge Friday threw out charges against an 11-year-old Anaheim boy accused of helping his mother kill his grandmother, despite a prosecutor's argument that the youth was a clever assassin's apprentice acting out of hatred.

After two days of testimony, Pasadena Juvenile Court Judge Sandy Kriegler dismissed the claim that the youth had aided his mother, Victoria Elizabeth Jacobs Madeira, in the Oct. 14 stabbing and shooting of Roma Jaul Jacobs at her La Canada Flintridge home.

The youth was believed to be the state's youngest murder defendant since 1981.

Now let's see how we can fan the flames of conflict in our story. Let's proceed character by character, relationship by relationship. Lynn is our protagonist. Is her relationship with her son saccharine sweet? On the contrary, it is and has been stormy. Yes, there's genuine love beneath the dark clouds. Marty has had problems at school and in his choice of companions. Lynn has leaned on him hard to avoid losing him to the unsavory characters who haunt their streets. Perhaps we begin our show with an angry confrontation between Marty and Lynn in which she forces him to abandon his projected gang affiliation.

After the shooting of the grandmother, Lynn is protective of Marty but she's filled with doubt. Could he possibly have committed the crime? He swears he is innocent but doubts (internal conflicts) start to tear her apart.

Marty doesn't confess because he feels he will lose his mother's love, especially after their past battles. He's at war with himself: Should he tell the truth or shouldn't he is probably the biggest conflict in the story. He also has conflicts with his grandmother, with the law, and in a loving, teasing fashion, with his younger brother, Rick, whom he feels closer to than anyone in the world, including his mother. When Rick is wounded in the drive-by shooting, Marty is absolutely devastated and willing to go to almost any lengths to get money to help him.

Initially, everyone is at war with Grandma Millie. Marty and Rick openly dislike her. Lynn conceals her true feelings, trying to get the boys to show respect for their grandmother. But they understand intuitively that Lynn doesn't like her much either.

During the time that Lynn and Lieutenant Brent are falling in love, she fights her emotions because he represents the enemy, the justice system that is allied against her son. Another internal battle.

Even Brent, a comparatively minor character, must fight his own attraction to Lynn when she confesses to the shooting and he is obliged to take her in. Perhaps he will battle other members of the police force who are quick to condemn her.

There seems to be no need in our story for Lynn's brother Phil. We certainly have sufficient battles to fight without him. Almost every character in our story generates conflict. Scenes should bristle. Our screenplay may not win awards, but it should prove entertaining. Let's give it a working title. Let's call it "Over the River and Through the Woods."

CHAPTER HIGHLIGHTS

➤ In screenplays, antagonists fight to keep protagonists from reaching worthwhile goals, thereby creating conflict.

➤ Conflict appears in all well-written screenplays and in almost all scenes.

➤ The type and degree of conflict in scenes vary enormously, thereby preventing any feeling of repetition. Variety includes teasing, shouting, physical violence, and internal or unspoken conflict.

➤ Conflict divides into four categories: conflict with others (sheriff versus desperado), conflict with one's environment (fighting a wind storm or society), conflict with the supernatural (fighting ghosts or demons), and conflict with self (fighting fears or conscience). Most screenplays include more than one category of conflict.

➤ Conflict with self provides screenplays with character richness. Writers often have difficulty revealing inner conflicts. Dialog is their most obvious form of expression. Sometimes writers create characters to symbolize the two sides of an inner conflict, as in *Dr. Jekyll and Mr. Hyde.*

➤ When detectives gather clues, their scenes can degenerate into bland question-answer patterns. The addition of conflict makes such scenes entertaining. By creating obstacles to a character's goal, the writer adds tension.

➤ Contrast in characters usually creates conflict. When characters share the same attitudes, they are, in effect, the same character. Entire movies, plays, and TV series have been based on contrasting characters.

➤ When warplanes fight each other without character involvement, the action quickly becomes boring, demonstrating that conflict must play between characters. Audiences relate to people.

➤ If audiences relate only to people, the emotionally involving Disney animals and *Star Wars'* robot R2D2 seem a contradiction. But these characters exhibit definitive human characteristics; therefore audiences can relate to them as people.

S CRIPTWRITING PROJECTS

EXERCISES DESIGNED TO
SHARPEN YOUR NARRATIVE SKILLS

EXAMPLES OF CONFLICT

1. Invent a story premise (a sentence or two) using each of the following:
    - Conflict with others
    - Conflict with nature

- Conflict with society
- Conflict with the supernatural
- Conflict with self

2. Recall a feature motion picture or TV show that demonstrates each of the above categories.

INVENTING CONFLICTS

Write the following scene two ways: (1) without conflict of any kind and (2) with whichever type of conflict you feel is most appropriate. Select any legitimate locale. Make the characters as realistic as you can, perhaps modeling them after people you know. Don't worry about correct script format; we'll get to that in Chapter 10. For now, use any format that feels comfortable. Be as specific as you can. Include all actions and dialog. After writing both versions, compare the length of version 1 with that of version 2.

> David and Linda are college students who have fallen in love. They discuss the practicality of taking their Easter break together at a remote and romantic vacation resort.

CONTRAST

Stephanie and Eric are junior executives in a midwestern department store.

1. Devise two or three essential contrasts in their characters that will create conflicts in their scenes and that may be powerful enough to generate a major screenplay problem.

2. Write a short story (two to three pages) that dramatizes one of these contrasting character elements.

CHAPTER 5

The People Who Inhabit a Screenplay

Think of motion picture or television shows that stand out in your memory. What do you remember best about them? Chances are, you remember one or two of the principal characters.

You may recall certain characters because they were colorful or unique or because of unusual deeds they performed. More likely, you remember them because they generated powerful emotions. A child aroused your sympathy; a heavy made you angry; a presence from another planet made you afraid.

Sometimes screenwriters begin their stories with an emotionally involving character in mind, allowing that character's personal goals, flaws, or obsessions to determine which direction the plot will take. Some writers claim that if you know a character well enough, he or she simply won't allow you to create inappropriate incidents or to follow story paths that contradict the character's basic nature. More commonly, it's the other way around; most writers develop their plots first, concentrating on story construction, and then search for the characters that will make that story work. In the twenty years I've worked with professional writers, I've found only one or two who began their creative thinking with a character rather than a story line.

Regardless of whether a character is invented to help the plot or the plot invented to dramatize a character, you need to follow certain fundamental principles if your character is to emerge believable, dimensional, and emotionally involving. In this chapter we will examine those principles in six discussions:

➤ **CONCEIVING CHARACTERS**: ways in which writers add flesh and sinew to skeletal character concepts

➤ **REVEALING CHARACTERS**: how writers reveal their characters to audiences — the face behind the mask

➤ **MAKING CHARACTERS GROW**: reasons why pressures inevitably change characters, including two different kinds of character progression

➤ **PLOTTING PROBLEMS**: answers to these problems sometimes lie in the nature of the characters

➤ **WRITER REVELATIONS**: personal techniques for developing characters as described by Frank Pierson, one of Hollywood's most prestigious writer-directors

➤ **OVER THE RIVER AND THROUGH THE WOODS**: adding character biographies to our developing newspaper story

Conceiving characters

An actor receives a motion picture script; she will play the part of a small-town doctor obsessively interested in money. Now she faces the task of developing a characterization.

How does the actor accomplish this? First, of course, she reads the script to glean all of the information the writer has provided. The character's actions and dialog provide substantial clues. Then she digs into her memory to recall all the doctors she has known, both in real life and in fiction, including novels, motion pictures, TV shows, newspapers, and magazines. She recalls the people who resemble the scripted role, either physically or psychologically.

Fragments emerge that might form the external picture of such a character, recollected bits and pieces from the reservoir of memory. These fragments might include ways of walking, posture, patterns of speech or vocal quality, clothing styles, hairstyles, personal habits, and mannerisms. Other fragments might concern the internal nature of such a character, such as moral or ethical code, personality, attitudes, thought processes, and personal goals, both in life and within the screenplay. If the actor is dedicated, she goes into the character's world, studying the residents and their life-styles. She then pieces together whichever collected fragments seem to fit or enrich the scripted character, building a composite image that, during rehearsal, will acquire dimension and life.

Screenwriters build a character in much the same way as actors: from their entire background experience. But the type of in-depth study just described does not happen at the outset. It occurs only after a writer has spent days, weeks, or months devising a plot structure and deciding what characters and what character traits are needed to make the story work.

Only after writers have worked out the basic story line do they begin to examine their characters in depth. Once they decide on the essential nature of their principal characters, they prepare a **biography** (bio), or **backstory**, examining significant aspects of the characters' past lives.

Biographies create the environment and incidents that shaped the characters and led to their actions in this particular story. In the example of the doctor obsessively interested in money, the writer should search the doctor's background to determine what circumstances were responsible for such an obsession. Perhaps she came from a poverty-stricken family; money was a god worshiped by her parents. Perhaps the character worked to the point of exhaustion to finance her way through medical school, repeatedly falling ill, flunking out because of her illnesses, watching other, wealthier students move ahead. Later she reenrolled and scraped her way through the difficult regimen. Now, bitter, she is determined to get her share, more than her share. She pursues wealthy men, courts her most successful patients. Yet, despite this one obsession, our doctor is a decent, compassionate woman.

Lajos Egri divides the study of a character's background into three categories: physiology, sociology, and psychology.* In preparing biographies, writers might do well to use these convenient, all-embracing categories: (1) physiology: a character's entire physical dimension (appearance, health, dwelling, car); (2) sociology: a character's place in society (family, friends, job, church, clubs, education); and (3) psychology: a character's internal world (temperament, moral code, personality, fears, drives, sense of humor, imagination).

Students sometimes grumble at the need to write biographies; they are anxious to begin their scripts and feel that the task is unnecessary and time consuming. Experienced writers understand that time spent writing biographies will be more than repaid. Why? Because the writer won't have to stop and wonder in each scene how characters will act or react. Biographies help writers avoid countless wasted hours writing scenes that go in wrong directions, that must be thrown out, reconceived, and rewritten. Because biographies build a comfortable familiarity between writer and character, they ensure consistency between scenes and honesty in plot development.

REVEALING CHARACTERS

Once your characters have assumed dimension, they are ready to participate in the action of your screenplay. As they fight battles, fall in love, run from fearsome antagonists, and achieve triumphs and defeats, they will reveal their nature to an audience. If you truly know your characters, you won't need to concern yourself with how to demonstrate or explain their many facets. Those revelations will occur almost automatically from the way your characters conduct themselves in interactions with others and with your screenplay's environment.

Characters reveal their nature to audiences in six ways: (1) their entire physical aspect, (2) their actions (or lack of actions), (3) their words (or lack of words), (4) their traits and mannerisms, (5) their effect on other characters, and (6) their names.

PHYSICAL ASPECT

In most screenplays, physical descriptions of characters usually are minimal, limited to name, age, and general appearance (for example, Joe Hayden, middle aged, wealthy). Why not include a couple of paragraphs describing the character? Because the producer or director must have some freedom in selecting actors for a role; also, the character's behavior from scene to scene provides

---

The Art of Dramatic Writing (New York: Simon & Schuster, 1946), pp. 49–59.

more significant information. It is better to show that Joe Hayden is brash through his actions or dialog than to spell it out in stage directions. It's always better to allow audiences to deduce character values than to hit them over the head with descriptions. In this way, audiences participate more actively as they search for character clues.

The fact that writers seldom include elaborate character descriptions in scripts doesn't mean they haven't done their homework. Experienced writers examine the physical aspects of characters in their biographies, aware that physical details often find their way into scenes and help bring a character to life.

Writers explore physical details either in biographies or in their imaginations. For example, they might ask such questions about Joe Hayden as: Is he fat? Sloppily fat or just nicely padded? Is he thin? Hungrily thin or elegantly slim? Is he bald? Is his hair neat or shaggy, long or short? Does he have a beard or mustache? If either, is it neat and trim or long and bushy? Does he wear spectacles? A hearing aid?

What kind of clothes does he wear? High fashion or old fashioned? New or old, clean or dirty, freshly pressed or rumpled? Are his shoes scuffed or are they shined? Wing tips or moccasins? Are there holes in the soles? Does he wear neckties? If so, are they wide or narrow, conservatively striped or covered with gaudy flowers? Does he wear bow ties?

What kind of car does Hayden drive? New or old? If old, has it been meticulously maintained or is it scarred and rusted? Is there a bumper sticker? What does it say? Does a good-luck charm hang from the mirror?

What kind of commentary would Hayden's bedroom provide? Is the room tidy or are clothes thrown on the floor in disarray? Is the bed made? What kind of pictures hang on the wall? Matisse prints, Playboy centerfolds, or rock posters? Are there newspapers or magazines on the nightstand? *National Geographic* or *The National Enquirer*? Are there pipes or cigars on the dresser? Ashtrays filled with cigarette butts? Is there stereo equipment? What kind of music? Rock, country, or classical? What color is the room painted? Are there lace curtains?

Even if such details never find their way into the script, they still provide writers with a vivid mental image that helps bring their characters to life in the screenplay. When writers have a crisp, clear picture in mind as they write, that picture is communicated to the reader through character actions, dialog, stage directions — and between the lines.

CHARACTER ACTIONS

We have seen that actions usually reflect a character's thoughts or feelings more accurately than words. In dialog, characters can cover their true feelings and pretend emotions they do not feel. Dialog may actually contradict their true feelings.

Actions sometimes reveal the true inner nature of a character, especially when those actions take place under pressure. When a man under fire on the battlefield stops to help a comrade, at great risk to himself, we recognize that here is a character worthy of our respect. On the other hand, if he encounters a fellow soldier who has been wounded and urgently needs help and then runs by, pretending not to see him, we regard the man with contempt because he obviously thinks only of himself. Lack of action can be as significant as action in determining the nature of characters.

Screenplays that are character studies often place characters in conflict with themselves. The protagonist is really two people or three or four. The audience speculates about which is the real character. Coward or hero? Wise person or fool? The climaxes of such shows usually place protagonists in a dramatic vise, forcing them to remove whatever masks the story has required them to wear.

Almost all of us wear masks. We try to present an image to our associates that is reassuring. Chameleonlike, we change our appearance and personality to suit the occasion, to appear as our associates want us to appear, to conform to their image. In an extreme example, Woody Allen's character in *Zelig* undergoes a metamorphosis each time he enters a new situation, becoming a mirror image of others in that environment. When employees begin work for a company, they usually change their dress styles to conform to the clothing worn by their bosses or associates. We wear a businesslike mask when confronting our boss or instructor, another mask when greeting parents, a third when flirting, and perhaps a fourth when we entertain friends. Which is the real us?

Throughout a screenplay, the spectator receives clues to the true nature of characters. But it is usually at the story climax, when characters are under acute pressure, that the audience receives the most revealing insights. This is when characters remove their masks, exposing their true selves. Under pressure, characters have no time for pretense; they must act in accordance with basic needs and drives. And audiences recognize the essential truth of such revelatory actions.

CHARACTER DIALOG

Although perhaps not as significant as character actions, the words spoken by characters nevertheless provide clues to their nature. Words that remain unspoken are equally valuable.

Is a teenage boy quick to tell a girl that he loves her or does he pretend disinterest, saying nothing? (But his constant glances in her direction reveal the truth!) Does a young wife report a rape to the police or does she remain silent, fearing it may destroy her marriage? (But she fingers the business card once given her by a police detective; the conflict rages within her.) Does a woman yell at her husband for ignoring household chores or does she remain silent? And does she remain silent out of timidity or out of love? Does an old man confess that he was responsible for a fire in the retirement home or does he clamp his mouth shut, allowing someone else to take the blame? In screenplays, unspoken words can be louder than spoken ones.

TRAITS AND MANNERISMS

Good writers are observers of the human condition. By studying the actions of people around you, you will become sensitive to the meanings of their traits and mannerisms. Many cover their insecurities or fears with smiles or glib phrases, but inevitably they reveal themselves, sometimes overtly, sometimes through small, virtually undetectable personal mannerisms. What does it signify when people constantly polish their spectacles? What do they reveal when they keep glancing at themselves in mirrors or combing and recombing their hair?

As you become a habitual people watcher, you will discover the foot tappers, the fingernail biters, the teeth grinders, the frightened few who hide behind their hands or dark glasses, the lip chewers, the hair twirlers, the blinkers, and others. Some of these mannerisms indicate nervousness or tension; some imply a more disturbed mental or emotional state. Body language also indicates mental state. Photographs taken during production of a TV movie in Utah show me repeatedly standing with my arms crossed protectively in front of my chest. The pose, totally uncharacteristic, revealed that I was unconsciously shielding myself from the harrowing pressures of a problem-filled production.

REACTIONS OF OTHERS

In the early stages of a screenplay, the audience slowly forms attitudes regarding the nature of a character. It studies clues from a number of sources. One source of clues is the reaction of other characters.

If the women in a small town despise a sexy young widow, for example, the audience will temporarily accept the women's attitude as its own. But as the story progresses, the audience will assess the nature of these women. If they are decent, sympathetic characters, the audience will hold to its initial impression: The widow is a reprehensible character. If, on the other hand, the story reveals that the women are mean minded, jealous because their husbands are attracted to the widow, then the widow may actually merit our sympathy. We cannot gauge the validity of reactions until we understand the nature of the peripheral characters.

The more we identify with a character, the more we tend to accept that character's attitudes as our own. When a sympathetic protagonist violently dislikes a character, for example, we tend to accept that hostility as our own, until a plot development redeems the character and proves our hostility unjustified.

CHARACTER NAMES

Names are only a partial clue to the nature of characters and are often untrustworthy. Consider the following characters. Who are they? What do they look like? What do they do for a living? Don't take time to think about each name. Write your instant appraisal on a scrap of paper.

Brad Steele

Sophie Schwartz

Ernest W. Farnsworth

Cecily Smythe-Wellington

Bubbles Branigan

What did you come up with? In my classes, students usually identify Brad Steele as macho, a hunk, very physical, very good looking; he's either a football player, a private eye, or the leading man in a TV series.

Sophie Schwartz has changed identity over the years. Originally she was stout, Jewish, middle aged, wore horn-rimmed glasses, and talked too much. Interestingly, she has metamorphosed, getting younger and better looking from semester to semester.

Students generally agree that Ernest W. Farnsworth is a businessman, perhaps a banker or a CPA, successful, gray haired or balding, middle aged, sometimes paunchy, carrying a briefcase. He changed identities briefly after Warren Beatty wore the Farnsworth name in *Heaven Can Wait*. Once the picture was forgotten, Ernest returned to his original businessman identity, revealing how instrumental our environment is in shaping name concepts.

Cecily Smythe-Wellington is a fiftyish English lady who wears sensible shoes, is incredibly wealthy, and is a bird watcher. Sometimes she emerges as a sophisticated high-fashion model.

Bubbles Branigan always works in one of three jobs: hooker, exotic dancer, or cocktail waitress. She's attractive, blonde, undereducated, but good hearted, and generously proportioned. Bubbles likes to chew gum.

This exercise demonstrates that character names create specific impressions that affect viewers' attitudes toward characters. These impressions usually arise from past associations or encounters. Many are personal, based on conscious or subconscious memories of friends or acquaintances who have the same or similar names. Other impressions are cultural. Some are associative. The name Brad Steele, for example, uses the associative principle: A brad is a nail, and steel is hard and impenetrable. Our subconscious minds put these characteristics together in evaluating a character. Therefore, Brad emerges as a tough guy, hard as nails.

An early television series, "Peter Gunn," deliberately used names that created associations in viewers' minds. A peter is a slang expression for a penis.

And a gun, in Freudian terms, is also a symbol of the male organ. Although audiences may be unaware of the source of this association, recognizing it only subconsciously, the character name nevertheless took on attributes of maleness and virility. In 1971, Quinn Martin Productions launched a private-eye show starring William Conrad, an actor of considerable weight, both figuratively and literally. Recalling the Peter Gunn series, Martin named his detective Cannon. What is a cannon? It's another kind of gun, a fat one.

Some writers just take any name that comes to mind and affix it to a character. Others are more careful, aware of the associations created in viewers' minds. For whatever reason, many television series characters have colorless, WASP (white Anglo-Saxon Protestant) names (such as Gary Gordon, Steve Jennings, Carol Saunders) that create few associations. Many writers prepare lists of unusual or definitive names and update these lists continually. Some writers select names from telephone directories or books for naming babies. One writer I know consults a world atlas for offbeat and colorful character names.

Names also reflect how the writer personally feels about a character. Thus, you're revealing something of your own attitudes by the label you paste on a character. That label will affect casting and wardrobe decisions as well as the audience reaction. The role of a landlady, for example, would be cast one way if you named her Delilah Jones and another if you named her Sophie Schwartz. The audience might react positively if you named a character Steve Young and negatively if you named him Spike Bletchmer or Ivan Krokov. Because names add colorations to characters, you should exercise care and caution in their selection.

*M*aking Characters Grow

In the real world, when people undergo excruciating pressures (for example, fighting in Vietnam), they usually emerge somewhat changed. Imitating the real world, motion picture and television shows reflect the identical pattern. Obvious examples include *Hook*, in which an adult Peter Pan, at first addicted to the pursuit of money, fights the evil Captain Hook for the love of his children and learns to think like a boy again; *Rain Man*, in which a superficial wheeler-dealer grows into a dimensional human being, rediscovering love for his handicapped brother; and *Regarding Henry*, in which an amoral lawyer grows to appreciate his wife and daughter and life itself because of a bullet wound that wiped his mental slate clean.

In *City Slickers*, Billy Crystal and friends face a depressing midlife crisis, unsure of their future, dissatisfied with family and careers, unhappy with themselves. Participation in a cattle drive in which they are forced to face the challenges of nature and rely on their own primitive strengths enables them finally to sort out the pieces of their lives and discover what is meaningful.

These are perhaps atypical examples, stories in which the character arc is the reason for making the film. In other motion pictures, character change is usually more subtle. In *Silence of the Lambs*, for example, Jodie Foster's character matures, gains greater understanding of both her psychopathic ally and the serial killer she is trailing. She is clearly wiser at the end of the film — and more aware of her own frailties — than at the beginning.

Screenplay characters cannot suffer the crises that a writer creates for them without being affected in some degree, perhaps for the better, perhaps for the worse. Character growth increases the sense of reality in a screenplay. It also adds to the audience's sense of fulfillment; all the turmoil has accomplished something.

Although character change is healthy, excessive change can be unbelievable, especially if it happens overnight. In real life, good people don't easily or quickly turn bad; bad people don't quickly or easily reform. When a character does an instant flip-flop in films, changing 180 degrees at the end of a show ("Oh, what a fool I've been!"), audiences are quick to realize that the change is dishonest, motivated more by the writer's need for a happy ending than by the circumstances of the screenplay.

When a criminal reforms in real life, it usually is due to a succession of events. Cumulatively, like water wearing away a stone, the criminal comes to accept a new pattern of behavior, a new standard of morality. At the end of a movie, if a character performs a single act suggesting the beginning of personal change, the audience will accept that the progression has begun. Viewers will provide the remainder of the scenario from their imaginations.

Another kind of change often occurring in movies or TV shows does not represent a real character arc. In this case, the change happens not in the character but in the audience. This pattern is sometimes called **peeling the layers off an onion** because it provides the audience with additional bits of information as the show progresses, information that changes the audience's perception of a character.

Such a pattern often occurs in espionage films. At the outset we meet a character who appears to be despicable, but we gradually learn that the hateful behavior has been deliberate, that he or she is really good. If you have seen Hitchcock's classic *North by Northwest*, you may remember that Cary Grant falls in love with Eva Marie Saint and later is shocked to discover that she is the mistress of an evil foreign spy. (A layer is peeled off the onion.) Later, you learn that Eva Marie is actually an American espionage agent who is risking her life to gain evidence against the evil spy. (Another layer is peeled off the onion.)

Peeling the layers off an onion is a technique also used in story construction. A simple incident leads to the gradual unfolding of an elaborate plot. A young man parks his car at the curb while his companion runs into a store to pick up a videocassette. He waits and waits and she doesn't return. Finally, puzzled, he enters the store and asks about his friend, but the manager claims she never entered. "Damn it," the young man exclaims, "I saw her come in here." The manager tells him he's welcome to look around. The young man explores every cranny of the store; his friend has totally disappeared. He calls the police to help him, but they seem disinterested. Gradually, layer by layer, the young man discovers that the record store is being run by the police as an undercover exchange for stolen merchandise. His friend is an undercover policewoman, and her disappearance was engineered by her police bosses because she was in deadly danger. You get the idea.

Notice that even in this bizarre story pattern, we return to our first-act basis for screenplay drama: a person with a problem. Someone we care about has a goal (to find his friend) and an antagonist (the police) fights to prevent him from reaching it.

Resolving
PLOTTING PROBLEMS

Plotting a narrative structure can be difficult work. Writers sometimes spend weeks attacking a story problem, twisting and bending plot elements in an attempt to find logical, believable solutions. Sometimes the answer to such problems lies not in plotting but in the nature of characters.

Most writers begin plotting with a rough concept of their characters. That initial concept often remains locked in their minds until exhaustion or desperation forces them to abandon it. When writers back themselves into corners, sometimes only their characters can extricate them.

If a writer needs Mike to commit an illogical act—betray or abandon someone dear to him—logic provides no clear-cut answer but changing Mike's nature might. If the writer transforms him into a restless character, uneasy when life remains static or becomes too comfortable, Mike might now perform the deed that the writer requires. If the writer needs Julie to deliberately steal her best friend's lover, and Julie is a trustworthy, sympathetic character, logic provides no answer. If the writer transforms her into a woman whose psychological makeup compels her to destroy those around her, Julie will answer the writer's needs. Her compulsion might be concealed beneath a facade of innocence and frailty. Julie might be totally unaware of such a compulsion until forced to examine her own history.

Screenplay writers generally think of plot first and character second. Such a tendency is eminently practical, except when writers accept their initial character concepts without bothering to explore them further. Lack of character exploration deprives screenplays of the depth and richness that only dimensional characters can provide.

"OVER THE RIVER AND THROUGH THE WOODS": A STORY FROM A NEWSPAPER ITEM

Since Chapter 1, we have been constructing a screenplay story based on the following article from the *Los Angeles Times*.

Murder Charge Against Boy, 11, Is Thrown Out

By LORI GRANGE

TIMES STAFF WRITER

A judge Friday threw out charges against an 11-year-old Anaheim boy accused of helping his mother kill his grandmother, despite a prosecutor's argument that the youth was a clever assassin's apprentice acting out of hatred.

After two days of testimony, Pasadena Juvenile Court Judge Sandy Kriegler dismissed the claim that the youth had aided his mother, Victoria Elizabeth Jacobs Madeira, in the Oct. 14 stabbing and shooting of Roma Jaul Jacobs at her La Canada Flintridge home.

The youth was believed to be the state's youngest murder defendant since 1981.

Because Chapter 5 deals with character, let us examine briefly the three major characters in our story. There isn't space for complete biographies of each. Instead, we'll do capsules.

Lynn Hatcher is our protagonist, thirty-two, attractive, Eurasian, the mother of Rick, ten, and Marty, thirteen. She has a lovely smile, but she doesn't smile often. Lynn's Caucasian husband died four years ago in an industrial accident, leaving her with a $10,000 settlement from the company and little else. Since his death she has struggled to feed the boys and maintain their small apartment. The task has been difficult because Rick has had continuing medical problems. He was born prematurely and nearly died. Lynn's mother-in-law once claimed in a moment of anger that Lynn was being punished for worshipping the wrong god.

Lynn adored her husband; his death was devastating. She keeps their wedding picture on her dresser. They married in spite of his mother's bitter opposition. Religious and racial differences turned Millie Hatcher against Lynn. More than that, the two women never liked each other.

Lynn's bitterness at the death of her husband has mellowed somewhat. She's a patient, loving mother but she's lonely, feeling that she is living between cultures. (Her mother was Chinese, her father American.) Although Lynn is Buddhist, she makes sure that her sons understand their father's religion. For a year they attended Sunday school at the neighborhood Lutheran church.

Lynn works in the shoe department at Nordstrom, earning a modest salary; she's assistant manager. She hates where she lives, a small apartment on the edge of gang-ridden east Los Angeles. She's trying to save enough money to move to a better neighborhood. After her apartment was twice robbed by street hoodlums, Lynn bought a small handgun for protection.

Marty Hatcher, thirteen, is short and stocky. A trace of his mother's heritage can be seen in his almond eyes. Marty's a nice kid but he has a temper. He's been in fights at school and once threatened a bully with his mother's gun. (His mother grounded him for three months after he was sent home from school, forbidding him ever to touch her gun again. She eventually knocked off a month for good behavior.)

Marty's defensiveness grows from several causes. He's shorter than others in his class and neighborhood; though bright, he doesn't do well in school; he feels a strong adolescent surge of sexuality and yet the girls totally ignore him. He welcomed the sense of belonging that a street gang promised but refused membership after his mother loudly protested.

In spite of her tough discipline, Marty adores his mother. Since the death of his father four years ago, Marty feels highly protective toward her. He is now the Man of the House and Lynn encourages this attitude, asking his counsel when making family decisions. His protectiveness extends to his younger brother, but it alternates with anger and impatience growing out of age-old sibling conflicts. They share the same bedroom; Rick is neat, Marty is a slob. Rick likes to sleep; Marty's awake at dawn; Rick stays at home, reads, is introverted; Marty can't wait to get out of the apartment. Despite their differences, Marty feels real love for his younger brother. He socked him once, hard, in a burst of anger and then started to cry and beat his own hand against the wall until it started to bleed.

Marty has been angry at Grandma Millie for some time. He feels she is rich (she isn't) and that she should help her son's family. He had one angry confrontation with her six months ago, and she kicked him out of her house. He hasn't seen her since — until the day that he takes his mother's gun and goes to see her, sure that he can force her to contribute a few thousand dollars to help with Rick's medical expenses.

Marty feels that the drive-by shooting is his fault. It would never have happened, he believes, had he not defected from the gang. He thinks that it is his responsibility to secure money for Rick, and somehow, by God, he's going to get it.

Millie Hatcher is not rich. She has some money that she has carefully nursed through the years. Bad investments several years ago cost her almost half her husband's estate. She's extremely insecure about finances, knowing that her limited bankroll must sustain her for the rest of her life, perhaps another twenty years.

Millie is in her late sixties, tall, slender, a very social woman who plays bridge three afternoons a week. She colors her hair honey blonde; it's almost white beneath the color. Most of her friends are richer than Millie. She tries to keep up with them as best she can, to pretend that she's as well off financially as they are.

And Millie is bitter about her son's marriage. She's the first to admit that she's something of a bigot. It galled her that her son married a Chinese woman. (Her father would have called Lynn a "chink.") In the beginning, when her son was alive, Millie tried hard to be kind and loving. But after his death (which somehow, unreasonably, she blames on Lynn), Millie backed off, seeing Lynn and the boys only occasionally, doling out a few dollars now and then — and finally abstaining altogether. She realizes that she should feel more pride and love for her grandsons, but, to be perfectly honest, she doesn't.

CHAPTER HIGHLIGHTS

➤ Writers conceive characters from the reservoir of personal experience. In most cases, writers create characters to meet specific plot needs. A few writers, however, begin creative thinking with specific characters or relationships and then devise a plot to dramatize them.

➤ Once writers have decided on their primary characters, they then develop a biography for each, a three-dimensional history that shapes a character to meet the plot demands. Biographies enable writers to bring characters to life.

➤ Writers reveal the nature of characters through their physical aspect (appearance, posture, clothing, car), their actions or lack of actions, what they say or don't say, their traits and mannerisms, the reactions of other characters, and the names that writers give them.

➤ In real life, acute pressure tends to change people, sometimes greatly. In well-written screenplays, protagonists also change because the writer places pressure on them. A second kind of progression (peeling the layers off an onion) gradually reveals new bits of information about a character so that the audience constantly changes its perception.

➤ Character names often create specific responses in audiences based on past associations with those names. Thus, writers should be careful in creating names. By their choices, writers reveal something of how they feel about a character.

SCRIPTWRITING PROJECTS

EXERCISES DESIGNED TO SHARPEN YOUR NARRATIVE SKILLS

BIOGRAPHIES

Select one of the characters pictured above and create a five-page biography about him or her. Think of specific incidents that may be revealing. If you want, include bits of dialog that may define the character. Consider the following specific aspects, but do not limit yourself to them:

1. *Early years.* Where did he or she grow up? Relationship with parents? With siblings? Was the family religious? How much schooling did the character have? When did he or she first have sex? What was/is the character's attitude toward sex? Was the character as a child shy, outgoing, fearful? IQ level? Special talents? (Musical? Artistic?) Special childhood problems?

2. *Recent years.* What is the character's present occupation? Past occupations? What does the character do for fun? Favorite motion pictures or TV shows? Married or unmarried? Relationships with opposite sex? What kind of car? Clothes? Personality? Favorite food or beverage? Favorite magazine? What is the character's goal in life? What is he or she most afraid of? Special interests or hobbies? Liberal or conservative in views? Bigoted? Moral? Immoral? Vices?

PLOT ORIENTATION

Christie Marie Crawford, seventeen, apparently has everything going for her. She's attractive, bright, and personable, yet her behavior in recent years seems inexplicable, and her wealthy, socially correct family is deeply concerned. Last night, Christie's father was called to the police station; his daughter had been picked up for soliciting. Three months ago, she started living with a handsome but uneducated foreigner who had been in jail twice, both times for armed robbery. Before that she was thrown out of a fashionable girls' school for cheating.

Although we can't always explain all details of a character's behavior, we can discover and explore some of the most basic motivations. Ask yourself: What circumstances in Christie's background would make her behave in such an aberrant way? What past incidents or relationships might make her recent actions understandable and (perhaps) inevitable? Writers are students of human behavior. Here's your chance to play psychologist. See if you can provide (in not more than a page) a logical explanation for Christie's actions.

*W*RITER REVELATIONS

IN SEARCH OF CHARACTERS

Writer-director Frank Pierson began his career in television, writing and producing some of the industry's most successful shows, including "Have Gun, Will Travel" and "The Man from U.N.C.L.E." Later, in the motion picture field, his scripts for The Ballad of Cat Ballou, Cool Hand Luke, *and* Dog Day Afternoon *were celebrated by critics, enjoyed high box-office grosses, and won numerous industry awards, including an Oscar.*

In the following essay, Frank Pierson provides insights into the development of his colorful and unique characters. In particular, he details his steps for Dog Day Afternoon *in building the character of Sonny from a name in a newspaper story to a fascinating and complex character.*

*W*e call him or her an *actor*, not a speaker or an orator. We look always for the action that drives the story, and the action comes from the feeling heart of the character. . . .

Character Is the Driving Force of a Story

There are those of us who begin a film by constructing a plot and then try to find characters whose conflict will cause that plot (and no other) to happen. I prefer to begin with a character whose drives touch some unconscious aspects of myself and then proceed to work out a story that dramatizes this character's dilemma, by finding complementary characters whose drives are in conflict. Of course, one cannot make this choice rationally, because of its unconscious nature. You have to feel a deep sympathy and alliance, a harmony with the character. The best writing is done when one can literally feel the body rhythms of the character, when one can walk and move and dream like the character. It is a kinesthetic empathy, experienced not in the brain but in the bones and muscles.

From Will to Personality

In real life we have a deep unconscious knowledge of the people around us, a sense of their character so immediate and powerful and automatic that we all experience little scenes like this.

YOU have just entered the room, and OTHER glances up. . . .

> OTHER
> What's wrong? You have a bad day?

> YOU
> No. I'm fine. I'm okay.

> OTHER
> I don't know. You seem.... You came in the room
> like you were upset.

> YOU
> I'm fine. Why would I be upset?

> OTHER
> I don't know—you were walking kind of angry.

Other can't put her finger on what was different about You; she just knows it. There were unconscious clues she picked up: intuition. That's how well you know people in your life, and it's the way you must know your characters before you can write them. So that you could put them into any situation, anywhere, any time, and you could write their reactions and their dialog, if any, without stopping to think.

I go into such detail about psychodynamic considerations because the creation of a character is the creation of a personality. And we know and recognize and react to personalities at both a conscious and unconscious level. Yet there is a method by which one can approach creating a character who has many levels and into which an actor can work and produce his own version of that character, including the unconscious.

I never not write; if I can't think of what happens next, I write improvisational scenes, ones that may have nothing to do with the plot or the events at hand, that expand my feeling and understanding of the character. I am creating a life for him or her. I imagine "what if" the character had to change a tire on the freeway in the rain? Would this character bump along and tear the tire to shreds until she reached an off ramp? Would she spare the tire and risk her life changing it in the center divider? Would she do it right by the fast lane out of bravado, feeling a manic excitement at the danger? Or because she's just numb and oblivious? How would she talk to her daughter who tells her she thinks she's pregnant? How would she feel in these situations? These improvisations expand our picture of the character beyond the boundaries of the screenplay.

It also helps to find the contradictions and quirks, the conflicting motives within the character that are part of what makes the difference between stereotype and a personality with unique rhythms and style. Most screenplays are so flatly characterized that without names for the characters, it would be difficult if not impossible to know who is speaking. If you don't believe it, try this sometime. Black out the character names on the page and read the dialog. Try to figure out who is speaking. If you can't tell by the rhythm of speech, the writer should take up another line of work.

Biography

Sometimes during production, the writer is asked to write a biography of the character. When the question comes from executives, it usually means they want a history of events, which is useless to the actor and to the director, if he's any good (though it may help the production designer, who needs to know what kind of clothes might hang in the closet and the kind of college pictures that might be around the house).

A useful biography is written in the present tense. She is rich or poor, drives an old car or a new car, jogs or is sedentary, works or idles, and so on. But this is marginally helpful to the actor or the writer still in the formative stages, trying to find his character.

What is needed is a biography of feelings: How does she feel about being rich or poor, having an old car or a new car? We know a hell of a lot more about a woman if we know she jogs though she hates it than simply to know that she jogs. The next question is why does she hate jogging?

It isn't important that she graduated from Radcliffe in 1968 summa cum laude or that her mother died in Hingham, Massachusetts, in 1978 and the whole family was there. What's vital is how she felt when her mother died and that she hated going to the funeral because her father would be there. It isn't important that she was fearful of her father because he abused her when she was young. What is important is that what she fears is the conflicted mixture of feelings that are aroused by her father's presence. This is a sick and sad and confused character, but you only know in what ways she is confused and sick and sad if you know how she feels.

A completely different woman given the exact same history of incestuous abuse might have been traumatized into numbness and indifference; in the presence of her father, she goes cold and flat. The first woman is hot and mercurial, lashes out in venomous attacks, alternating with childish seductiveness, followed by shame and depression. The key to the difference is the difference in their feelings.

I try to write a biography, if that's the word for such a document, in emotional terms, with as few concrete facts as possible. We are trying to construct the emotional lines of the story; the facts can come later, and they tend to get in the way now. "Her mother dies; she feels a sense of relief, without any sadness. Always when she visits 'Mumm' she feels as though all her vital processes stop, and she can only wait until she escapes so that she can breathe again. She feels as though she is suffocating while she waits for 'Mumm' to make up her mind." And so on.

Not a word of geography or date or specific event. Feelings. This is actable. It also generates an idea of how to write this character, because if you know how she feels in major life crises, you intuitively know how she would act in any related situation that calls up these emotions by association. Those emotions will drive the action, and those actions will drive the scene and the story forward. You can imagine how she will deal with a submissive man or a domineering man, with a mother who can't understand how she can work with small children still in the house, with an auto mechanic who tries to take advantage of her presumed passivity and ignorance; you'll know the shadow that passes over her mood when she sees a hearse, and so on.

This sort of biography provides the writer and actor with the sense memories the character carries with him or her everywhere in life, which are the unconscious source of feeling and action. The actor can use these as a key to finding his or her own corresponding sense memories to use in working into the character.

A Practical Example

Dog Day Afternoon was advertised as a true story but was extensively fictionalized in order to make it a story as opposed to a documentary recreation, a series of events one after another in chronological order. I had to find a story driven from within, by personality.

For me, *Dog Day* began with a huge pile of clippings, news and magazine reports of a bank robbery motivated by the need of the homosexual wife of the robber for a sex-change operation. I also had a huge pile of transcripts of tape-recorded interviews with all of the various people involved, the hostages the robber held in the bank, the various cops and FBI people who eventually captured him and shot and killed his partner, with the robber's family and friends, his homosexual wife, and his heterosexual wife. It was overwhelming.

The incident exercised a morbid fascination. It came at an earlier and more innocent phase of the TV revolution; it came on an afternoon in one of New York's unbearable heat waves when people will do almost anything for distraction. The robbers were (in that day before police took control of reporters' coverage) able to appear on the television news shows, and Sonny, as we called him in the movie, took full advantage. Millions watched, thousands actually got in their cars to go to the scene, including some hundreds (one police officer thought thousands) of off-duty police.

The first problem in dramatizing this event was to identify what it was that was so fascinating. It was tempting to believe that the public event was the interesting aspect, a television first, as it were. But this is the stuff of documentaries; it was an interesting color of the action, and certainly provided a good deal of the specific actions and backgrounds and could be exploited for stage business. But this is not drama.

The problem lay in the character of the hero. In all of the material I was supplied (and backed up by further interviews I did myself), there was nothing from Sonny. He was involved in a contract dispute with Warner Brothers and wouldn't talk to me. (He had signed a legal release, however, so we were free to depict him as a character.) I had a biography. It was in the newspapers and the tapes — it was all event. I knew the bare bones of his history, where he'd gone to school, that he'd been a rather conservative young man who'd been a Goldwater delegate at a Republican convention, that he had a wife and two children who loved him, that he once worked in a bank and so knew how banks worked and where things were kept. I knew his height and weight and that he looked a lot like Al Pacino. I knew he'd married a man (Ernie) in a Catholic church ceremony, without getting a divorce from his female wife. I knew he'd been unable to keep a job regularly as his life grew more and more chaotic. I knew his homosexual wife grew exasperated with him as he was sexually demanding and jealous. I knew his heterosexual wife was exasperated with him for all kinds of reasons. I knew he'd gone into the bank to steal money because he thought a sex-change operation as a birthday present would make his homosexual wife happy.

His behavior in his life and in the bank was riddled with contradictions, quixotic gestures of kindness alternated with raging defiance, noisy outbursts of anger with sudden quiet. The tapes of those who knew him, especially those who knew him best, were wildly confusing. Even within the same tape. It was as though each person was describing a different man, and some, several different men.

I could find no way to write the story around him, and yet I couldn't see who he was in a way that would let me write him. He was a stranger to me. Some weeks went by in this way, and I was getting nowhere. I was on the verge of giving up and telling my agent to get me out of the assignment.

I knew what was wrong. I could not find in this character anything I could understand and identify with, that would let me feel the way he felt and understand why he did the things he did. It was impossible to imagine the things I would have to make up to create the story.

A story doesn't exist, except as a series of unrelated incidents, unless there is some driving principle, a will driving the action, that makes all of the incidents inevitable. The fact that Sonny robbed a bank to get a sex-change operation for Ernie would seem to satisfy the criterion of a will that drives the action. But it was not enough to give a sense of his style, of how he would go about it, of why the hostages rather liked him, and so forth.

I set myself an exercise, a little like a quiz crossed with improvisation. I asked myself what kind of man could produce such contradictory responses from those who knew him? And what did his relationships with all of these people have in common?

I saw that in each case the person had loved him and that in every case he or she felt betrayed. When I began to see this, I dug deeper into their testimony: In each case, in a way peculiar to that particular case, he made a promise, tacit and unspoken but nonetheless a kind of emotional contract with the person involved, which, given the circumstances of his life, was impossible to fulfill.

For example, his heterosexual wife had grown enormously fat. But he refused to allow her to call herself fat; he pretended — even went to preposterous lengths — to pretend that she was in fact thin. So of course, since she was forbidden to diet (it would be a tacit admission that she was fat), she grew fatter, and the pretense grew like a lie in their lives to a proportion that she dimly perceived; she grew angrier and angrier. All these people loved him and yet they were all angry at him because he based his relationship to them on false premises that grew out of promises he made that nobody could keep.

The final promise was robbing the bank to get money for the sex-change operation, which turned out to be a televised fiasco in which people would get killed. Ernie was not grateful; he viewed it as typical of the kind of disaster that Sonny created around him, with all the best intentions. Then it struck me that Sonny conceived of himself as a magician with the power to make dreams come true, to fulfill hopes and ambitions. He loved the needy and unfulfilled, and he went through life trying to fulfill their dreams of themselves, to make them whole. And once they were whole, they could give back to him the love he had given to them. But this was an impossible dream. All he was able to do was fan their hopes. He was a convincing dreamer because he believed the dream was real. And when the eventual disaster materialized, he was blamed for letting them down. Instead of love, he got back from everyone waves of anger and resentment.

Now of course this is wholly imaginary. I never met the real-life Sonny, and I have no way of knowing if this is an accurate psychological portrait. But it made sense of a vast pile of unrelated facts. And of course I didn't think of this fictional Sonny as being so articulate and aware that he would know this about himself; it was the way he acted in the world. Once I knew this about my fictional Sonny, I knew how to write him. I knew what he would do or say in any situation I could put him into.

I knew he would be considerate and worried about the needs of his hostages, down to getting them food and medicine and allowing them to go to the bathroom. I knew he would even try to see into the needs of the cops and intuit their actions from their needs as he understood them. A character like this would grow sly and very smart about reading people's real intentions and subconscious attitudes. I knew that at times the strain of trying to handle everyone else's problems and manage his own would tell; he would break out and accuse them all of ingratitude for his prodigious efforts. He would at times be bitter and sad and feel unappreciated. But he would also feel proud and in control, almost arrogant in his feeling that he understood everything and that everybody else understood nothing.

I now had a will driving the story that went far beyond the mere stipulation that a man robbed a bank to raise money for a sex-change operation for his lover. I understood why he would do it; and the schizoid disintegration of his personality from repeated failure in the past explained why he was so out of touch with reality.

From that moment, I could write the screenplay almost without effort. Until that understanding, I couldn't write a word.

If You're Lucky

You write with the dialog sounding in your ear, the rhythms of the characters' movement swaying you like seaweed in the tides, or like partners in a dance, the tempo and flow of images unspooling in your mind like the movie you want the actors and director to make for you.

The characters are no longer invented shadows; they are known to you like brothers and sisters, capable of making you cry and laugh, of dusting your skin with cold fear. They have become so real that they act before you can think.*

*Copyright © 1986, Frank Pierson. Reprinted by permission.

CHAPTER 6

Dialog

Throughout the theater's long history, speech remained the dramatist's primary creative tool, communicating characters' thoughts and emotions and describing incidents that occurred offstage. To be sure, characters performed certain deeds onstage: killing, stealing, kissing, fighting. But incidents of considerable dramatic significance often happened elsewhere. Ships were launched, wars were fought, kingdoms fell. Because of their size or scope, such events simply could not be performed on a stage. Occasionally, too, events occurred offstage because they were too heinous to view.

The entertainment world has expanded considerably in the past hundred years. Audiences have discovered the exhilaration of viewing Roman chariot races, of seeing Atlanta burning, of watching the Red Sea part. They have found such firsthand involvement more satisfying than hearing those events described by witnesses. Twentieth-century screenwriters understand that they can awe, inspire, provoke, dazzle, mystify, or shatter audiences by transporting them to where the action is, whether it takes place in Singapore, medieval England, or a galaxy far, far away.

Surprisingly, however, beginning screenwriters often revert to an earlier stage-bound tradition, talking about incidents rather than showing them. TV drama is often guilty of this, and writers (like everyone else) tend to be brainwashed by what they see. As their abilities mature, however, screenwriters discover that creating events or incidents is as much a part of their art as creating speeches and that no dialog is often superior to much dialog, no matter how skillfully that dialog may be written.

There are occasions, of course, when only dialog will perfectly express ideas or emotions — when awkward, fumbling words appropriately articulate young love or when explosive words ideally express anger. The effectiveness of those words will vary in proportion to the writer's talent and the use of certain established principles that we will discuss in this and the next chapter.

In the following pages we will examine:

➤ **DIALOG'S PURPOSE**: defining characters, providing the audience with information, and advancing the plot; a comparison between dialog and character action

➤ **CHARACTERISTICS OF EFFECTIVE DIALOG**: including vernacular speech, economy, simplicity, invisibility, and progression, with examples from motion pictures and television

PURPOSE

Dialog has three primary functions: (1) to reveal or suggest the nature of each character, (2) to provide the audience with information, and (3) to advance the plot. Dialog also performs a fourth function that will be described in Chapter 8: revealing thoughts and emotions.

DEFINING CHARACTERS

The writer's choice of spoken words — and even the arrangement of those words — helps define the nature of characters. People raised in the slums, for example, use certain phrases in voicing a concept; those raised in million-dollar mansions and educated at Ivy League colleges use other phrases. For many years, motion picture and television shows stereotyped their heavies (bad guys) by having them speak ungrammatically and use such New York East Side words as *dese*, *dem*, and *dose* (*these*, *them*, and *those*). Thus, if a character entered a room with a speech such as "All right, youse creeps, up wid yer hands!" audiences readily deduced that this was not a college professor.

In scripts by inept writers, all characters speak in similar patterns. It is often possible to switch character names above speeches, giving one character's dialog to another. Fine writers, on the other hand, study their characters carefully, preparing biographies that define physical, psychological, and sociological histories before beginning their scripts. Such writers understand how scripted characters think, what their moralities are, what they fear most, what their personalities reveal, and the style in which they speak. Their characters have individual speech rhythms, patterns, phrases, and ideas that are unique to each character and therefore unsuitable for any other character.

What characters say in dialog (and what they *don't* say) constitutes one of the primary ways in which audiences come to understand their essential natures. In addition to defining characters, dialog also conveys information about the story.

What does the following scene* from the motion picture *Misery* tell you about the character of Annie Wilkes? (Note: The format is William Goldman's; it is not typical.)

PAUL. He's been dozing but now his eyes flutter awake as we

CUT TO

THE DOOR. It opens and ANNIE enters, comes to his bedside.

---

*Reprinted by permission of William Goldman, Stephen King, and Castle Rock Entertainment.

CUT TO

PAUL. Hard to see. He squints up as we

CUT TO

ANNIE, CLOSE UP, and her face is ashen pale, the cords in her neck stand out. One vein pulses uncontrollably in the center of her forehead. She brings her hands up to her face—they're rocklike fists. They open, close, open, close—

> ANNIE
> (screaming)
> You... you... you dirty bird.

CUT TO

PAUL, staring up at her, trying to move away on the bed—

> ANNIE
> She can't be dead. MISERY CHASTAIN CANNOT BE DEAD!

> PAUL
> Annie—Annie, listen—

> ANNIE
> Oh—oh you dirty birdie—how could you?—

> PAUL
> —Annie, in 1871 women often died in childbirth, but her spirit is the important thing and Misery's spirit is still alive—

> ANNIE
> (screaming again)
> —I don't want her spirit! I want her! And you murdered her!

> PAUL
> (screaming back)
> I didn't—

> ANNIE
> Then who did?

> PAUL
> (quieter)
> No one—she just died—she slipped away, that's all.

CUT TO

ANNIE, and again her fists are rocks and they're raised high and they could come crashing down on his crippled form but then at the last moment, she turns with a cry and if Orson Welles destroyed the room in <u>Citizen Kane</u>, that's what Annie does now.

She picks up the water pitcher, grips it tight and spins with it like a discus thrower, finally releasing it up at the ceiling where it shatters, and then she's got the water glass in her hands and she heaves that against the wall and then next she picks up the bed-table—it's not a feather but it might as well be as she launches it all the way across the room and then she chases it down, picks it up again, smashes it, holding it by the legs, against the wall, until it's splinters and every other thing in the room she grabs and rips and kills and

CUT TO

PAUL, terrified, watching it, helpless to do any damn thing but that, just watch and finally

CUT TO

ANNIE, her back to PAUL. She stops, taking great gasping breaths. Then, finally, she turns, head on her chest like some powerful red-eyed bull, and wordlessly, she advances across the room until she hovers right on top of him and he could be dead in a blink, you can tell that from her eyes.

> ANNIE
> (her voice surprisingly
> soft at the start)
> I've seen a lot of deaths in my time—so many deaths—sometimes patients go screaming and sometimes they slip away—but characters in books, Paul, <u>they do not slip away</u>—

CUT TO

PAUL. Frozen. Helpless—whatever comes, comes.

CUT TO

ANNIE

> ANNIE
> I thought you were good, Paul, but you're not good. You're just another lying old dirty birdie and I don't think I better be around you for a while—I don't think it's safe or wise, so I'm going now.
> (she turns)

>   PAUL
>   Where?
>
>   ANNIE
>   A place. I need to think. Good-bye, Paul; you'd
>   better hope nothing happens to me, because if I
>   die, you die

Annie's dialog defines her as a woman of strange contrasts: Unwilling to use swear words, she is still capable of terrifying violence and childlike in her wants and needs. A single scene gives us incredible insights.

PROVIDING INFORMATION

Information that audiences need to know in order to understand the circumstances of a story is called exposition (as discussed in Chapter 3). Such information emerges in screenplays primarily in two ways: from visual information (newspaper headlines, billboards, handwritten letters, uniforms that define a profession, photographs, symbols) and from dialog. Of the two, screenwriters tend to use dialog more often, not because dialog is preferable to visual exposition but because it usually is more convenient; appropriate visual material is not always available in a scene and it is not usually as explicit as dialog.

Beginning writers sometimes have difficulty conveying information through dialog, since speeches may sound artificial, as if the character is expressing ideas or facts solely for the audience's benefit.

ADVANCING THE PLOT

When a teenage son dedicates himself to becoming a rock musician and his father determines to steer him into the family business, they may face each other angrily. As a result of their verbal confrontation, the son may resolve to leave home forever, the father may disown him, or each may recognize the depth of the other's needs (and love) and accede. Such scenes obviously advance the plot; they are stepping-stones as we move through a story. Even though their content is largely dialog, such scenes represent significant narrative action. Characters undergo changes; they make decisions that affect the screenplay's progression.

We saw earlier that dramatizing an important event is usually preferable to having characters discuss it. Yet many of these visual events emerge from, or climax, a succession of dialog scenes, such as the father-son confrontation. Thus, dialog represents a major portion of most screenplays. If you have access to motion picture scripts, study them. Reading the material of top screenwriters will stimulate your imagination, acquaint you with script form and style, and make you eager to write your own screenplay. In addition, you will discover that most of the scene content is dialog.

CHARACTERISTICS OF EFFECTIVE DIALOG

Many nonprofessionals believe that the best dialog is that closest to reality, that screenplay speech closely parallels the speech of everyday life. This is not so. Remember, screenplays create not reality but the *appearance* of reality. As scriptwriters, we practice sleight of hand whenever we put words on paper, trying to convince audiences that the dialog they hear represents actual speech from real people. But, of course, that dialog has been carefully contrived to meet the rigorous demands of our scenes and our story. In farce or in fantasy, the need for any semblance of reality often disappears.

Beneath a surface illusion of reality, effective dialog must meet these fundamental qualifications: (1) vernacular speech, (2) economy, (3) simplicity, (4) invisibility, and (5) progression.

VERNACULAR SPEECH

A writer I know arbitrarily picks a key scene from somewhere deep in his story and dramatizes it in detail *before* he begins his script. Why? Simply to hear how his characters talk, to listen to the kinds of words they use.

Each character in a script has his or her own speech pattern. Choice of words, sentence structure, and speech rhythm will usually reveal something of a person's nature, origins, workplace, and personality.

We form our **vernacular speech** (as well as our attitudes) from the people closest to us. The word *vernacular* refers to native speech patterns, such as those acquired from a particular locale or from our parents. If our parents use the word *ain't* a lot, chances are that we will, too. If they speak with a southern or foreign accent, so will we.

As we grow up, we make friends in our neighborhood and in school. We absorb some of their words, phrases, and speech patterns. Our vocabularies grow and change as we study new subjects. Our speech is modified again when our parents move to another state. We discover in high school that certain trendy words and phrases will make us appear sophisticated—and so we add them to our vocabulary.

Trendy words and phrases can make a screenplay appear current, yet the writer should exercise caution in using them. Motion pictures are released sometimes two or three years (or more) after completion of a screenplay. Words that were in vogue when the script was written may be hopelessly outdated when the picture is released.

When we enter the business world, we absorb the esoteric words or phrases from that world, and almost without our realizing it, they become part of our vocabulary. Oil-well drillers, computer programmers, gene splicers, and race-track touts all have their vernaculars: legitimate as well as slang words that add color and individuality to their speech.

Words, sentence structure, and speech rhythm all reflect the nature of the person speaking. In the following scene from *Citizen Kane*, note the difference in speech style and word choice between imperious Kane, speaking as if to a child, and his volatile, undereducated wife.

> KANE
>
> You're in a tent, darling. You're not at home.
> And I can hear you very well if you speak in a
> normal tone of voice.
>
> SUSAN
>
> I'm not going to have my guests insulted, just
> because you...
>   (in a rage)
> If people want to bring a drink or two along
> on a picnic, that's their business. You've got no
> right...
>
> KANE
>   (quickly)
> I've got more than a right as far as you're
> concerned, Susan.
>
> SUSAN
>
> I'm sick and tired of your telling me what I
> mustn't do! And what I...
>
> KANE
>
> We can discuss all this some other time, Susan.
> Right now...
>
> SUSAN
>
> I'll discuss what's on my mind when I want to.
> I'm sick of having you run my life the way you
> want it.
>
> KANE
>
> Susan, as far as you're concerned, I've never
> wanted anything — I don't want anything now —
> except what you want.

                    SUSAN

What you want me to want, you mean. What
you've decided I ought to have—what you'd want
if you were me. Never what I want.

                    KANE

Susan...

                    SUSAN

You've never given me anything that...

                    KANE

I really think...

                    SUSAN

Oh, sure, you've given me things that don't
mean anything to you. What's the difference
between giving me a bracelet or giving
somebody else a hundred thousand dollars for a
statue you're going to keep crated up and never
look at? It's only money.

                    KANE

Susan, I want you to stop this.

                    SUSAN

I'm not going to stop it!

                    KANE

Right now!

                    SUSAN
                  (screams)
You never gave me anything in your life! You
just tried to... to buy me into giving you
something. You're... it's like you were bribing
me!

                    KANE

Susan!

                    SUSAN

That's all you ever done... no matter how much
it cost you... your time, your money... that's
all you've done with everybody. Tried to bribe
them!

                    KANE

Susan!
          (MORE)

                              KANE
                     (continuing; quietly)
             Whatever I do — I do — because I love you.

                              SUSAN
             You don't love me! You just want me to love
             you. Sure, I'm Charles Foster Kane. Whatever
             you want, just name it and it's yours. But you
             gotta love me!

Without a word, Kane slaps her across the face. He continues to stare
at her.

                              SUSAN
                         (continuing)
             You'll never get a chance to do that again.
                     (he stares at her
                     silently; then)
             And don't tell me you're sorry.

                              KANE
             I'm not sorry.*

It is control more than any other characteristic that distinguishes Kane's
words from those of his young wife. His speeches seek to repress the surging
emotions beneath. Susan's words, on the other hand, spew out in all directions,
intemperately, with occasional lapses in grammar. Notice that Kane's final
violent action is a far more accurate barometer of his feelings than are his
words. If the character names were removed from each of the above speeches,
there would be no problem determining which person was speaking.

How do writers find the appropriate speech colorations for characters such
as Kane and Susan? Some writers simply dream them up from their own
imaginations. Such a practice is satisfactory much of the time. For characters
whose backgrounds are familiar to the writer, such an easy solution suffices.
But for principal characters from unfamiliar worlds, writers must do their
homework.

Ideally, if a writer wants to learn how oil-well drillers speak (as well as
other aspects of their lives), he or she should enter their world, live with them —
absorb the color, smell, grit, and atmosphere of that world — talk to drillers,
meet their families, soak up the esoteric words and phrases that color their
speech. Directors do this. So do actors. Before Jane Fonda began work on the
movie *Coming Home*, she spent weeks in Veterans Administration hospitals,
talking to disabled vets from the Vietnam War, learning their deepest fears,

what made them laugh, the nature of their physical problems, and how they dealt with those problems. Before director Arthur Hiller began production on *Making Love*, a film about the gay community, he spent days in that community, visiting its bars, interviewing its inhabitants, talking at length with a psychiatrist whose clientele was primarily gay about the emotional and physical problems facing those committed to a homosexual life-style.

Firsthand research inevitably enriches a script, giving its dialog a pungent reality. It is a good idea to take a tape recorder along on interviews to preserve the interviewee's actual words and phrases as well as the style, accent, and pattern in which they are spoken. Writer-researchers should also note the personal details that characterize the interviewee: clothing, posture, way of walking. Perhaps the interviewee will agree to read a first-draft script, checking it for accuracy, correcting words or phrases that seem wrong or dishonest.

Many beginning writers are timid, reluctant to impose on a total stranger. In truth, most people like nothing better than to talk about themselves. They are flattered when a writer — even a student writer — wants to use their experiences in a script or wants to create a character using them as a model. Usually they are delighted to cooperate.

When it's impossible to enter your characters' world or to interview an inhabitant of that world, one final option remains: the public library. Check out some books or other materials that describe your character's milieu, and soak up as much of it as you can. You'll find yourself better able to recreate it honestly if you have done your homework.

A word of caution: Sometimes writers become so excited by the world they have discovered that they cram their material into every scene and every speech. The research begins to take a foreground position, and the story dims. Remember that research is intended to provide honest background color. And that's where it must remain — in the background.

ECONOMY

The next time you go to a party, listen critically to some of the conversations. You will discover that people repeat themselves endlessly, that they include irrelevant or meaningless details, that they wander all around a subject before making a point. If you were to present those conversations as entertainment, you'd discover that the audience would quickly grow restless and leave the theater.

Effective dialog usually is lean. The fat has been trimmed away. Unnecessary speeches, sentences, and words have been mercilessly deleted.

Some professionals recommend the following screenwriting pattern: When you commit a scene to paper, write it fully, not censoring your thoughts, allowing the full, free flow of ideas to be recorded. Yes, the speeches will be fat and filled with clichés and repetition. Yes, the scene will run far longer than its content dictates. Then, ideally, you should lock the pages away in a desk drawer for a day or two, allowing the scene to "cool" and giving you time to gain objectivity.

When you write a scene or an essay, you probably write in a fever of excitement. (Many professionals believe that such excitement is necessary to function creatively. They play **mind games** to light creative fires, finding some aspect of a project that will challenge and stimulate them.) You become emotionally caught up in your work, and it becomes difficult to be truly objective regarding its strengths and weaknesses.

A day or two later when you take the scene out of the drawer and read it again, you will probably be disappointed. The magic has disappeared. The good ideas are buried in a debris of unnecessary words. So you pick up a pencil and set to work correcting your excesses. You go through the scene, speech by speech, word by word, eliminating the fat, removing clichés, finding better words to express your ideas, looking for character actions that will express thoughts visually, without the need for explanation. The six-page scene suddenly becomes three. You read it again and discover another trim or two that will tighten speeches, giving them more impact. And now, in astonishment and delight, you discover that the scene has gained new power and strength, largely because you have removed the clutter. You have transformed a mediocre scene into a good scene, primarily through the exercise of dramatic economy.

Compare the *Citizen Kane* scene as it was originally written (page 118) with the following version that appeared in the completed film. Note how the film version retains all of the essential story information yet is tighter and probably more pungent. The scene begins in the middle of Susan's tirade, eliminating some of the early lines.

                         SUSAN
          Oh, sure, you gimme things that don't mean
          anything to you.

                         KANE
          You're in a tent, darling. You're not at home.
          I can hear you very well if you speak in a
          normal tone of voice.

                         SUSAN
          What's the difference between giving me a
          bracelet and giving somebody else a hundred
          thousand dollars for a statue you're going to
          keep crated up and never even look at? It's
          money. It doesn't mean anything. You never
          really give me anything that belongs to you —
          that you care about!

> KANE
>
> Susan!

For contrast, the film cuts away here to a brief glimpse of the party: music, food, expensive merrymaking. Then it cuts back inside Kane's tent.

> KANE
>
> (quietly)
>
> Whatever I do—I do—because I love you.

> SUSAN
>
> You don't love me! You want me to love you. Sure, I'm Charles Foster Kane. Whatever you want, just name it and it's yours. But you gotta love me!

He slaps her. Hard.

> SUSAN
>
> Don't tell me you're sorry.

> KANE
>
> I'm not sorry.

This shortened version of the *Citizen Kane* scene reinforces the concept of beginning a scene at the latest possible moment and cutting away as soon as it has completed its message.

When dialog abandons economy, when characters voice every aspect of a thought, every nuance of their feelings, the writer leaves no room for the audience to contribute. When characters suggest or imply an idea rather than laying it out in explicit detail, audiences then may fill in the blanks from their imaginations.

SIMPLICITY

Most people most of the time speak in simple, declarative sentences, using short, one- or two-syllable words. Why? Because when we speak to friends, we aren't trying to impress them with the size of our vocabularies or our ability to frame elaborate sentences. In our private lives, we express thoughts in the easiest way possible. When we become shocked or angry, the phrases come tumbling out helter skelter, sometimes awkwardly or without structure; sometimes we become almost inarticulate. At such moments we don't search for fancy words; we grab for those within easy reach.

In our working environments, on the other hand, we use the esoteric terms of our professions. Doctors speaking to other doctors use a clinical language that would be incomprehensible to outsiders. Computer programmers, bacteriologists, pipefitters, and TV technicians normally use esoteric language in their workplace, and screenwriters properly use such jargon when staging scenes in a professional environment. Most of the time, however, outside of their working environments, doctors, scientists, and college professors use short sentences and simple words. At the dinner table with their spouses and children, they say "Pass the bread" or "How was your day?" or "I hate cauliflower" just like everyone else.

Most of us speak in contractions, shortening *do not* to *don't* because it's a faster, easier way to communicate ideas. When we use the longer form, "I do not care," people think we're being formal or pretentious.

Examine the words of a high school student and his psychiatrist in this portion of a scene from *Ordinary People*. Sixteen-year-old Conrad, who recently tried to kill himself, has come here in tears, shattered because a close friend has just committed suicide. Notice how simple the speeches are; they contain short sentences, contractions, and mostly one- or two-syllable words.

> BERGER
>
> Things are beginning to happen to you. You're coming alive and don't tell me you don't feel it.

> CONRAD
>
> Well, it doesn't feel good.

> BERGER
>
> Well, it is good, because it's you, wonderful, beautiful you, just as good as anyone, believe me. I'm your friend, I love you. It <u>is</u> good. You're alive.

> CONRAD
>
> (starts to sob)
>
> I was beginning to think so.

> BERGER
>
> Then what happened? What started all this?

> CONRAD
>
> (crying, having trouble talking)
>
> Karen... in the paper. She killed herself.

> BERGER
>
> Oh, Jesus.

> CONRAD
>
> But she was okay.

                    BERGER
          (gently)
No, she wasn't.

                    CONRAD
She said she was okay.

                    BERGER
She wasn't.

                    CONRAD
Into everything at school, and happy, doing <u>A
Thousand Clowns</u>. She told me it was better,
that she was better. I believed her.
          (pause)
It isn't fair.

                    BERGER
No. It isn't fair.

                    CONRAD
Well, what is it, a joke?

And he lowers his head and just bawls. Berger watches him.

Conrad looks up as he continues to cry and half laughs and shrugs at
his inability to stop the tears.

Berger watches another moment, then moves next to him. He puts his
arms around him and embraces him as Conrad continues to cry.

                    CONRAD
I know it's late and you're tired... But I gotta
talk... I gotta talk 'bout her.

                    BERGER
Okay. We'll talk about her.

                    CONRAD
And Buck.

                    BERGER
And Buck.

                    CONRAD
And everybody.

                    BERGER
Everybody.

>   CONRAD
>   I'm so sad. I'm so scared... and sad...
>   (suddenly very angry)
>   And I'm so angry.
>
>   BERGER
>   Everything, you're everything.
>
>   CONRAD
>   (still crying)
>   I don't know what I would've done if you hadn't
>   been here.
>
>   BERGER
>   You're welcome.
>
> Conrad continues to sob. Berger holding him.
>
>   CONRAD
>   Do you really love me?
>
>   BERGER
>   (holding him)
>   I love you, my friend. Count on it.
>
> VERY TIGHT ON BERGER
>
> His compassion.*

For those who believe that fancy words are the key to effective screenplays, this deeply moving scene should be argument enough. The simplicity of the speeches underscores their honesty, thereby giving impact to their emotion.

INVISIBILITY

In his *Art of Dramatic Writing*, Lajos Egri relates a story about the completion of Rodin's statue of French author Honoré de Balzac.† Despite the fact that it was four in the morning, the great French sculptor excitedly awakened some of his students, asking them to view the completed masterpiece.

Each student in turn studied the sculpture and exclaimed at the incredible beauty of the figure's hands: "Only a God could have created such hands. They are alive!" After several such reactions, the sculptor's face darkened. As his students watched in horror, he grabbed an axe and chopped the offending hands

---

*Courtesy of Alvin Sargent and Wildwood Enterprises, Inc.

†Lajos Egri, *The Art of Dramatic Writing* (New York: Simon & Schuster, 1946), pp. 30–31.

off the statue. "Fools!" he cried. "I was forced to destroy those hands because they had a life of their own. They didn't belong to the rest of the composition. Remember this and remember it well: No part is more important than the whole!"*

When audiences watch a well-made motion picture or television drama, they get caught up in the story and emotionally involved with its characters. In time, they forget that they are seated in a movie theater or living room. It's only when viewers become aware of some artifice, sculpted hands that attract too much attention, that they realize the work has been contrived, that they have been living in a manufactured world. Such awareness inevitably jolts them out of the dream.

When writers show off — "Hey, look at me! See how brilliant I am!" — they destroy the illusion that they have worked to achieve. When writers with a gift for clever, sophisticated banter place their witticisms in the mouths of unsophisticated characters, for example, the mismatch calls attention to itself. The audience might think "How clever! What a marvelous writer!" But they have become aware of the writer's existence — and so the writer has defeated him- or herself.

All screenwriters tend occasionally to fall in love with lines they create. But if the line is wrong for a character, if it calls too much attention to itself, it must be hacked off, just as Rodin hacked off the statue's offending hands. Author Ernest Hemingway always distrusted lines that he fell in love with and inevitably eliminated them, simply because they called attention to themselves.

The principle of invisibility also holds true, of course, for directors, actors, composers, art directors, or any of the other artists in film or television. Awareness of directorial touches, scenery that attracts undue attention, or any musical intrusion — all will destroy the illusion, forcing audiences to withdraw their emotional involvement.

PROGRESSION

In Chapter 3 we saw that progression is intrinsic to screenplay narrative — a sense of growth, a climbing action, a building in tension from scene to scene and from act to act up to the story climax.

Progression also is necessary in dialog; lines of dialog must develop from the *least* important to the *more* important to the *most* important thought. For example, "A few of the soldiers had been wounded. A few had lost limbs. A few were becoming dust on some forgotten battlefield." Or, "The mayors of half a dozen cities attended the convention. A few senators also appeared. And, on the final day, the president himself showed up."

*Ibid.

When we express a sequence of thoughts in everyday life, our instincts usually guide us to use this dramatic pattern. We save the best for the last. So accustomed are we to this progression of ideas that when we reverse the normal order, it frequently becomes laughable. In his *Art of Dramatic Writing*, Egri recalls a classic line that warns against murder since it may lead to drinking, which in turn may lead to smoking, which may lead to nonobservance of the Sabbath!*

*C*HAPTER HIGHLIGHTS

➤ In the theater, dialog is the dramatist's primary tool. Major events often play offstage because of spatial (or other) limitations. Despite the fact that movies and television can effectively depict such events, many beginning writers allow characters to describe events in dialog, thereby undercutting their impact.

➤ Dialog has several purposes: (1) to define characters, (2) to provide information, and (3) to advance the plot. As in life, dialog is not always an accurate barometer of a character's thoughts or nature. People lie; they exaggerate; they conceal weaknesses. Because of these behaviors and because dialog often is merely ritualistic, actions sometimes reveal a character's nature more accurately than words.

➤ A primary characteristic of effective dialog is economy. In real life, speech often is cluttered with repetition and meaningless detail. But screenplays do not create life; they create an appearance or compression of life. Screenplay dialog eliminates unnecessary words.

➤ Another characteristic of effective dialog is simplicity. Most people speak in simple, declarative sentences composed of one- or two-syllable words. When people express thoughts or emotions, they use whatever words come most easily to mind. We imitate real-life speech patterns when writing dialog.

➤ Characters' backgrounds influence their patterns of speech, rhythms, accents, and choices of words. Because different people express thoughts differently, dialog cannot be interchangeable. Ideally, the writer creates a specific vernacular pattern for each character. Skilled writers research their characters, studying their speech and environment.

*Ibid., p. 242.

➤ The writer's goal is to draw the spectator into a movie or TV show by creating a sense of illusory participation. The moment writers call attention to themselves with flashy dialog, they rupture the illusion, forcing spectators to withdraw their participation. Genuine artists create a cloak of invisibility — art that conceals art.

➤ In real life and in screenplays, speeches tend to build from the least important, to the more important, to the most important thought. Such progression is the hallmark of well-written plays, acts, scenes, and speeches.

CHAPTER 7

More About Dialog

TECHNIQUES AND TABOOS

When composers write music, they rely on certain respected, almost mathematical principles of structure and harmony. Successful painters, poets, architects, and sculptors also rely on established aesthetic and structural principles. And, although some will deny it, successful screenwriters, consciously or unconsciously, follow time-honored principles and techniques when creating their dialog.

Many claim that they write intuitively, from gut instinct, that they create their best dialog simply because it "feels right." But intuitive feelings often derive from experience, from observation and study, from discipline, from screenplays that failed and those that triggered box-office bonanzas. Most screenwriters may not be able to articulate in so many words the techniques described in this chapter and Chapter 6, but they will use some of those principles and techniques in every screenplay they write.

This chapter includes:

➤ **TECHNIQUES FOR EFFECTIVE DIALOG**: Saying the Words Aloud, Playbacks, Tag Lines and Tag Business, Making the Audience Work, Injecting Conflict, Avoiding Clichés

➤ **CHARACTERISTICS OF BAD DIALOG**: studying an inept scene and analyzing why its speeches are inadequate

➤ **WRITER REVELATIONS**: personal techniques for creating effective dialog as described by distinguished writer-executive producer, George Eckstein

Techniques for Effective Dialog

When creating dialog, writers practice certain techniques so their speeches will have the appearance of reality, provide impact, and ensure maximum audience response. These techniques include: (1) saying it out loud, (2) play-backs, (3) tag lines, (4) making the audience work, (5) injecting conflict, and (6) avoiding clichés.

SAYING IT OUT LOUD

Pick up a novel or short story and say some of the dialog out loud. If you're listening critically, you will discover that many of the speeches sound unnatural. Why? Because most novelists aren't screenwriters. Their dialog has to read well, of course, but it doesn't have to stand the test of being spoken aloud.

Effective movie or TV dialog must sound spontaneous; it should appear to have occurred to the actors at that very second. Many writers achieve this sense of spontaneity by saying words out loud before committing them to paper.

When we write dialog, we become actors. We assume a character's thoughts, emotions, and point of view; we crawl into a character's mind and imagine what he or she would say or do in each plot situation. We speak the words aloud, tentatively, exploratively, trying to determine if they are correct for a particular scene or mood. Sometimes, when we are really "into" a character, we shout angrily or whimper or sob — whatever the scene requires.

When listening critically to the words we speak (which isn't as difficult as it sounds), we must both examine them and ask questions: Are the words easy to say or are they awkward? How may we rearrange them to make them simpler, easier for an actor to articulate? Are the words honest? Do they sound legitimate for a character in a specific situation? Do they carry the proper emotional weight?

At first you may feel self-conscious acting out the content of a scene, striding up and down angrily, pounding the desk, whispering love words, or sobbing. Such behavior in the presence of others becomes embarrassing. The solution is to seek privacy and then to lose your inhibitions. Remember that many top professionals write their best dialog by "becoming" a character and improvising that character's speech. So can you.

USING PLAYBACKS

Repetitions of lines of dialog or significant pieces of business are called **playbacks** because they (obviously) play back on earlier moments. In burlesque and comedy, such repetitions are known as **running gags**.

When jokes or pieces of business are repeated throughout a story, they become funnier. When lines of dialog or key pieces of business are repeated, the repetition evokes memories of emotions that were triggered by the original moment. This emotionality tends to grow, to take on added colorations each time significant dialog or business is repeated. A classic example is Humphrey Bogart's line from *Casablanca*, "Here's looking at you, kid," first uttered when he and Ingrid Bergman shared an idyllic love affair in Paris. When she reappears years later in Bogart's Café Americain, after having (apparently) deserted him, Bogart repeats the line, this time in bitterness, an ironic commentary on a love gone sour. When, finally, the lovers have reconciled and Bogart selflessly sends Bergman to America with another man, he repeats the line for the final time, gently, in love and respect, evoking tears from audiences wherever the film is shown.

Good writers don't let anything go to waste. When they discover a particularly trenchant line of dialog, they find ways of using it again, in another scene or another situation, playing back on the original line in humor or irony or tragedy. In *Ghost*, for example, Patrick Swayze repeatedly says, "Ditto," when Demi Moore tells him she loves him, apparently embarrassed to say the words himself. The repeated word becomes the source of humor between them — and some frustration to her. At the end of the film, when he returns as a ghost and finally makes contact with her, he declares for the first time that he truly loves her; now she utters the familiar word "Ditto," and audiences become choked up. The word recalls all of its earlier utterances, and the repetition here, with humor and deep affection, makes it curiously moving.

PUNCTUATING WITH TAG LINES
OR TAG BUSINESS

Many professional writers — particularly comedy writers — provide a final punctuation for scenes, an after beat, a final payoff that either signifies completion or creates a surprise twist in the action. These **tag lines** don't occur at the end of every scene, of course. Such a pattern would become boring. But when used selectively, they provide an effective closing, or curtain.

Sometimes tag lines use the playback principle. For example, in Rod Serling's "Requiem for a Heavyweight," ex-boxer "Mountain" McClintock gets acquainted with a young woman at a bar frequented by prize fighters. During the scene, McClintock plays a song on the jukebox. As they listen to the music, he stares at her, smitten, and explains, "Them are violins." Later in the scene, the line reappears.

> GRACE
> There isn't much else, is there—besides
> fighting?
>
> McCLINTOCK
> (thoughtfully)
> No, no, there isn't, I guess. I'm ... I'm sorry.
>
> GRACE
> Don't be. It's just that there is so much more
> for you that you'll be able to find now.

They look at each other and both smile. The music is playing, and they are both aware of it suddenly.

> GRACE
> Hey, Mountain—
>
> McCLINTOCK
> Yeah?
>
> GRACE
> Them are violins.

They both laugh. CAMERA PULLS AWAY from them as they continue to talk.

The repetition of McClintock's line, "Them are violins," concludes the scene with humor, warmth, and a feeling of closeness between two characters whom we like. The line also provides a punctuation, the period at the end of a sentence.

Sometimes a final tag question becomes an arrow that points directly toward the upcoming scene, that *propels* us into the upcoming scene. An obvious example: "How do you suppose Jill will take it when she hears the bad news?" And we cut to a close-up of Jill as she reacts at the beginning of the next scene.

Tag lines are used more often in comedy than in serious drama. Writers such as Neil Simon use them to provide a final "kicker" at the end of an act, to send the audience out laughing. Here's an example from his *The Sunshine Boys* in a sketch titled "The Doctor Will See You."*

> WILLIE
> Open wider and say "Ahh."
>
> PATIENT
> Ahh.

*Used by permission of Random House, Inc.

WILLIE

Wider.

PATIENT

Ahh.

WILLIE

A little wider.

PATIENT

Ahhh!

WILLIE

Your throat is all right, but you're gonna have some trouble with your stomach.

PATIENT

How come?

WILLIE

You just swallowed the stick.

CURTAIN

The final punctuation of a scene sometimes emerges in the form of business rather than dialog. A man tells his wife he is leaving her, that he has fallen in love with a client. He gives her the bankbook for their joint account. When he leaves, the camera remains with the wife as her eyes moisten. Then she picks up the bankbook and hurls it after him.

When the owner of a company fires one of his oldest employees, claiming financial problems and promising a handsome settlement check, the employee smiles understandingly. As soon as his boss leaves, however, the employee stares at the pencil he is holding and abruptly breaks it in half. Such payoff action, or **tag business**, not only punctuates the sequence but also gives us insight into the employee's feelings. Character business is also valuable because it makes the audience interpret the action and thereby participate.

MAKING THE AUDIENCE WORK

In the 1930s and 1940s, much of the success of good radio drama arose from the fact that listeners were forced to supply missing elements from their imaginations. Because radio drama provided only sound, listeners furnished their own scenery, costumes, and faces.

Novels and short stories also require us to use our imaginations. The printed page provides neither pictures nor sound, and therefore we invent images, calling them forth from the reservoir of our experience. That is one reason why motion pictures adapted from novels frequently don't measure up to our expectations. No writer or director can create scenes as vivid as those seen in our mind's eye. When writers use dialog that reveals everything and conceals nothing, they prevent viewers from contributing. Such writers defeat their purpose, which is to involve the spectator. Writing dialog is something like the connect-the-numbers games in children's coloring books. Boys and girls see a pattern of numbers and then take a pencil and connect them. Once connected in the correct order, the numbers reveal a picture, perhaps a clown or dragon. When writing dialog, good writers present only the numbers. They allow audiences to fill in the spaces for themselves, completing the picture in their imaginations.

In *Pretty Woman*, after Julia Roberts has left Richard Gere to return to her street profession, he gives a stunning ruby necklace to the hotel manager, for return to the jewelry store from which it had been borrowed. The manager, enormously impressed with Julia Roberts's beauty and character, says to Gere, "It must be difficult to part with something so beautiful," apparently referring to the necklace. The audience "connects the numbers," understanding that the manager actually refers to Julia Roberts. They are moved by the manager's line because they had to participate to appreciate its meaning.

In the motion picture *All That Jazz*, writers Robert Alan Aurthur and Bob Fosse introduced a series of hallucinatory sequences, photographed through a fog filter, that featured a gauzily gowned Jessica Lange in a bizarre theatrical dressing room. The dialog never defined her character for us. Yet, because her sequences usually followed the protagonist's heart pains or other physical discomfort, audiences came to realize that she represented death. If Roy Scheider (the protagonist) had bluntly identified her as such, audiences would have cringed in embarrassment.

In that same film, Scheider's heart attack is presented not in the expected fashion, with the protagonist grabbing his chest and doubling over in pain or with someone exclaiming, "Good heavens, you're pale and sweating. Are you all right?" Instead, the heart attack is revealed through a sudden and alarming absence of dialog sound, even though characters near Scheider are laughing or speaking. All that audiences hear are the exaggeratedly loud sounds of his breathing, coughing, stubbing out a cigarette, or closing a book. Audiences are forced to fill in the blanks for themselves, completing the grim picture.

When we supply material from our memories or imaginations — material that the writer has artfully omitted from dialog — we become more deeply involved with the characters and in the unfolding of their story. Because we enter the creative processes directly, we become vulnerable to a scene's emotional thrust; we find ourselves unaccountably moved by a poignant moment, often surprising ourselves by the sudden rush of emotion.

The ending of *E.T., the Extraterrestrial* demonstrates this principle. When E.T. is about to leave his friend, Elliot, and travel back to his own planet, Elliot begins to cry. Seeing the tears, E.T. utters a single word, "Ouch." Because audiences must dig into their memories to decipher the word's meaning (and because of its gentle humor), the moment becomes enormously moving. Audiences recall that Elliot cried earlier when he hurt his finger. At that time he said, "Ouch." Unfamiliar with our language, the little alien associated the word with tears. In the film's final moments, when E.T. raises his finger to wipe away Elliot's tears and murmurs "ouuuchhh" even the most sophisticated audiences become misty eyed.

The dialog from *E.T.* is effective because it makes audiences participate. At the opposite pole is dialog that sounds uncomfortable or embarrassing because it does not make audiences work. Producers and writers refer to blunt, obvious, and heavy-handed dialog as **on the nose**. Such dialog leaves no room for interpretation; it dumps information into the audience's lap. Would the moment have been as poignant if Elliot had pleaded, "Don't leave me, old friend! We'll never see each other again! It's never going to be the same here without you!"? This is not to suggest, of course, that dialog should be deliberately unclear or confusing. There's a vast difference between confusing dialog and speeches that permit audience interpretation. E.T.'s use of the word *ouch* is neither unclear nor confusing. We will examine other examples of on the nose dialog later in the chapter.

When writers devise dramatic content that is beneath the surface, that audiences must work to figure out, they succeed in creating genuine involvement. An episode of "The Fugitive" TV series demonstrates this principle. The series concerned a former pediatrician, Richard Kimble, who was unjustly convicted of killing his wife. On the way to the death house, he escaped.

For one award-winning segment, writer George Eckstein created the character of a testy old criminal lawyer, the best in his field, who had been crippled in an automobile accident. Confined to a wheelchair, no longer able to practice the profession he loved, he now taught graduate law classes at the local university. But he bitterly resented the students, almost blaming them for his fate. They, in turn, resented his harsh manner and critical barbs.

In this episode, the lawyer, G. Stanley Lazer, stages a mock trial in which he attempts to convince Kimble to turn himself in to the authorities so that Lazer might represent him in a new trial. What follows is a portion of the climactic scene* where Lazer makes his summation to a jury composed of students, apparently pleading for his client but actually pleading for understanding and compassion for himself.

INT. CLASSROOM - LAZER AND JURY - DAY

Lazer wheels himself slowly across the floor in the direction of the jury. He stops and regards them expressionlessly. He speaks directly and honestly. Gone are the whiplike sarcasm, the bombast, the acid, and the anger.

*Used by permission of the Taft Entertainment Co.

                          LAZER
          I suppose I should have taken this opportunity
          to attack the state's case in some slashing
          display of rhetoric—to cloud the real issues
          with some sort of legalistic doubletalk. However
          the district attorney has left little room for
          this.
                      (to jury; sincerely)
          And I have too much respect for the
          intelligence of you gentlemen to expect success
          from such a tactic.

ANOTHER ANGLE

The student district attorney and his assistant exchange glances.
Lazer's remarks seem out of character.

LAZER AND JURY

                          LAZER
          But I should like you to consider, if you will,
          the defendant himself. What manner of human
          being are we judging here today?
                      (beat)
          A member of one of the great professions, he
          now stands before this court even as the most
          humble supplicant. And what he asks from you
          is only this... compassion.

INT. ANTEROOM - MED. SHOT - DAY

Kimble, watching the TV set, begins to understand what Lazer is doing.
(NOTE TO READERS: The mock trial is being televised on closed circuit
by the university's TV department.)

INT. CLASSROOM - LAZER AND JURY - DAY

                          LAZER
          He is a man whose very vocation demanded a
          dedication beyond that required of the ordinary
          man. And, perhaps, he gave too much...
          shutting out that which should have been most
          important to him—family, friends... and even
          humanity.

ANGLE ON JURY

The twelve law-school students listen to Lazer's words, moved by them.

CLOSE ON LAZER

> LAZER
>
> Then, suddenly, he was thrust out of the only
> life he knew—unable then to do the very work
> that, for him, made <u>any</u> life meaningful. He
> was exiled to a world he hated—hated only
> because it was strange to him, and because...
> because memories of mountaintops had blinded
> him to the beauties of the valley. He had such
> an abundance of hate that he built a wall of it,
> a wall so high that no man could extend a
> hand over it in friendship.

ANGLE ON DISTRICT ATTORNEY

The DA's assistant leans across the table to him.

> ASSISTANT
> (low)
> He's not talking about Kimble.

> D.A.
> He never was.

LAZER AND JURY

> LAZER
>
> He is alone now, his wife—a lonely woman—
> taken from this earth in a pointless and insane
> moment of violence. And though the woman
> was dead, the man still selfishly scratched at
> his <u>own</u> wounds, until he was marked by scars
> that cut deep into his very soul.
> (a pause)
> This, then, is the man you are asked to judge. I
> commend him to your mercy.

The room is hushed as Lazer turns from the jury and wheels himself
back to the defense table.

The richest dialog frequently plays on a number of levels. The surface level is obvious; layers beneath the surface must be inferred by the audience. In the Lazer scene, the audience must see past Lazer's defense of his client and recognize that he is defending himself. In the writer's first draft, the explanatory lines "He's not talking about himself" and "He never was" did not appear. The executive producer, worried that vast numbers of the audience would miss the subtext, insisted that they be included. But even they are not totally on the nose. They are certainly more oblique than stating, "Why, he's talking about *himself*!"

INJECTING CONFLICT

Conflict is not a dialog technique and does not properly belong in this section. And yet conflict is such an essential part of dialog that we include it here, if only briefly.

Several of the scenes we have examined in this chapter are deceptive in that they contain little or no conflict. Recall that in Chapter 4 we saw that any scene improves when it includes conflict. The partial scenes from *Ordinary People* and "The Fugitive" are payoff moments, satisfying because audiences endured a lot of anguish to get there. Such payoff moments are the gold at the end of the rainbow, more rewarding because of the difficulty of the trip. Were the story lines less filled with conflict, the triumphant moments would not be so exhilarating.

But the "difficulty of the trip" is what screenplays are all about. It is up to writers to contrive dialog that will allow viewers to worry. If a boy teases a girl, gently, lovingly, good-naturedly, the teasing still represents conflict and is far more intriguing to audiences than if the two simply stare at each other moonstruck and whisper sweet nothings. If a police detective and his burly prisoner joke with each other, apparently good-humoredly, and the audience knows that their banter covers deep-seated feelings of hostility, they will watch fascinated, awaiting the moment when buried anger erupts into violence. When husband and wife holler at each other, perhaps actually throwing shoes or hairbrushes, and the audience understands that such actions are merely off-center expressions of love, the writer has devised still another demonstration of conflict.

As these examples show, dialog conflict takes many forms; it may be humorous or serious, spoken or concealed, loving or angry. Dialog in any scene should contain the seeds of conflict to make the outcome questionable — and therefore more intriguing.

AVOIDING CLICHÉS

When we can anticipate the line a character will speak or the direction a plot will take, our interest promptly diminishes. When we expect one direction but the film takes another, we pay attention, intrigued by the writer's inventiveness and the exhilaration of traveling a new path. **Clichés** abound: in casting, the same actors playing the same parts again and again, especially the heavies; in action, car chases that end with one car going over a cliff and bursting into flames; in music, love themes that feature time-worn and recognizable phrases and fulsome violins; in dialog, policemen who pull guns and shout, "Hold it right there!"

Because television spews out such quantities of drama, week after week, month after month, year after year, it creates clichés almost continuously, making life difficult—and challenging—for writers. The first thoughts that pop into our heads are usually clichés. *Beware of first thoughts.* Recognize them for what they are. Search for ways to surprise your audience with fresher lines of dialog and unexpected plot directions.

Don't think less of yourself if you write clichés. Almost all writers—even the most experienced pros—commit that sin when putting words on paper. But experienced pros inevitably read over their material, recognize the hackneyed phrases, and promptly delete them. Every writer makes mistakes in a first rough draft. The sin is allowing those mistakes to remain.

CHARACTERISTICS OF
BAD DIALOG

Sometimes it's helpful to study what not to do. The following dismal scene attempts to include as many types of ineffective dialog as possible. You may have seen more disastrous scenes on television. I doubt it.

BAD SCENE

INT. LUXURIOUS CONDO - ANGLE ON MIRROR - NIGHT

MICHELE TAYLOR, 23, sexy, applies lipstick. She looks in mirror and whirls, stunned to see her overweight husband, HUGH, entering the condo, a frown on his porcine face.

> HUGH
> (evenly)
> So this is where you go—all those evenings
> you tell me you're "bowling with the girls."

                    MICHELE
                  (shocked)
Hugh! I'm so... so surprised to see you! You
promised to stay home, wash the dinner dishes,
pay the bills, feed the baby....
                  (drops lipstick)
You're making me nervous, Hugh.

                    HUGH
I've upset your apple cart, haven't I, Michele?
                  (staring at her)
Do you know what I think? I think you're
meeting someone here. I think you have a
secret lover!

                    MICHELE
                  (in apparent shock)
Secret lover! Hugh, that's insane. Why should I
want a lover? I have everything: a handsome
husband, an adorable baby, a beautiful home, a
garden with a fish pond, a wardrobe second to
none, a police dog named Prince that protects
us from prowlers...

                    HUGH
Shut up!
                  (shaking head sadly)
Michele, you should know you can't pull the
wool over my eyes.

Hugh whirls as he hears a DOOR CLOSING.

                    HUGH
                  (suspicious)
What was that? It sounded like it came from
the closet.

                    MICHELE
I didn't hear anything.
                  (urgently)
Hugh, please, let's go home!

Hugh takes a revolver from his inside coat pocket.

                    MICHELE
                  (shocked)
Where did you get that gun?

MICHELE
(shocked)
Where did you get that gun?

HUGH
(grim determination)
If I find somebody in that closet, Michele, I'm
going to kill him. I'm going to shoot him. I'm
going to put a bullet in his no-good body. Do
you understand me, Michele?
(starts toward closet)
I'm going to put him out of his misery.

MICHELE
(desperate)
Hugh, please! Don't look in that closet!

HUGH
(aiming gun, loudly)
I'm aiming my gun. I'm going to pull the
trigger. One, two...

The closet door suddenly bursts open and a MALE FIGURE runs out,
down the hallway and out of the rear door. Hugh looks at Michele
triumphantly.

HUGH
If you weren't meeting a lover, who was that,
Michele?

MICHELE
(grasping at straws)
Didn't you recognize him? That was my... my
brother. My brother, George.

HUGH
(dubious)
Brother?

MICHELE
(confidently)
Of course. You must have met him at our
wedding. My brother, George.

HUGH
No. I don't remember any brother.
(wanting to believe)
But he... he did sort've look like you.
(MORE)

> HUGH
> (continuing)
> Michele, why didn't you tell me you had a
> brother? I'm sorry that I doubted you.

> MICHELE
> (gently)
> Don't be sorry, darling. But I do resent your
> feeling that I'd pull the wool over your eyes.

As they start out, arm in arm.

> HUGH
> (contritely)
> I'm such a fool, Michele. Can you ever forgive
> me?

They exit. CAMERA HOLDS as the Male Figure reenters, crosses to the bar, and pours himself a stiff one.

> FADE OUT

In studying why dialog in the preceding scene appears inept, we will examine (1) dialog cues, (2) character names, (3) clichés, (4) dishonest exposition, (5) lack of progression, (6) radio lines, and (7) the concept of playing against dramatic values.

DIALOG CUES

Actors resent being told too frequently how they should read lines. Directors, too, resent the writer pasting a road map on every speech. The content of speeches and the narrative context usually provide all the clues necessary.

In the above scene, almost every speech contains cues to the actor, instructions in parentheses, most of which are totally unnecessary and should be deleted. Occasionally, certain dialog may be misunderstood by the reader or a specific interpretation may be crucial to the development of a scene. In such cases dialog cues are essential. But as a general rule, avoid them or use them sparingly.

CHARACTER NAMES

When you talk with members of your family or with friends, do you call them by name each time you address them? "Good morning, Debby." "Did you finish your homework, Debby?" "How are you feeling today, Debby?" "That's good, Debby." After a while, such repetition becomes ludicrous. And yet, for some reason, many beginning writers tend to overuse character names in dialog.

Writers should use character names whenever characters make their first appearance in a script. When an audience watches a show, it doesn't know who the characters are or the nature of their relationships. It's up to the writer to identify characters for the audience. When a character first appears in a script, another character (preferably one we already know) should call him or her by name and, if possible, identify the new character's relationship to others. Thus, "Hi, Bob!" (turning to Nicole) "Honey, this is my best friend, Bob." Or, "Nicole, I'd like you to meet my mom."

Of course, it's perfectly all right to use character names occasionally, as we do in everyday life. It's their overuse that becomes offensive.

CLICHÉS

In our bad scene, clichés abound: "I've upset your apple cart"; "Second to none"; "You can't pull the wool over my eyes"; "Put him out of his misery." So do other expressions — "It's no wonder"; "I'm such a fool"; "Can you ever forgive me?" — that sag from weariness, abused phrases that threaten to become clichés at any second.

Clichés are stains on any form of writing: essays, novels, poems, and research papers. From the time we write our first English compositions in grade school, teachers warn us against trite or hackneyed phrases. Such clichés reflect a lack of creative thought, a laziness, an unwillingness to search for a fresher way of expressing an idea. Because we have heard clichéd phrases so often, they have lost much of their meaning.

Sometimes merely changing a word or two will convert a cliché into a fresher way of expressing a thought. The answer often lies in eliminating the offensive words. Let's examine a couple of clichés and see if we can improve them. After Michele's line, "You're making me nervous, Hugh," he replies, "I've upset your apple cart, haven't I, Michele?" First, let's eliminate the cliché altogether. Perhaps he just stares at her, saying nothing. Notice that the moment becomes more interesting because the audience now must supply some of the missing material. If we feel that Hugh needs a reply to "You're making me nervous," he might enjoy her discomfort, mocking her with, "Aw, I'm so sorry, Michele. It hurts me to see you uncomfortable."

The scene's second major cliché is "Michele, you should know you can't pull the wool over my eyes." How can we express the idea more simply, more honestly? Well, what does the phrase "pull the wool over one's eyes" mean? Simply to keep a person from glimpsing the truth, right? How can we express that thought in simpler, more honest words? This time I'll allow you the honor of providing the answer. After you've wrestled with alternative lines of dialog, consult the suggestion in the Scriptwriting Projects section later in this chapter.

Clichés are the mark of an inexperienced writer. They will creep into your scripts the moment your attention wanders. So be vigilant! Keep your eye on the ball and your nose to the grindstone!

BLATANT EXPOSITION:
UNNECESSARY WORDS

What's wrong with the scene's first two speeches? Why do they sound awkward and inept?

> HUGH
>
> So this is where you go—all those evenings
> you tell me you're "bowling with the girls."

> MICHELE
>
> Hugh! I'm so shocked to see you! You promised
> to stay home, wash the dinner dishes, pay the
> bills, feed the baby....

One reason those speeches sound awkward is that they contain unnecessary and dishonest words. Whenever characters express ideas that both already know, it's usually because the writer has inserted the information solely for the audience's benefit in an awkward attempt at exposition. In a moment of confrontation, would Michele (or anyone!) actually itemize chores that Hugh had promised to do? Of course not. The extraneous words are ludicrous and should be stricken from the scene.

Similarly, many of the words in Hugh's opening speech are dishonest, lame exposition that the writer has inserted solely for our benefit. Just trimming away some of the fat would help. Thus, Hugh might say, "So this is where you go bowling," and the line would become more honest. Critics could object that some audience members might misunderstand or be confused by the reference. Most viewers would figure it out, however, and would enjoy the line more because they had. Dialog should not be confusing. But neither is it necessary to spell out the meaning of every word. Other examples of unnecessary words appear throughout the scene. Michele's reaction at Hugh's appearance ("I'm so surprised to see you!") is merely explaining the obvious. If the actress is not totally lacking in ability, we will see her surprise. It's always preferable to demonstrate an emotion rather than talk about it. Play it, don't say it!

Michele's recitation of all of the riches in her life lacks any trace of believability; it's doubtful if even the most inexperienced writer would overstate so grievously. And Hugh declares no less than three times that he is going to shoot Michele's lover. The major flaw in these speeches and others is that they violate the need for dialog economy.

LACK OF PROGRESSION

Two of the scene's speeches contain another flaw: They lack progression. As we saw in Chapter 6, good dialog builds from the least, to the more, to the most important thought. When that natural order is reversed, statements become ludicrous.

When Michele states that she doesn't need a lover because she has everything and then itemizes them, beginning with husband and baby and ending with her police dog Prince who defends their home against prowlers, the items decrease in importance. When Hugh draws his revolver, he voices his anger most strongly when he says, "I'm going to kill him." Then in successive restatements, he moves backward, ending lamely with the cliché, "I'm going to put him out of his misery." Such reversals of the normal speech progression inevitably become comedic. Read again Lazer's final speeches in "The Fugitive" scene to see how they build in ideas and importance.

RADIO LINES

When Hugh takes a revolver from his pocket, Michele reacts in shock and asks, "Where did you get that gun?" Aside from being stupid (who cares where he got the gun?), the line demonstrates another symptom of bad dialog. I call such lines **radio lines** because they come from another era.

During the 1930s and early 1940s, writers of network drama found practical answers to intrinsic problems. Because listeners couldn't see what was happening, writers had to provide auditory clues, either through sound effects or dialog. As a result, actors often spoke such lines as "Why, Henry, your coat's all torn! Have you been in a fight?" or "That black sedan at the curb — isn't that your brother's?" or "Where did you get that gun?"

Because television and film are visual media, they do not require such spoken crutches. Radio lines comment on the obvious, describing what we can see. Yet, inevitably, they find their way into scripts. When they do, grab your trusty pencil and edit them out.

PLAYING AGAINST DRAMATIC VALUES

Lines that are blunt and obvious allow little or no audience participation. As mentioned before, industry writers and producers label such lines *on the nose*. One of the reasons why audiences would cringe in embarrassment from our bad scene is that so much of its dialog is on the nose: It states the obvious in the most conspicuous way. But the problem goes deeper. The scene itself is melodramatic; its content intensifies sentiment and exaggerates emotion, much as bad soap operas do. A sensitive professional writer would recognize the scene's melodramatic nature and would try to play against that **melodrama**. A prime example in the scene are the lines: "If I find somebody in that closet, Michele, I'm going to kill him. I'm going to shoot him. I'm going to put a bullet in his no-good body!" Professional writers might veer in another direction with a line such as "Why would I want to hurt him, [acidly] a nice guy like that?"

Playing against simply means taking another, perhaps opposite approach to a scene or a line. When a melodramatic scene contains sentimental or exaggerated dialog, each excess compounds the other and the melodrama is exacerbated. On the other hand, if a scene that is potentially melodramatic is written with extreme simplicity and honesty, the writer is playing against the potential melodrama. The scene moves to a level of reality that audiences can relate to. One of the reasons why so many heroes of westerns and adventure thrillers (for example, Clint Eastwood) tend to speak in simple, monosyllabic phrases is that their authors try to play against the potential melodrama by not allowing their protagonists emotional excesses.

Simplicity and honesty play effectively against melodrama. So does humor. William Goldman's use of humor in *Butch Cassidy and the Sundance Kid*, for example, prevents the action from becoming melodramatic and simultaneously lifts the film far above its genre (westerns).

Screenwriters frequently use humor when emotions threaten to get soggy. Such writers play against sentimentality by adding a value that seems to contradict the sentiment, thereby preventing overstatement. Lately, even this device threatens to become stereotypical.

The following scene from the television movie "Brian's Song" effectively demonstrates the use of dialog lightness in a tragic situation.* In his Emmy-winning script, writer William Blinn dramatized the love that grew between two stars of the Chicago Bears football team, Brian Piccolo and his black roommate, Gale Sayers. Their friendship eventually ended with Piccolo's death from cancer. In this scene, Sayers comes to the hospital to visit his friend in what will be their last moments together. (Wives Joy and Linda are also present.)

GALE AND BRIAN

Brian's hand comes up from the sheet in greeting. Gale takes the hand in his. His eyelids are fighting a terrible weight and his words come slowly, breath on a ration.

> BRIAN
>
> Hello, Black Magic.

> GALE
>
> You are so bad... a racist, that's all you are.
> Bigot from head to toe.

> BRIAN
>
> Believe it, man.

*Excerpt from *Brian's Song* © 1971 by Screen Gems, a division of Columbia Pictures. Used by permission of Columbia Pictures and William Blinn.

GALE
(after a beat)
How's it going, Pick?

BRIAN
It's fourth and eight, man... but they won't let
me punt.

GALE
Go for it, then.

BRIAN
I'm trying, Gale... Jesus God, how I'm
trying...

Suddenly an agonizing spasm rips through his frame as a thousand
screaming nerve ends are consumed by the cellular inferno. Brian's
head snaps back, his hand convulses on Gale's. Tears spilling down her
cheeks, Joy leans close to her husband.

Seconds go by, terrible instants of impotent love. Then, slowly, Brian's
body relaxes and his head touches the pillow. Joy blots the perspiration
from his brow. His eyes go to Gale.

BRIAN
Remember that first year... couldn't get a word
out of you...

GALE
Couldn't get you to shut up...

BRIAN
Remember how you got me with those mashed
potatoes...

GALE
You deserved it, the way you sang that dumb
fight song. Twice you did it... at camp, and
that time down in my basement.
(beat)
And that 32 trap play, remember that?

BRIAN
Yeah... how could I forget?

There is a pause. Brian's look turns reflective. He smiles.
(MORE)

> BRIAN
> (continuing)
> You taught me a lot about running, Gale. I
> appreciate it.

> GALE
> I wouldn't be running if I hadn't had you
> pushin' me, helping me.

> BRIAN
> I'll get you next training camp...

> GALE
> I'll be waiting...

> BRIAN
> Yeah...
> (a sigh)
> Gale, I'm feeling kind of punk. I think I'll sack
> out for a while, okay?

> GALE
> Sure thing.

ANGLE TO THEIR HANDS

As Gale gently lets go of Brian's hand, which falls limply back onto the
sheet. Gale's hand rests on the other for a beat, then he moves away.

FULL SHOT

As the nun opens the door for Gale and Linda. He stops, looks back, his
voice choked. Linda holds his arm tightly, her eyes shine with tears
held in check.

> GALE
> See you tomorrow, Pick...

TIGHT ON BRIAN

He turns his head toward Gale, brings his gaze into focus. He lifts the
hand closest to the door and gives a "thumbs-up."

> BRIAN
> If you say so...

The humor, mostly banter or teasing, lifts the scene above cheap melodrama.
Most of us seldom express love overtly. Often, such love is expressed
obliquely—and teasing is an effective way to voice it. Young men and women
in the workplace frequently kid each other about their style of dress or hairstyles or the work they are doing. Such banter, often mocking or deprecating,
can be an indicator of attraction.

*C*HAPTER HIGHLIGHTS

➤ Many professional writers voice their speeches aloud when composing dialog. They immerse themselves in their scenes, experiencing their characters' emotions.

➤ The repetition of key lines of dialog increases their emotional effect. Such lines acquire the colorations of earlier renditions, building richness and evoking audience emotions. Parallels occur in the reprising of musical themes, locales, or pieces of business.

➤ A curtain line or piece of business at the end of scenes often provides an effective punctuation. Use such tag lines only occasionally to avoid redundancy. They are far more common in comedy than drama.

➤ When ideas are dumped overtly into an audience's lap, they create little involvement. Involvement increases whenever the writer forces viewers to participate, adding material from their imaginations. Obvious dialog is called "on the nose." Skilled writers try to avoid such heavy-handedness through oblique lines of dialog or by allowing viewers to reach conclusions on their own.

➤ Dialog, like other screenplay elements, requires conflict for effectiveness. Conflict may be internal or external, humorous or serious, physical or spoken, loving or angry.

➤ When audiences can predict plot, character actions, or dialog, they quickly lose interest. Such clichés make scripts seem amateurish. Even professionals write clichés in their first drafts. But inevitably they find and eliminate them. The following are characteristics of bad dialog:

1. *Excessive cues.* They create resentment in actors and therefore should be used sparingly.

2. *Overuse of character names.* Names should be stated, however, when characters are first introduced.

3. *Stereotyped lines.* Clichés in plot, characterization, music, or casting should be avoided.

4. *Dishonest exposition.* This occurs when characters speak lines of exposition solely for the audience's benefit.

5. *Lack of progression.* In any statement of ideas, thoughts should build in importance. When speeches reverse the normal order of progression, they become laughable.

6. *Radio lines.* These describe what audiences can see and are therefore unnecessary.

➤ When dialog becomes melodramatic in a scene that is itself melodramatic, one excess compounds the other and the result is often soap opera. Similarly, in tragic situations, when dialog is on the nose and sentimental, the scene becomes embarrassing. The answer often is to play against excesses by taking a different direction with the dialog (for example, using humor in a tragic scene).

*S*CRIPTWRITING PROJECTS

EXERCISES DESIGNED TO SHARPEN YOUR NARRATIVE SKILLS

VERNACULAR SPEECH

Write three telephone conversations, all with essentially the same content (described below) but each expressed in the words of a different character. Three sample characters are a feisty truckdriver, a teenage hooker, and a Presbyterian minister. You may use these characters or you may select your own. If you select your own, choose characters from widely divergent backgrounds.

Note that you will be writing only one end of each phone conversation; the words of the person on the other end will not be heard, they will be inferred. Speeches will reflect the differing character backgrounds.

In each conversation, the character will inform his or her brother that the brother's wife has been in an automobile accident and has just died. This is a difficult subject to discuss; the characters will probably struggle to express their thoughts. To make them real, you must consider the nature of each character (personality, background, style of speech) and the relationship that each has with his or her brother. Consider why these characters know of the sister-in-law's death before the brother does (for instance, the brother is out of town).

Select an appropriate name for each character and a name for each brother. Choose a locale for each telephone conversation that feels legitimate. Make the scenes as vivid as you can — and as honest. If such honesty involves the use of X-rated language, so be it. Caution: To create differences between characters, some writers tend to overstate, to create caricatures rather than legitimate people; try to guard against such a tendency.

CLICHÉS

List a least six clichés that you discover either in your speech or the speech of friends. Find alternate (and fresher!) ways of expressing each of these timeworn phrases. Alternate ways of expressing the cliché on page 143, "Michele, you should know you can't pull the wool over my eyes," might include:

1. Michele, I may not be bright but I'm not blind!

2. Michele, don't lie to me.

3. You still think I'm Mr. Gullible, don't you?

READING DIALOG OUT LOUD

Select half a dozen examples of dialog from novels or short stories, preferably from emotional or critical moments. Read them out loud. Compare them for ease of articulation, honesty, and believability. You will probably discover that while some novelists write excellent dialog, the majority write speeches that sound literary, lacking in reality or spontaneity.

Rewrite the novelist's dialog into speeches that reflect the characteristics of effective dialog described in Chapter 6. Read them aloud and compare them with the novelist's original speeches.

MAKING THE AUDIENCE WORK

Situation: Thirteen-year-old Penny takes her mother to her junior high school's open house. Penny's a bright, sensitive, somewhat timid girl, proud of her work in art class and anxious to have her mother, Sharon, meet her teacher. Entering the classroom, Sharon is shocked to discover that Penny's teacher is a man she had an affair with several years ago.

Both the teacher, Doug Hinton, and Sharon immediately recognize each other, but they may not speak freely because of Penny's presence.

The assignment here is to write a scene in which the subtext becomes more important than the text—in which looks, gestures, innuendo, or references to student paintings convey a hidden conversation that Penny is totally unaware of.

Assume either that Sharon is now divorced or that her husband is working and therefore unable to attend the open house. It's too easy to send Penny away so that Sharon and Doug can converse freely with each other. They may try to send Penny away, but she must remain at their sides.

Write the scene in two to three pages, playing it either for gentle comedy or for honest dramatic value. Assume that the audience understands all of the background. Use your imagination to determine the nature of the Sharon-Doug love affair and its resolution.

ADVANCING THE PLOT

Write the father-son confrontation described on page 116 in Chapter 6 with two different endings. Assume that the father's business is a restaurant that has been in the family for two generations. Secret awareness that his health is failing gives urgency to the father's words. The father, Walter, is fifty-two, emotional, bright, and a little stubborn.

The son, Randy, nineteen, has worked vacations in his father's restaurant and found it unsatisfying. He's an excellent musician, a drummer who has composed half a dozen original songs. A member of Randy's musical group has secured an audition with a major recording company. Rehearsals for this event precipitated the confrontation.

You may play the scene anywhere you choose. Build it as legitimately as you can — in three to four pages — but with two different endings, each of which must grow inexorably out of the scene's content. Select two of the following options: (1) Walter angrily throws his son out of the house; (2) Randy agrees to give up his musical career, at least temporarily, and work for his father; or (3) Walter understands the depth of his son's need for a musical career, conceals his ill health, and allows Randy to pursue his dream.

USING PLAYBACKS

Study your Sharon-Doug (mother-art teacher) scene or your father-son confrontation and see if you can create dialog or actions capable of repetition for dramatic effect. Perhaps such lines will provide a tag for your scene, playing back on an earlier moment either for emotional impact or humor.

For example, perhaps early in the argument with his son, Walter says, "Randy, you're dreaming! You're as big a dreamer as your mother was!" At the scene's conclusion, after the two have reconciled their differences, the father might play back on his earlier line as he hugs his son by stating huskily, "You're a dreamer all right. Just like your mother. But, hell, I married her, didn't I?"

$\mathcal{W}$RITER REVELATIONS

SOME OBSERVATIONS ON DIALOG

George Eckstein has been a writer, producer, or executive producer for some of television's best movies and continuing series. Among his movies for TV are "Masada," "Duel," "Tailgunner Joe," "Amelia Earhart," and "The Bad Seed." His TV series include "The Name of the Game," "Banacek," "Sunshine," "The Fugitive," and "The Untouchables."

If his tennis were as good as his writing, he'd be playing yearly at Wimbledon and Forest Hills.

$\mathcal{T}$he following are some random thoughts that I hope will be of practical value:

1. *Exposition.* Every writer I know would agree that exposition is the single most troublesome area in dramatic writing. The backstories of the leading characters, details of time and place, the familial or professional relationships of the characters, what has gone before in terms of plot development, the technical aspects of the law, medicine, advertising, or any of the myriad professions or trades with which a script may deal — all these and more may have to be communicated to an audience that, like most of us, has a low threshold of boredom. Unfortunately, there is no easy path to the land of graceful exposition. There are, however, a few road signs.

   a. *Show Instead of Tell.* If any piece of exposition can be communicated visually, it's for the better. A clock, a sign on a door, a piece of business, specific wardrobe or props, personalized set decoration — any of these can be used as shortcuts to help the audience understand what it needs to know without the characters verbalizing.

      A man carrying a lunch pail comes out of a shabby cottage, warmly kisses a woman in the doorway, rumples the hair of a couple of children, puts on his hard hat, climbs into a battered 1956 sedan, backs out of his driveway past his mailbox with the name "Peters" on it, and continues down the street past other vintage cars. A single, silent shot, but we have already been introduced to the family unit and we know their name, the nature of their domestic relationship, their economic status, and the general period in which the story takes place. If there is lettering on the side of the car that says "Peters' Plumbing Company," we will learn even more. And if, instead of the above action, the man slams out of the door, leaving a tearful wife and two bewildered children looking after him, we may learn something entirely different. Particularly, if he is carrying a suitcase instead of a lunch pail. Again, any information that can be transmitted visually will be just that much less you will have to incorporate into dialog, and there will almost always be more than enough of that.

Some years ago I produced a ninety-minute *Movie of the Week* called "Duel." It was a pure chase film involving a diesel truck and a car. Fearing that the audience expected a "talking" picture, we wrote in a great deal of "voice-over" interior monolog for the driver of the car. Later, when the director and I were obliged to add another fifteen minutes of film for the purpose of theatrical release, we cut about half of this dialog out of the picture and it played much better. I would still like to go back and cut another 50 percent, and I'm certain that the director (a Mr. Spielberg) would concur.

b. *Gradual Is Better.* It is always a great relief for the writer to finish the exposition in order to get on with the story or the exploration of relationships. Consequently, there can be a tendency to try to condense all of the expository material into one scene near the beginning of the script. This is dangerous on several counts. First, the scene will sound like exactly what it is—a boring recital of facts. Second, there is the risk of overloading the audience's circuits. The viewer is there to be entertained, not to be educated or challenged as to his capacity for data retention.

When planning exposition, it might be wise to ask yourself two questions. Does the audience need to know this fact now? And, perhaps more important, does it need to know this information at all? It is usually better — and more dramatically viable — to learn about characters as the story progresses. None of us is drawn to a person who tells us his whole life story in the first five minutes after we've met him. Character revelation and plot development are both more effective and more easily assimilated if they aren't thrust on us all at once. Obviously, the audience shouldn't be confused or disoriented from lack of information, but if there are sufficient screen dynamics to hold its attention, then "expository gradualism" is the best policy.

Sometimes, of course, there are facts we never have to learn. A writer may construct a fascinating history for a character that helps the writer understand the character's needs, values, and attitudes, but the audience doesn't have to share all of those details in order to become emotionally involved. Research may reveal some surprising historical or cultural details that captivate the writer's imagination. But unless those details further the story or assist in character exploration, save them for games of Trivial Pursuit. Because there is always so much necessary exposition to worry about, we cannot clutter our scripts with dispensable material. Avoid unnecessary exposition — even at the expense of your own pride in letting the audience know how brilliantly you invented the character's background or how well you did your homework.

c. *Conflict and Action.* I usually find it easier to reveal expository information within a scene of conflict. For some reason, an emotionally charged scene allows a more graceful insertion of what otherwise could emerge as blatantly obvious and tedious material. The operating principle, of course, is that there is something else going on to distract the audience from realizing they are merely being briefed. However, a conflict scene should not be manufactured just for this purpose—unless it tells us something else about the relationships or aids in the story progression.

Another way to clothe offensively naked exposition is to play it during some form of action. Walking and driving scenes obviously will play better than two people standing or sitting still. And two people engaged in some colorful work or play activity (such as washing a car or playing touch football) can effectively ease any expository pain. The trap here, of course, is that the peripheral activity may be so interesting that the audience will pay no attention to the expository dialog. It's a delicate line, but no one ever said exposition was easy.

2. *Economy.* A writer friend of mine lives by a cardinal rule: "If it occurs to you to cut it, cut it." Although he applies that rule to his entire script, it is also a valid axiom with respect to dialog itself. And sometimes it can be a very difficult rule to apply. Writers, by definition, use words as their working tools, and we take great pride in our use of language. We can also fall helplessly in love with a given line or turn of phrase, and it's hard to sacrifice something you love. But a dramatist has to be made of sterner stuff than a novelist or poet. Thomas Wolfe would have made a terrible playwright. (As a matter of fact, he did.)

Even Lord Byron failed in his efforts for the stage. But dramatists, although they may shamelessly indulge their literary conceits in stage directions, must always be true in dialog to the characters they've created. A writer who comes up with an immortal gem that would ring false in the mouth of a character would be well advised to take it out of that character's mouth and bank it on a 3″ x 5″ card for a later and more appropriate withdrawal.

a. *Handles.* Many writers, myself included, have a weakness for these. "Handles," of course, are those extraneous words and phrases that usually begin a line. "Look," "Well," "You know," "The point is," "Anyhow," "By the way," and so on. (The rather bizarre comedian Professor Irwin Corey became famous for strolling on stage, balefully surveying his audience, and introducing his monolog with the single word "However.") Despite the sure knowledge that handles only constitute excess verbiage, I still find them difficult to abandon. Sometimes I include them to give a sense of reality to the dialog; sometimes I feel they aid the rhythm of a particular speech; and sometimes they seem to operate as a transitional device to separate thoughts or change the subject within a scene. There are occasions when I have guiltily caught myself using them in horrendous combinations, such as, "Look, anyhow, the point is, we're leaving." The best advice is to omit handles as often as possible. And the sad probability is that the actor will either get rid of them himself or substitute his own.

b. *Use the Actor.* Screenplays are written to be filmed (or videotaped), not to be read or merely heard. In other words, the writer has the benefit of performers, including their faces and their body language. I will usually make it a habit to go through a finished draft and examine each line to see whether or not I can substitute a silent reaction for it. A shrug can easily replace an "I don't know"; a nod, a "yes"; a head shake, a "no." A look down or away may silently say "I'd rather not talk about it" or a frown may substitute for "You're wrong" or "You're out of line." A character may angrily stride to a door and fling it open instead of ordering the other character to "Get out of here!" A smile is usually better than "I can't tell you how happy I am." There are countless other examples, but I think I've made my point.

c. *Good Talk Isn't All Bad.* In light of some of the preceding as well as the very valid admonitions of Alan Armer in this (and the preceding) chapter, it might appear that dialog is the cross a script must bear and that we must strive to lighten the load. But, remember, the ability to speak (and the thumb, of course) is what distinguishes humanity from the lower species. Whether dealing with comedy or drama, conflict is an essential ingredient, the cornerstone of dramatic writing. A character may be in conflict with other characters, with the elements, with mysterious malevolent forces — or with himself. And language is often the best — sometimes only — way to dramatize the heart of that conflict and illuminate the characters, particularly when the work introduces articulate protagonists and antagonists.

Obviously, it depends on the nature of the material, but good dialog can be just as exciting as a barroom brawl or the most imaginative car chase. Granted, reliance on the art of dialog is a rare cinematic commodity in this age of McLuhan, but let's not write it off entirely. Playwrights such as Tom Stoppard, David Rabe, Edward Albee, Alan Aykbourn, and Simon Grey have shown us how the brilliant use of speech can electrify a theater audience. Surely we could use a little of that in films — instead of our increasing dependency on technology and physical violence. Woody Allen, Robert Bolt, and a few others have shown the way, and it's a road not necessarily fraught with peril.

3. *Miscellany.* Almost everything else I could write about dialog has been covered by Alan Armer, but there are a few brief points I would like to add that pertain to the profession of film and television writing.

a. *Rhythm.* Although a difficult area to articulate, every line of dialog has a certain rhythm, and each character has a distinctive rhythm to his speech. If it's not there, you hear criticisms of "stilted," "wooden," and the like.

I find it of great benefit while writing to read each line aloud to myself — and then each scene — and finally the entire script. Very often you will find that there is a lack of flow or a certain stiffness to a particular speech that is easily correctable. If you have a speech that may be subject to a different reading from the one you intend, feel free to cue the reader or performer by means of a parenthetical direction or by underlining the desired emphasis. But don't do it when it's not essential, or you run the risk of insulting the actor or director. As a rule, they are highly intelligent contributors and will discern your intention. I also find it helpful, when possible, to attend casting sessions and rehearsals. Hearing the dialog read by a fresh voice will frequently reveal a lack of rhythm in a certain line or provoke constructive dialog changes.

b. *Adaptations.* Do not be intimidated by the original author of a work you're adapting for film. It is one thing to respect the material, but it can be fatal to consider it sacrosanct. Remember that the original writer was not writing for film, and translating any work from one medium to another requires substantial changes. And remember also that many prose writers, Pulitzer Prize winners included, do not necessarily have a good ear for dramatic dialog.

c. *Defensiveness.* In writing for television or film, you unfortunately have to check your pride of authorship at the door. Yes, you can and should fight for what you believe in, but in the absence yet of anything resembling the Author's League contract for playwrights, you have no real defense against the superior clout of the producers, directors, or stars. They will normally own the script and, consequently, have the legal right to do whatever they want to it. Sometimes it's the better part of valor to do what you can to protect your material without alienating those more-powerful-but-necessary collaborators. Walking off a project because you feel the material is being trashed can be extremely counterproductive. If you can hang in there, you at least have a chance of diplomatically blocking the actor or director when he decides to junk a particular line and replace it with the nearest cliché.

d. *Originality and Surprise.* After a script is finished, I will read it through again, this time examining each line as to its predictability. There is nothing quite as depressing as the thought of the audience, at home or in a darkened theater, saying the words along with the characters on screen. Always look for a fresh way to say everything. And that's not a bad thought on which to end my rambling. Or to hang on my wall, for that matter.*

*Used by permission of George Eckstein.

CHAPTER 8

Revealing the Subtext

WHAT SCENES ARE ALL ABOUT

*I*nstant quiz: What are movies, TV shows, or stageplays all about? Narrow it down. What are individual scenes all about? Dialog? Plot? Character? Conflict? All of the above? None of the above?

If you said, "All of the above," you were right. But only partially. Study a key scene in any well-written screenplay. Read it two or three times. Paraphrase its content. Cut through to the bottom line and you'll discover that the basic content of most scenes (and most drama) is the *thoughts and feelings of its characters*. That's a tough concept to grasp, so let's talk about it.

In any scene, characters say things and do things: dialog and actions. But what they do and what they say are merely ways of externalizing what they are thinking or feeling. Think about it. What characters do and what they say are merely ways of expressing what's going on inside their minds and hearts. Sometimes the things they say or do reveal feelings they don't even know exist. When we cut through the surface, we get to the scene's underpinnings, the source: the emotions of its characters. The screenwriter's often difficult job is to find ways of *externalizing* those inner thoughts and feelings, expressing them either in dialog or in visual terms that an audience can see and appreciate.

Novelists have it easy. When they want to describe what a character is thinking or feeling, they simply blurt it out: "John's mind was in a turmoil. He wondered how Barbara would take the news that he had been fired. He remembered the last time he had come home with bad news, how her mouth had tightened at the corners. . . ." For screenwriters, externalizing thoughts or emotions is somewhat more difficult.

Beginning writers sometimes put emotive descriptions in their screenplay's stage directions. For example, "She remembers Joe, the lavender-eyed boy who jilted her, and her heart fills suddenly with sadness. She feels hollow, empty, and for the first time very much alone." Such words create a vivid picture for those who read the script, but the audience sitting in a motion picture theater or in front of a TV set cannot read those words. Audiences know only what they see or hear on the screen. Descriptions on a script page may help an actor or director to understand what's happening inside a character, but the successful screenwriter must find ways of externalizing those thoughts and emotions, dramatizing them visually or through sound so that the audience can recognize and react to them.

The ways of externalizing a character's thoughts and emotions are surprisingly varied, although they are most commonly revealed through dialog. In this chapter we'll discuss:

➤ **INADEQUACIES OF DIALOG**: how spoken words are often meaningless or actually contradict a character's feelings

➤ **DON'T TALK ABOUT IT, SHOW IT!**: Actions not only speak louder than words but are also more emotionally involving

➤ **TURNING CHARACTERS INSIDE OUT**: how to externalize thoughts and feelings through dialog, body language, business, and pathetic fallacy

*I*NADEQUACIES OF DIALOG

The most obvious way of revealing emotion is for characters to talk about it. One character tells another, "I'm feeling sad today" or "I'm so angry I could cry." But dialog is just one of several ways to reveal emotions, and it is not necessarily the best.

Former CBS vice president Tony Barr conducts a workshop in North Hollywood for professional film and television actors. One of the exercises he presents to students is a short scene whose dialog is banal, capable of various interpretations.*

> HE
>
> Good morning.
>
> SHE
>
> Good morning.
>
> HE
>
> How do you feel?
>
> SHE
>
> Great.
>
> HE
>
> I'm sure.
>
> SHE
>
> What do you want for breakfast?
>
> HE
>
> Whatever.
>
> SHE
>
> I'll fix you some scrambled eggs.
>
> HE
>
> Fine.
>
> SHE
>
> You going to work this morning?
>
> HE
>
> Have to.

*As described by Tony Barr in *Acting for the Camera* (Boston: Allyn & Bacon, 1982), pp. 68–74.

                    SHE
Oh.

                    HE
Do you want me to stay home?

                    SHE
It's up to you.

                    HE
Can't.

                    SHE
Like I said, it's up to you.

Tony Barr asks his students to play the scene several times for his studio cameras. For each enactment he gives them a totally different preparation (emotional attitude). The first time he suggests that they have just returned from their honeymoon and days of passionate lovemaking. For the second enactment he suggests that the husband came home at four o'clock in the morning after an affair with his secretary and the couple fought bitterly. For the final enactment Barr suggests that they learned only yesterday that the husband has a terminal illness.

In all three versions, of course, the words are identical. The actors on their own, without direction, seek to express the emotion behind the words. Even with relatively inexperienced actors, the difference in performances is astounding. In the first (honeymoon) version, the dialog emerges as sensuous, steamy, filled with innuendo. The actors cling to each other, touching. The camera is close, suggesting their intimacy.

In the second (angry) version, words are clipped, brittle, revealing depths of resentment and bitterness. Husband and wife remain apart, separated by the breakfast table. Guilt makes it difficult for the husband to remain seated; he paces agitatedly. He does not look at his wife.

In the third (tragic) version, actors sometimes play the heartbreak overtly; sometimes they try to conceal it, allowing the pain to appear only occasionally in a broken word or phrase. Sometimes the wives choose to play gentleness. Sometimes they pretend that nothing tragic has happened or try to ignore it and discover that they cannot, turning abruptly away from their husbands to conceal their tears. But whichever attitude the actors choose, the underlying emotion dictates not only their vocal colorations and facial expressions but also their physical movement in relation to each other, their closeness, and the specific "business" they select. We'll talk more about business later in this chapter.

Although the dialog is identical in each, the three enactments emerge as totally different scenes, underscoring the principle that dialog is sometimes unimportant; *it is the emotion beneath the dialog that counts.* That's the bottom line. That's what most scenes are really all about.

In screenplays as in real life, dialog is sometimes an accurate expression of thoughts and feelings and sometimes not. You may be shocked to hear this (brace yourself), but many people lie. They try to conceal personal weaknesses or misdeeds. They try to protect loved ones. They try to gain power or physical possessions. They may not even realize they are lying and thereby protecting themselves from fears or anxieties. "Aren't you afraid, Mike? He's a lot bigger than you." "Hell, no, he'll never touch me!" Audiences must assess the truthfulness of dialog, just as they assess the nature of the characters who speak it. Dialog helps us to evaluate characters; the nature of those characters, in turn, helps us to evaluate their dialog.

Sometimes actions totally contradict dialog. When eight-year-old Ricky comes home from school and his mother asks how his classes went, he might answer, "Fine." But his agitation and fidgeting, his inability to look her in the eye, and his eagerness to get out of the room all betray that answer. It is his actions that speak the truth, not his words. Similarly, in the motion picture *Klute*, Jane Fonda played a call girl. In one scene she pretended great passion while engaging in sex with a client. Her spoken words and moans all seemed to substantiate her passion — until she glanced furtively at her watch.

Sometimes dialog has little relationship to the content of a scene. A young woman at a party reluctantly makes conversation with a predatory male companion. As they talk, her eyes seek out a distinguished looking gentleman across the room. When he returns her glance, smiling, clearly interested, she rolls her eyes upward, unseen by her companion. Her look clearly signals that she is unhappy and seeks relief. Moments later, the distinguished gentleman arrives and rescues her. In such a situation, the dialog between the woman and her predatory companion provides nothing more than an accompaniment to the scene's significant content: the eye contact between her and the man across the room.

Many of the words we speak in everyday life have no literal meaning. They are merely part of a ritual. When you pass a friend and mutter "How's it going?" or "Whatta ya say?" usually you're merely acknowledging that person. When you say "Good morning," you're not commenting on the weather. Your words imply recognition and acceptance. You are "stroking" the other person. In screenplays as in real life, words don't always mean what they say.

Consider the statement "I love you." When a sincere character genuinely in love says these words, they might be taken at face value as an expression of the heart. But when a young man on the prowl in a singles bar says them, they represent words of convenience, spoken lightly with ulterior purpose. And yet there's no deception here; both speaker and listener understand that the dialog is symbolic, part of a ritual, with no real basis in honest emotion.

$\mathcal{D}$ON'T TALK ABOUT IT, *SHOW* IT: VISUAL STORYTELLING

When silent films needed dialog, art cards flashed briefly on the screen revealing the characters' words. Transitions also were occasionally spelled out for audiences. "Came the dawn" was one frequently used. But the most effective silent films used few if any such cards, relying instead on the abilities of actors to convey emotion through facial expressions, body language, or through their actions.* Writers of those early films did not have the luxury of sound, so they were forced to rely on their imaginations, to invent actions or incidents that would help them tell their stories. Many of those silent films have become classics in the art of dramatizing a story in purely visual terms. To be sure, characters in those films spoke to each other occasionally but in most cases the audience didn't need to understand their words to understand the plot.

Telling a story solely through the actions of characters seems to carry more power than dramatizing it through dialog. Perhaps the reason is that actions compel us to interpret their meaning, and therefore we become more deeply involved. When we must figure out *why* a character performs an action, we have to run the question through our minds and come up with answers. Thus, we participate in the dramatic process. When we find answers, sometimes we are unaccountably moved; we cry or become angry. The more we participate, the more successful the writer has been in arousing our emotions. Jenny Flynn discovers a locket that once belonged to her mother. Her face becomes hard, angry when she sees it, and she promptly flings it into a wastebasket. She stares at the wastebasket for a long moment, and then her face softens and she retrieves the locket, stares at it, holds it to her cheek, and then places it tenderly back in the drawer where she found it. Because we have to interpret the meaning of Jenny's actions, we become more deeply involved than if she had merely voiced her conflicting feelings in words.

When writers dump information in our laps ("on the nose" dialog), it frequently caroms off us; we receive the information but do not need to process it. We don't participate because the thinking has been done for us. Because there's less participation, there's ultimately less emotional impact. We'll discuss this concept in more detail in the "Business" section later in this chapter.

If you think visual storytelling is easy, try it sometime. You will probably find yourself resorting to dialog before you've completed the first page. One of the exercises I give students in my screenwriting classes is to create a complete little story (two to four pages) totally without sound. No dialog. No narration.

---

*An excellent example is F. W. Murnau's *The Last Laugh*.

No subtitles. To make the project even more challenging, I demand that they eliminate "talking heads" shots in which characters speak to each other without our hearing their words.

Examples of such a story might involve a chase sequence in which a timid secretary who has worked late discovers that she is being followed by a sinister figure as she walks home on darkening streets. Or a student who has overslept on the morning of a final exam, who races the clock and overcomes horrendous obstacles to get to school on time. Or a wife returning home from a business trip who discovers evidence that her husband has been unfaithful while she was away. She packs her suitcase, takes the baby from his crib, and leaves.

Try it. Try writing a visuals-only script. You'll find it's stimulating and a challenge to your imagination. Such a project is described in greater detail at the end of this chapter.

TURNING CHARACTERS INSIDE OUT

Because the real content of most scenes is the emotions of its characters, we need to examine the various ways in which we can externalize those emotions, dramatize them visually or audibly so that audiences can become aware of them.

Figure 8.1 illustrates the emotions that lie below the surface and some of the many ways of revealing them to audiences. On the following pages we'll discuss: dialog, body language, business, and pathetic fallacy.

DIALOG

The most obvious purpose of screenplay dialog is identical to the purpose of dialog in everyday life: to express ideas or emotions. "How are you feeling, Mom?" "Darling, I think I'm in love with you." "Take me to your leader." Monologs, seldom used today, are also a conduit to the inner character. But gestures, posture, movement, mannerisms, and facial expressions also are conduits, sometimes revealing thoughts and emotions more vividly or more accurately than any dialog we might contrive. Researchers tell us that most communication is nonverbal.

Had evolution veered in a different direction, we might not use dialog at all. Evidence suggests that primitive humans primarily used sign language for interpersonal communication, providing emphasis with a few well-chosen grunts. At one point in their development, humans were forced to choose between hand gestures and primitive dialog. Because speech left their hands

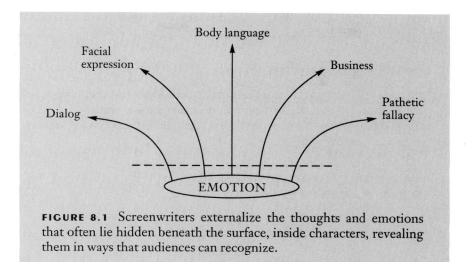

FIGURE 8.1 Screenwriters externalize the thoughts and emotions that often lie hidden beneath the surface, inside characters, revealing them in ways that audiences can recognize.

free for other purposes (hunting, fishing, preparing meals), most primitive tribes opted for dialog and against sign language.

Despite the premise that actions are sometimes more eloquent than words, please remember that nothing in this text is intended to undercut the beauty or effectiveness of well-written dialog. Producers respect and mass audiences applaud writers whose speeches re-create the real world, whose dialog advances the plot, defines dimensional characters, and vividly exposes their thoughts and emotions.

BODY LANGUAGE

One character shuffles down the street, shoulders slumped, head down; another strides rapidly, head erect, shoulders back. Without dialog or lengthy descriptions to assist us, we can make immediate and probably dead accurate assessments of each of those characters and their states of mind solely from their body language.

The term *body language* applies to a character's posture, physical attitude, manner of movement, gestures, even facial expressions. And all of these, of course, provide valuable clues to the character's mental or emotional state. Unlike authors of novels, screenwriters provide only clues, usually brief, sometimes only a word or two. Their descriptions usually are external, dealing primarily with what the camera sees and the microphone hears, seldom with the inner state of characters. Writers' descriptions are limited to two screenplay areas: *stage directions* and dialog *cues*.

A TYPICAL STAGE DIRECTION

Terry enters the room and looks around apprehensively. Sure enough, Magruder is here, standing by the mantel, arms folded, smiling maliciously at her. She turns away, clearly frightened, and starts to exit, but he crosses quickly and takes her arm.

DIALOG CUES, WITHIN SPEECHES, BETWEEN PARENTHESES

TERRY
(pulling away)

Let go of me!

(starting to cry)

I said let <u>go</u> of me!

The best writers are observers. They're sensitive to the interaction between people, their changing moods, and their body language. They recognize efforts to conceal embarrassment or pain, to stay cool in threatening situations. They know intuitively that one day they will use these observations in a screenplay: the way a woman looks at a man she wants, the way she puts a hand on his arm, the way he responds, making eye contact. Writers recognize how some people deliberately avoid eye contact with others to avoid involvement, how some smile when embarrassed or uncomfortable, how young men slick their hair into place before meeting young women, how older men make the same gesture, but to conceal thinning hairlines. Good writers write about what they know, and the ways in which humans interact and communicate lie at the very heart of a successful writer's knowledge. As I've indicated, most communication is nonverbal. Body language therefore represents a substantial part of human communication.

BUSINESS

The personal actions that characters perform during a scene are called **business**. When you spell it "busyness," the word defines itself. Examples of business include lighting a cigarette, combing hair, applying lipstick, pouring a drink, making a sandwich, reading a newspaper, or washing a car.

We know that dialog is usually the most convenient way of expressing inner feelings. But there are many occasions when dialog must be ruled out. For example, sometimes characters want to conceal their emotions. Or perhaps a character is alone, with no one to confide in. On such occasions, business frequently provides the audience with insights into what characters are thinking or feeling.

If the writer has given story significance to a symbol, then the way in which the character relates to that symbol becomes extremely revealing. If Denise's lover has given her a giant panda bear, for example, then her feelings about her lover can be dramatized through her actions with the panda. When Denise's lover proposes marriage, she returns home ecstatic. When she hugs the bear, she is, in effect, hugging him. If Denise learns that he has secretly been dating her best friend, the news creates pain and anger. Perhaps she responds by throwing the bear away. In effect she is throwing away her lover.

Photographs also are symbols but less effective than other physical objects because they are "on the nose," so obvious in their message that they rob the audience of the chance to figure out its meaning and thereby participate. Remember, when audiences are forced to interpret, they become involved; the more actively they participate, the more emotion they will experience. If Denise says, "I hate him. I never want to see him again!" there will be little audience involvement. But if she goes to her bedroom, takes the panda off the bed, hugs it tenderly for a long moment, her eyes moist, and then gravely deposits the animal in a trashcan, the scene will be poignant; audiences will be moved.

Business performs other valuable functions. One of a screenwriter's most significant tasks is to make the audience accept the contrived world as reality, to make people believe. When husband and wife come home from work and talk, they seldom stand in the center of the room facing each other. On the contrary, they usually busy themselves with a dozen normal, everyday activities. The husband removes his coat and tie, throws them on a chair, goes through the mail, and drops into an easy chair to read or watch TV. The wife kicks off her shoes, pours herself some wine, makes telephone calls, or leafs through the newspaper. Their conversation is interspersed with seemingly unimportant activities, but these activities are important because they help bring the scene to life.

Additionally, business helps screenwriters define their characters. What characters *do* suggests who they *are*. Their actions provide the audience with clues to their personalities, attitudes, and mental states. One woman may plant flowers in her garden while playing a scene with a neighbor. This woman obviously cares about her home and its appearance. Another might play the same or similar dialog while wolfing down junk food and watching soap operas on TV. It is essentially the same scene, yet the activities make totally different comments on the two women's characters.

Business usually provides more dependable criteria for assessing a character than his or her spoken words. Business may, in fact, actually contradict a character's dialog. A wife's declaration of love for her husband is invalidated when she ignores him to apply fingernail polish. A college student acts flip and unperturbed when a young woman refuses to date him. Outwardly he is Mr. Cool. But his fingers relentlessly twist and bend the cardboard cover of his notebook, giving us a more accurate picture of his feelings.

In *Sleeping with the Enemy*, the husband's careful aligning of towels on a bathroom rack or food cans on a kitchen shelf gives us almost as valuable insights to his obsessive/compulsive personality as the violent actions he takes against his wife.

PATHETIC FALLACY

Strange words. One definition (and there are others) is *nature reflecting the inner state of characters*. I'm slightly enlarging the scope of that definition to mean *the external reflecting the internal*.

Sounds like heavy stuff, doesn't it? One of those stuffy, esoteric phrases you encounter in graduate film theory classes. Actually, pathetic fallacy is a pretty simple idea.

How many times have you seen burial scenes in movies or TV shows in which it was raining? Remember the small cluster of raincoat-clad mourners gathered around the grave and carrying umbrellas? Why do you suppose it was always raining in those scenes? Because the weather was a reflection of what was going on inside the characters. The dark, dreary day mirrored their sadness at losing a loved one, and the rain was externalizing their unshed tears. That's not such a heavy idea, is it?

Nature reflecting the inner state of characters. The external reflecting the internal. Two youngsters enter a haunted house. Is it a bright, sunshiny spring day? Or is it a dark night with thunder and lightning reflecting the turbulence inside the young people, mirroring their fears and simultaneously making the audience nervous?

Notice that two elements are at work here. Nature is reflecting the inner state of characters and simultaneously is working on the audience so that it will experience the same emotions the characters feel. (We call that identification, remember?) In *Poltergeist* a screeching windstorm echoed the boy's fears as he lay in his bed and stared nervously at the gnarled tree outside his window, its branches outstretched, reaching for him. The wind's howl made us almost as nervous as he was and set the stage for his sister being sucked into the poltergeists' frightening Other World. Would that sequence have been as jarring on a clear, moonlit night? In *Jagged Edge* the brutal killing that begins the film takes place to the accompaniment of rain, thunder, and lightning, commenting on the dark deed being dramatized and simultaneously setting our nerves on edge.

Watch comedy shows on television. Are they shadowy and dimly lit? On the contrary, they are almost always "high key," brightly lighted, mirroring the upbeat world the characters live in and simultaneously creating an upbeat atmosphere that lifts spectators' spirits and puts them in the mood to laugh.

One television series I produced, "The Untouchables," played almost all of its scenes at night because night was the appropriate background for shows exploiting fear and violence.

When we discuss pathetic fallacy, we include *all* of the elements that reflect the moods and emotions of our characters. There are many and they extend far beyond the forces of nature. Some are obvious, some are not. *Music* is perhaps the most evocative of filmic elements. It reflects the characters' emotions, sometimes comments on those emotions, and evokes similar emotions in audiences. When a young couple meets at a Chinese restaurant and falls in love, the composer establishes a love theme. Months later, after the young man has been tragically killed, the love theme is repeated, this time in a minor key, reflecting the young woman's heavy heart and evoking audience tears. Some screenwriters refer to specific songs or musical themes in their scripts; most do not.

Costumes are another element that reflects character emotions; a young woman with a heavy heart usually does not wear brightly colored clothes. When all of the characters are dressed in funereal clothes, their wardrobe (together with the setting) helps to create a dreary atmosphere, and that atmosphere becomes an outward projection of the characters' emotions, almost as if it were a point of view shot.

Settings also comment on the actions and characters working within them. Beginning writers often give insufficient thought to the locales for their scenes. Locales contribute strongly to the color and character of stories and enrich their dramatic values. Avoid drab settings such as offices or living rooms. If you must use such a locale, look for ways of making it special, fitted to the style and personality of your characters.

In the heat of writing, we tend sometimes to grab at the first setting that occurs to us. Not a good idea. Always take a moment to stop and reconsider. When creating a scene, look for a locale whose character will contribute to the action, that will reflect the emotional positions of your cast. Preparing episodes of one TV series I worked on, the production staff would spend literally hours pondering the appropriate settings for certain scenes. When in doubt, select a colorful setting over a drab one. What if you're writing about drab characters? That's easy. Don't.

CHAPTER HIGHLIGHTS

➤ Beneath the surface level — what characters do and what they say — lies the real scene content: their thoughts and emotions. Dialog and actions are merely ways of externalizing thoughts and emotions so that the audience can become aware of them.

➤ Dialog is the most common conduit to thoughts and emotions. It can cover or contradict real feelings or it can become merely a verbal accompaniment to a scene's significant content.

➤ Showing is usually superior to telling. That is, dramatizing an event is usually more effective than a dialog description. Actions are often more emotionally involving than dialog because audiences must interpret their meaning.

➤ There are many ways of externalizing a character's thoughts and emotions. *Dialog* is the most obvious but not always the best. Other ways include *body language* (posture, physical attitude, manner of movement, gestures, facial expressions); *business*, the personal actions that characters perform during a scene; and *pathetic fallacy*, in which the entire outer world (weather, wardrobe, music) reflects the inner state of characters.

SCRIPTWRITING PROJECTS

EXERCISES DESIGNED TO
SHARPEN YOUR NARRATIVE SKILLS

FINDING THE PERFECT
DRAMATIZATION

Your protagonist has just achieved a major goal. What does he do? What does he say? Where do you play the scene?

It is the end of the second act. Your protagonist has lost the woman he loves to a despicable enemy. Again, what does he do; what does he say; where do you play the action?

How do you dramatize *joy* or *anger* or *loneliness* or *sadness*?

These questions cut to the heart of what this chapter tries to communicate. Successful writers search for the optimum ways of dramatizing a character's emotions. By optimum, I mean incidents or happenings that will most vividly, most accurately, most powerfully externalize those emotions in terms an audience can understand and, more importantly, *feel*. But for an audience to feel those emotions, the writer must feel them first.

> Being able to write about your feelings in a way others can share is as important as the ability to reason. Speaking about an emotion in the abstract, "I feel sad," does not convey the uniqueness of your experience or the quality of your sadness.
>
> Imagine that you are [writing a screenplay] where a child is feeling lonely. Without having a child say "I am lonely," how can you indicate

by visual and sound effects that the child is feeling lonely? Where is the child? By the ocean? In the woods? In a city alley? What time of day is it? What sounds might you hear? Trees creaking? Foghorns? An owl hooting? Sirens and gunshots? Wind through the trees? Would there be shadows? Bright lights? Fog drifting in? Would the child be alone or with others — or with an animal? Your emotions affect how you perceive the world. You might see things differently in the same location depending on whether you were feeling lonely or happy.*

Take a pencil and a piece of paper, relax in an easy chair, and let your mind free associate. Jot down descriptive words or phrases that make *you* feel lonely, that connote to you the sense of utter aloneness that the quotation refers to. The words or phrases don't have to be coherent; they just should suggest (as vividly as you can) the emotion of loneliness.

This kind of creative thinking will help you find the locales and incidents that properly dramatize your characters' emotions in the next screenplay you write.

Try the exercise again for each of these emotions:

- Rage/fury
- Exhilaration (incredible happiness)
- Sadness at the death of a loved one

VISUAL STORYTELLING

Write a three- to four-page script — in proper screenplay format — that tells its story entirely through the actions of its characters. This will be a silent film: no dialog, no sound effects, no music. The script should tell a complete little story with its own beginning, middle, and end.

You may not use title cards or subtitles at the bottom of the screen. You should avoid "talking heads," or characters speaking to each other even though we are unable to hear them. Such scenes are always awkward in a visuals-only project.

When characters are together in a scene, it's almost inevitable that they will speak to each other. Hint: Either keep your characters apart or tell the story of a single character.

This is a difficult project — but a valuable one. The difficulty lies in finding a viable concept. Once you have the concept, the actual writing is a breeze.

If you have questions regarding format, see Chapter 10.

Good luck!

*From Elizabeth McKim and Judith W. Steinbergh, *Beyond Words: Writing Poems with Children: A Guide for Parents and Teachers* (Green Harbor, MA: Wampeter Press, 1983), pp. 54–55.

CHAPTER 9

Elements of Entertainment

Some movies break the rules. They're structured awkwardly. They lack conflict or progression. Their screenplays would barely earn passing grades in film-school writing courses. And yet they work. They're fun to watch. Occasionally, they break box-office records. (The James Bond films often fall into this category.) Why?

One answer is that successful movies usually contain certain time-honored elements that please audiences. We find those elements in Greek myths, Grimm's fairy tales, ancient Apache legends, and folk ballads. We find them in the Bible and in tomorrow's music videos.

These elements delight us on a primitive level. Their appeal is mostly sensual; they are salted peanuts — tasty and hard to resist. Their use is by no means restricted to scripts that break the rules. Their presence in all scripts creates entertainment value beyond that engendered by the story itself. But they are not drama and they do not replace it.

These **entertainment elements** are valuable tools that not only help enhance the look of a show but also often help writers solve practical storytelling problems. For example, writers often have difficulty with exposition, conveying essential story information to an audience. But if the writer sugarcoats the exposition, it becomes easier to swallow. More specifically, if the writer provides elements of spectacle, conflict, sex, or humor in expository scenes, the audience will enjoy being entertained and will remain unaware it's being spoon-fed.

In the first act of most screenplays, it is usually the hero's problem that hooks an audience. Yet sometimes the writer needs time to establish a foundation for the problem, so it becomes impossible to initiate it until late in the act. How can the writer hold the audience's attention all of that time? One way is to create scenes with such entertainment value that audiences cannot lose interest.

This chapter examines the elements of entertainment in five discussions:

➤ **SPECTACLE**: dazzling audiences with sound, motion, and color

➤ **THE MALE-FEMALE RELATIONSHIP**: stimulating audiences through appeal to their sex drives

➤ **SYMMETRY AND ORDER**: gratifying audience needs for equilibrium and harmony

➤ **HUMOR AND SURPRISE**: providing freshness and discovery through the unexpected and releasing tension through laughter

➤ **CURIOSITY**: attracting audiences to intellectual subject matter and to the grisly and macabre (morbid curiosity)

SPECTACLE

Although the word *spectacle* literally refers only to the visual, **spectacle** as used here includes sound, creating a dynamic triad of sound, motion, and color.

When we are babies, we're closest to a pure animal state; civilization has not yet changed us. Our first reactions are natural, primitive, inborn. From infancy we're fascinated by sights and sounds that appeal primarily to the senses. Consider how a baby's toys incorporate the elements of spectacle: the rattle (sound), the mobile with slowly rotating plastic animals (color, motion), music boxes (sound), windup toys (color, motion), celluloid whirligigs that spin in the wind (color, motion).

As we grow older, the same spectacular elements continue to attract us. We set off firecrackers on the Fourth of July and watch as skyrockets explode in colored plumes across the sky. We hold kaleidoscopes to our eyes, observing the myriad color forms in constantly changing patterns. We line the streets to see parades with their costumed marching bands, strutting drum majorettes, and flower-festooned floats. We go to circuses to enjoy their clowns, trapeze artists, trained-animal acts, and garish music — an extravaganza of sound, motion, and color.

Producers use sound to enhance most movies and TV shows. Writers who watch their projects go from the editing room to the dubbing stage (where sound effects and music are added to the **sound track**) usually are thrilled at how much richer their story values play and how much more dynamic their project suddenly appears. All of the visuals remain the same, but the addition of screeching tires, sirens, footsteps, or flapping sails — with appropriate music — can transform a mildly diverting scene into an exciting one. Sound effects seem particularly potent when added to a show that exploits melodrama.

THE DARK SIDE OF SPECTACLE

Spectacle as defined here is not limited to the bright, the dazzling, the upbeat. It also contains darker elements of sensual appeal such as those in (1) the natural forces of thunder and lightning, raging fires, floods, and windstorms; and (2) the unnatural forces manifested by the contravention of natural laws. The second category includes such fantasy elements as magic and illusion, witchcraft, demonology, and ghosts and spirits. Such traditional magician's fare as floating a figure in air, sawing a woman in half, or making an elephant disappear continue to fascinate us because they defy logic and the laws of nature as we recognize them. Such entertainment is part spectacle (contravention of nature) and part puzzle. We gasp at a feat of levitation and simultaneously wonder how it is done.

If the term *spectacle* describes elements of sensual appeal, it seems odd that we would accept as appealing such spectacular creatures as witches, demons, and ghosts. One explanation is that in the entertainment world it is safe to be frightened by them. When science fiction creatures, poltergeists, or demons terrorize us, we experience a delicious fear. Why else would audiences flock to theaters to see so-called horror films? Our apprehension and shock become acceptable because the more practical side of our minds remains aware that we are spectators in a theater. When the terror grows too intense, a safety valve reminds us it is all make-believe. The terror is thus doubly enjoyed: We experience the thrill of an intense emotional experience, and yet we are secure in our comfortable seats. We may reassure ourselves at any time merely by glancing around the theater at other audience members and smile as they recoil from the screen's images.

SPECTACLE IN SCREENPLAYS

Beyond the structural uses described in this chapter's introduction, spectacle can enhance both narrative action and the playing value of scenes. Let's examine four screenplay areas in which spectacle may be applied: subject matter, settings, action, and climaxes. These areas necessarily overlap.

Subject Matter.   One reason why writers select certain characters for screenplays is because of the worlds they inhabit. It could be a lusterless, quiescent world, such as that inhabited by an old woman living alone in a drab, middle-class home. Or it could be a world filled with sound, motion, and color, such as that inhabited by a western sheriff, a race-car driver, or a professional magician. When you select characters, you're also committing yourself to their worlds, to the surrounding characters, locales, atmospheres, and urgencies of those worlds. When you tell the story of a magician, you know that certain scenes will play in theaters and nightclubs and will involve elements of mystification. When you write about a western sheriff, you're including the entire western milieu in your setting: saloons, canyons, ranches, and Indian villages. You're also including the elements of life and death.

There's nothing wrong with telling a small, intimate, human story, lacking in the glitzy elements of spectacle. Many fine writers prefer such focused storytelling. Intimate stories require sensitivity from writer, producer, director, and actor. If any of these four falls short, the structure may crumble. If the audience cannot become deeply involved in the central character's problem, there are no spectacular elements to fall back on to fan audience interest.

The element of spectacle, of course, never replaces screenplay drama; it merely adds a topping of whipped cream to make the pudding more appealing. Spectacle enhances whatever values already exist. As with other elements of audience appeal, it cannot compensate for content that is ill conceived.

Settings.   As writer, you are the creator. You have total control of who your characters are, what they do, and where they do it. Settings for scenes are more than backdrops. Settings interact with characters; they can contribute effectively to the scene's atmosphere, remain unseen, or actually undercut that atmosphere. Part of the reason for the success of *Star Trek*, *Aliens*, and *Star Wars* is that their awesome deep-space settings contribute significantly to their stories and create an atmosphere of wonderment and fear.

When you as writer decide to play a love scene, you face a number of creative choices, among them: What dramatic values will make the scene entertaining, different, fresh, unique? Your choice of locale figures strongly in that decision. For example, we've seen dozens of love scenes played in parked cars by a moonlit lake. Obviously, you would avoid such a clichéd setting. You would examine the worlds in which your characters live, searching for a locale that would logically be part of those worlds and that would enrich the scene in some way. If the young woman worked as a casting director, for example, the scene might play in a darkened projection room, sound turned down, images on the screen providing a delightful counterpoint to the lovers' words. The film images could depict a gun battle between gangsters or a slapstick comedy sequence with the laugh track clearly audible. If the young man were an actor, the screen footage could be of him, perhaps making love to a beautiful actress (adding irony), their huge faces on screen dominating the intimate scene between our characters.

Beginning writers often grab at the first setting that occurs to them, not realizing that another, more colorful locale might provide stronger dramatic values. A boy arrives home to tell his mother that he was expelled from school. He enters the house. The mother is in the kitchen or watching television. They play their scene. There's nothing wrong with this scene. It's simple. It's honest. But given a moment or two, the writer could think of a more effective setting. Perhaps the son encounters his mother a block from their home. Her car broke down and she's upset. She wonders why he's home from school so early, forcing him into his explanation at this inopportune time. Perhaps the mother runs a nursery school, and he meets her there, trying to tell his story but constantly being interrupted by youngsters who demand attention, cry, whine, and shout. It's usually possible to upgrade settings. The concern always is to make sure that the colorful setting is appropriate and honest.

Action.   Any scene that advances the plot contains dramatic action. Any scene in which a major character makes a decision changing the plot direction contains action. The word *action* doesn't necessarily translate to car chases or gunfights. Characters seated on a couch and talking can constitute an action scene — action without physical movement.

Interestingly, when a scene contains dramatic action, it usually also contains physical action (movement). If tensions build (as they do in most well-written scenes), it's almost impossible for characters to remain seated for long;

their emotions impel them to rise, to move about in agitation. Ted and Marcy sit on a couch. He tells her their relationship is over. Shocked, she cannot remain seated. She rises and paces, bewildered, her thoughts churning. And he rises and pursues her, trying to explain.

Physical action without dramatic action is pointless. But don't dismiss physical action too quickly — for it is a major component of spectacle.

Physical movement equates with energy. Physical action is visually exciting and seems (perhaps artificially) to create the illusion of dramatic action even when little dramatic action is taking place. Physical action energizes audiences. It's fun to watch.

One of the reasons why westerns remained a staple of the movie industry for almost thirty years was because they accentuated physical action: chases on horseback, saloon brawls, attacks by hostile Apaches, mine-shaft cave-ins, and heavies setting fire to a newspaper office. Overt physical action (as well as plot action) often meets the needs of impatient audiences.

Climaxes.   When screenplays reach their climactic moments, the writer usually tries to include all the entertainment values possible. Spectacle generally is a part of climactic action. How many TV shows have you seen that ended in car chases or gunfights? How many medical shows ended in an operating room? How many action-adventure movies ended in haunted houses, underground caverns, snake pits, quicksand, or on a monstrous planet in outer space? How many films or TV shows concluded with such spectacular events as fires, floods, earthquakes, avalanches, or wind- or rainstorms?

Experienced writers understand the need for spectacle. Over the years, they have covered such a wide spectrum of sound, motion, and color that many once-spectacular elements have become clichéd. A young writer recently told me, "If I see one more car go over a cliff and burst into flames, I'll smash my TV!" It becomes increasingly difficult to find fresh spectacular action or arenas in which to play story climaxes. Screenwriters deal with that challenge by expanding their creative horizons and searching for freshness. No one ever said that writing was easy. (Actually, bad writing is easy; it's good writing that is difficult.)

*M*ALE-FEMALE RELATIONSHIP

Because nature has implanted within us the curious and compelling force known as sexuality, many so-called rules of showmanship may occasionally be bent, broken, or knocked slightly askew. Graceless dancers, voiceless singers, and emotionless actors have attracted and held audiences because of sexual appeal.

In the American theater, the only plays able to survive extended engagements with just two characters have focused on a pairing of the sexes. These include "Two for the Seesaw," "Same Time Next Year," and "Voice of the Turtle." Viewers usually identify with the character of their own sex, vicariously experiencing the mating ritual. Such identification is so powerful that otherwise rigid rules of screenplay storytelling frequently go out the window. For example, the relatively routine situation of a boy and girl flirting at an amusement park might be extended considerably beyond the time that a non-sexual encounter would take. The 1930s comedy *Boy Meets Girl* attempted to reduce all drama to a formula: Boy meets girl, boy loses girl, boy gets girl. Although the formula appears simplistic, its countless variations still form the basis for many of our most successful plays and films, from *Romeo and Juliet* to the dozens of sex comedies that fill today's screens. In the 1930s the formula usually began with a "cute meet" in which the boy and girl encountered each other in an amusing or bizarre situation. For example, the boy (from a wealthy Philadelphia family) accidentally gets locked in an empty cage at the zoo. The girl (a reporter) happens along, sees him, laughs, takes his picture for her newspaper. He's furious. They meet a week later at an elegant party where she's posing as a waitress to get a scoop on a big news story. He exposes her. She drops her platter of hors d'oeuvres and stomps off in fury. Before long, they're in love.

Because the male-female relationship has been dramatized in countless variations, writers have ever-increasing difficulty avoiding clichés. Audiences have become so sophisticated that whenever an actor and actress of approximately the same age are cast together, expectations immediately arise that they will become romantically or sexually involved. If they do not, there's usually some disappointment.

The continuing challenge is to find new variations, new approaches, new reality for the male-female relationship. Writer-director Robert Towne created his own reality for the Jack Nicholson–Faye Dunaway relationship in *Chinatown* by using as minute a characteristic as a flaw in the iris of her eye as the trigger for their sexual awakening. (Towne had noticed such a flaw in the iris of his wife's eye.)

Such a moment gained honesty because it grew legitimately out of the character. Nicholson's character was somewhat in awe of Dunaway's, aware of her father's wealth and her position in society. He felt that he himself was flawed, professionally and personally. Therefore, the discovery of her flaw relieved and released him, enabling him to relate to her more overtly.*

The changes in today's society offer writers new directions for delineating the male-female relationship. The new prominence of women in the business

---

*As described by Robert Towne in "Images of a Writer," a PBS series.

world, for example, creates rich dramatic situations: women working in subordinate positions to men, men working in subordinate positions to women, sexual harassment, men and women competing for the same position, woman versus woman competing for the same executive, plus other variations.

SYMMETRY AND ORDER

In the motion picture *All About Eve*, a young actress flatters, browbeats, connives, deceives, and betrays others to gain a role. In time, she achieves great success, displacing theatrical star Bette Davis, whom she has betrayed. In the film's final moments, the actress (now a star) encounters another young hopeful who mouths much the same words she herself uttered earlier and who begins a pattern of flattery and deceit almost identical to the one she herself employed at the film's beginning. In the world of professional writers, a story that comes full circle, that concludes with a gambit similar to the one that began it, has become known as an **All About Eve ending**. The symmetry of such a pattern pleases audiences.

When a screenplay begins with a certain action, locale, or other narrative device and ends with the same device, the pattern is sometimes referred to as **bookends**; the similar beginning and ending enclose the central dramatic material. Examples include an opening and closing narration or an opening and closing in the present while the entire central portion has been told in flashback. In *The Princess Bride*, Peter Falk's opening and closing scenes in which he reads the story to his grandson become bookends for the central action.

Whenever themes — concepts, key lines of dialog, pieces of business — are repeated in the entertainment media, they create a sense of rhythm that is sensually gratifying. In music, such a recurring theme is called a **leitmotif** and usually is associated with a character or concept. Recurring themes tend to build audience familiarity and emotion with each replaying.

The song "As Time Goes By" in *Casablanca* demonstrates the leitmotif principle. Each replaying of the song recalls the idyllic Paris love affair between Humphrey Bogart and Ingrid Bergman and evokes in audiences the intense emotion associated with it. Each new playing takes on additional colorations as the story progresses from love to anger to bitterness and finally to a selfless love. The musical conductor took the theme originally played as **source music** — music that originates from a source within a scene (for example, a radio, TV set, or piano) — and wove it into the film's musical score, effectively stirring up audiences' emotions.

Writers use recurring themes in screenplays to achieve dramatic symmetry and to build response from an audience. Such motifs are not confined to music.

They occur in story patterns, dialog, pieces of business, settings, and visual imagery. Repetition of visual images — lines, forms, and colors — is more properly the concern of directors and cinematographers.

STORY PATTERNS

The *All About Eve* example demonstrates how story elements may be reprised to achieve a sense of roundness, or completion.

A television movie some years ago used flashbacks to achieve dramatic symmetry. A troubled young man repeatedly recalled fragments of an incident that had traumatized him almost to the point of destroying his life. Each time we saw the flashback, we glimpsed a few more of its details, until we finally witnessed the incident in its entirety. Repetition of the traumatic incident, beyond creating symmetry, also created a nightmarish sense of being caught in a maze, returning to a horror again and again.

Often, whodunits reveal only a portion of the killing that triggers the story. Then later, the incident is depicted again, this time in its entirety. The motion picture *A Soldier's Story*, for example, dramatized the shooting of an army sergeant under the opening titles. When the film replayed the incident later, revealing the identity of the killer, it created a satisfying sense of order. The audience revisited a previously incomplete scene. The missing piece of the puzzle had been added. Equilibrium had been restored.

Most screenplays change disequilibrium into equilibrium. This reestablishment of order probably provides much of drama's appeal. Traditionally, a ruthless antagonist fights to keep the hero from reaching a worthwhile goal. The problem worsens; the viewer's worry grows; the problem resolves; equilibrium is restored. Even in films that end unhappily, some measure of equilibrium usually is achieved. For example, the hero regains his honor or a wife finds new respect for her husband.

In police/private eye shows, a murder shatters the equilibrium. The protagonist gathers clues, risks death, makes accusations, and apprehends the killer, thereby repairing the rip in the social fabric. Curiosity, of course, is also a factor in whodunits, as we shall discuss later in this chapter.

DIALOG, BUSINESS, SETTINGS, COSTUMES

In Chapter 7 we called the repetition of lines of dialog *playbacks* because they recalled earlier moments and thereby evoked some of the emotions attached to those earlier moments. For example, a brother tells his younger sister "I'm too busy" every time she asks for a favor. Ultimately, when he needs the favor and she tells him coolly "I'm too busy," the playback (repetition) hits him hard.

The three words are curiously satisfying and effective because they recall the earlier incidents.

Dialog can provide writers with their most obvious opportunity to use repetition for effect. Less obvious and equally effective is the repetition of business, the personal actions a character performs.

In *Sleeping with the Enemy*, the abusive/obsessive husband insists that his wife straighten bathroom towels so that they hang evenly on a rack. After the wife has fled and found a happier life in another community, she wryly hangs her bathroom towels *unevenly*, symbolizing her joy at being free from his domination. After he has tracked her down, she discovers in horror that the towels have been carefully aligned, signaling his presence. Thus, business as slight as the aligning of towels can have major dramatic significance.

In the motion picture *Greystoke*, Tarzan encounters death again and again among members of his primate family. He registers grief each time by placing the animal's hand atop his head. Through repetition, we come to understand the meaning of the gesture. Through repetition, it gains emotionality. Late in the film, when Tarzan's beloved grandfather (a British lord) dies and the apeman repeats the same primitive grieving gesture, the effect is devastating.

Writers can also use locales as recurring themes. When lovers return to the small Chinese restaurant where they first met, the setting provides emotional overtones. Later in the story, when the young man has betrayed her, the woman revisits the restaurant alone. The audience's memory of happier scenes is stimulated as the musical score reprises the love theme. The waiter, unaware of her pain, asks where her boyfriend is tonight. The setting, dialog, and music all contribute to the scene's clichéd poignancy.

Even costumes may be used as a recurring theme. When an overworked, underpaid woman wears a certain, bright-colored dress every time she's unhappy, audiences come to understand the association. Late in the screenplay, her mood changes. Now she plans to quit her job and marry Mr. Wonderful. In haste, she starts to put on the bright-colored dress, changes her mind, grins, and throws it in the trash. Because of past associations, we understand exactly her state of mind.

*H*UMOR AND SURPRISE

Everyone loves to laugh. Writers with a sense of humor often create entertaining and salable material. Their scripts are fun to read. The obvious way of expressing humor, of course, is through scripts that are overtly comedic. Another is to find humor in dramatic screenplays, usually through the creation of characters with a bright sense of humor, using their bon mots to relieve the dramatic tension.

We saw in Chapter 1 that among a screenplay's most fundamental needs is a protagonist with whom we can become emotionally involved. One way to make audiences care about characters is to provide them with a sense of humor. Protagonists who wear a smile — who find humor in the commonplace, who are able to laugh at themselves or at misfortune — immediately become endearing. Recall the stereotypical heavy; he's often sullen, scowling, or sneering because writers want us to dislike such characters.

If your protagonist's personality doesn't fit your sense of humor, then find another character who does. If your style of comedy is brittle and sophisticated, then create a character whose brittle comments will rattle the walls and make audiences smile. Of course, it makes no sense to create characters just to evoke humor; characters must fulfill specific plot needs. But there's no reason why you can't modify or reshape an existing character to incorporate a sense of humor.

Chapter 11 deals specifically with writing comedy material. Read it. The chapter may provide clues that will help you understand the nature of comedy and some of its uses in screenplays.

CURIOSITY

Sometimes writers move an audience through a story by evoking a series of questions. Whodunits and other forms of mysteries typify such a structural pattern. We're puzzled and confused by events that seem to defy logic. We ask ourselves: Could the gardener have returned to the castle? Wouldn't someone recognize him? Would she have killed her lover? Why? Is the dead man really dead? We've never actually seen his corpse.

Curiosity represents the intellectual side of our psyches. Stories deriving solely from curiosity, therefore, seldom meet the primary requirement for screenplays: emotion. Mystery stories certainly can be dramatic, compelling our attention, dazzling us with many of the entertainment elements described in this chapter — but they are not drama in the traditional sense. We do not become emotionally involved with a protagonist, other than superficially. Audience-wise writers often try to include emotional elements in mystery and whodunit screenplays.

One facet of curiosity reflects our attraction to the grisly and the macabre. Morbid curiosity occasionally engenders real emotion. It can also be obsessive. See how spectators gather in excitement at the scene of an automobile accident and stare compulsively at the injured. Fascination with the grisly is part of our attraction to films such as *Silence of the Lambs*.

Fascination with the macabre sets up a curiously conflicting reaction in most of us: We are simultaneously attracted and repelled. Spectators of horror films sometimes cover their eyes during particularly gruesome moments, sneaking glimpses at the screen through cracks between their fingers. Psychologists tell us that our revulsion at the sight of a cadaver grows from this reminder of our own mortality. Cadavers occupy a shadowed niche in our culture that is labeled taboo. Like Pandora, we strive to see the forbidden.

As with other entertainment elements, morbid curiosity may be used in screenplays to compel audience attention. The grisly and the macabre are shocking. They are powerful. But their overuse or abuse can cheapen a screenplay. Wise writers often suggest rather than reveal, allowing the spectator's imagination to fill in grisly details. Events imagined can be far more shocking than those actually seen.

*C*HAPTER HIGHLIGHTS

> ➤ Certain elements of sensual appeal provide a screenplay with entertainment values beyond those created by plot. Such elements have delighted audiences since the beginning of time. They do not replace drama; they enhance it.

> ➤ One such element, spectacle, provides audiences with sound, motion, and color. We find spectacular elements in kaleidoscopes, fireworks displays, parades, and circuses.

> ➤ The darker elements of spectacle appear in the contravention of natural laws: ghosts, goblins, witches, and vampires. We enjoy such dark elements in TV shows or movies because it is safe to be frightened by them.

> ➤ Writers use the element of spectacle in their choice of characters, subject matter, settings, and scenic action.

> ➤ The male-female relationship stimulates audiences through appeal to their sex drives. Extensive use of this relationship has created plot clichés. Current social movements such as more women in the workplace may suggest new story directions.

> ➤ The element of symmetry gratifies the audience's need for dramatic rhythm and harmony. Reprising lines of dialog, settings, musical themes, business, and costumes evokes the emotions arising from their initial appearance.

> ➤ Audiences seek order. In whodunits, a murder ruptures the equilibrium. When the killer is finally unmasked, equilibrium is restored, gratifying the audience. All drama deals in attempts to restore equilibrium.

> ➤ Audiences love humor and surprise. One way of creating involvement with a protagonist is to provide him or her with a sense of humor. Chapter 11 deals specifically with comedy.

➤ Curiosity provides intellectual appeal; a mystery plot propels the audience along by asking puzzling questions. Morbid curiosity, on the other hand, provides emotional stimulation through attraction to the grisly and macabre.

SCRIPTWRITING PROJECTS

EXERCISES DESIGNED TO SHARPEN YOUR NARRATIVE SKILLS

LOCALE

Write the following three-page scene in two different settings. Take advantage of whatever atmospheric elements would normally be present in each. As much as you can, use those elements to enhance the dramatic values. Use proper script form. Include all dialog, actions, and business.

- Locale 1: A real estate office
- Locale 2: A sleazy waterfront (wharf) area

The scene: Stephanie has come to realize that her fiancé, Griff, is emotionally unhinged. In this scene, she tries to break off their engagement, with disastrous consequences. To justify the settings, let Griff be a real estate salesman in locale 1 and the skipper of a fishing boat in locale 2.

SYMMETRY

After you have written two versions of the preceding scene, try to inject the element of rhythm — repetition of form — into each. End the scene by reprising either a line of dialog or an action (piece of business) from earlier in the scene.

HUMOR AND SURPRISE

Although it may be difficult to inject humor into what will probably be a melodramatic scene, the element of surprise may fit nicely. Ask yourself: How can I give this scene an unexpected or twist ending?

MOVEMENT

Examine your scenes again. Do you feel you could play either version with your characters seated throughout? Try it with one version. The result may give you some laughs.

CHAPTER 10

Format and Style

*I*n the movies' earliest days, directors worked from rudimentary manuscripts, often no more elaborate than notes scrawled on a scrap of paper. Gradually, as the length and quantity of films increased, writers developed and standardized a manuscript form specifically suited to the camera-oriented medium. These film stories were variously referred to as screenplays, photo plays, scenarios, or scripts (short for *manuscripts*).

Aware that their screenplay would be photographed in camera angles, which later would be pieced together by a film editor, writers attempted to describe each scene in terms of these angles. These first-draft descriptions of camera angles were sometimes arbitrary as writers tried to visualize the dramatic action in their imaginations. The term *shooting script* usually implied that the director and production office had broken the screenplay down into long, medium, or close shots (plus other production information), which the director more or less followed.

Telling a story in a series of camera angles has remained the screenplay pattern until recent years, both in motion pictures and television films. Because directors usually select their own angles, rarely following those suggested by the writer, screenplay formats have become simpler and simpler, today usually omitting camera angles altogether.

Is correct format important? Yes and no. What is important is the story you tell, the nature of your characters — what they do and say. But if you want your script to look professional, you'd better make certain that its format is correct. Producers and story analysts have told me that when a screenplay is submitted to them, they are inevitably influenced by its presentation. Is it neatly typed? Are the words spelled correctly? Is the format professional? When scripts look amateurish, readers tend to expect the worst.

The screenplay formats described in this chapter are those most commonly used in motion pictures and television. They differ only in that television scripts still occasionally include camera angles; movie scripts generally do not. The described formats are not used for live TV production, three-camera sitcoms (situation comedies) staged before a live audience, or commercials. You may have seen screenplays that differ from the formats described in this chapter. Professional writers sometimes follow their own muse, especially in feature motion pictures.

This chapter examines:

➤ **DEVELOPING THE SCREENPLAY**: the three customary phases of script development — treatment, first draft, and final draft — plus a discussion of script distribution.

➤ **LEARNING THE SCREENPLAY LANGUAGE:** specific patterns found in most professional screenplays — banner headlines, stage directions, dialog, transitions, esoteric words and phrases

➤ **REVISING THE SCREENPLAY:** the most frequent causes of revision in TV and film and mechanics of revising

DEVELOPING THE SCREENPLAY

After writers have developed a story premise and detailed treatment, they then must create the screenplay, telling their story in a scene-by-scene progression, in specific character actions and lines of dialog. Screenplays describe what the camera sees and the microphone hears. They do *not* describe imaginings, reminiscences, thoughts, or emotions.

Screenplay length depends on several factors. Motion picture screenplays usually average between 110 and 120 pages. Most hour-long television scripts run between fifty-six and sixty pages in length. The per-page playing time varies; usually a script page averages between forty-five seconds and a minute.

Timing estimates cannot be absolute. A fight in a saloon, for example, might be described in half a page and yet might consume two minutes of screen time. Because comedies tend to play faster than drama, a half-hour dramatic show would require thirty pages while a half-hour comedy might consume forty or more. Further, some directors milk each scene for its dramatic values; their hour show might require only fifty-four pages. Directors demanding a more rapid pacing might require sixty. Some screenwriting texts insist mistakenly that a minute a page is an accurate assessment. According to Joyce Heftel who worked for years as a Script Supervisor and who has timed thousands of script pages and dozens of major feature films:

> Whoever created the minute-a-page myth has cost our industry millions of dollars. A minute a page is an exception. In fact, the range is more like 48 seconds to 65 seconds a page depending on the material.*

Writers of television scripts go through a standard series of developmental steps, as specified in the Writers Guild of America (**WGA**) contract. Usually, they receive three basic payments, each for a different phase of narrative development. The first phase deals with the treatment in which the story is described in prose, giving both writer and producer a chance to examine plot structure and characters and to discover strengths and weaknesses prior to the first-draft screenplay.

Sometimes treatments don't work. The WGA contract provides that producers may ask for one revision without having to pay for it but must pay for any additional revisions. I have produced episodes of television series in which we asked for (and paid for!) four or five treatments before we felt a story was solid enough to warrant going ahead with a screenplay.

---

*Joyce Heftel, "A Minute-a-Page — BAH, HUMBUG!" *POV* (*Point of View*), a publication of the Producers Guild of America, Fall, 1991.

The second payment in the standard WGA contract covers the writing of the **first-draft** screenplay. This is the draft the writer first turns in to a producer. Although it is labeled "first draft," it may actually be the writer's third or fourth draft, depending on how long he or she worked to solve creative problems before submitting it.

In spite of the best planning in the world, first drafts seldom are good enough. The third phase of the standard writer commitment covers the final draft, which usually is divided into two parts. The WGA contract specifies that producers may ask for a rewrite, which may be substantial in terms of restructuring plot or redefining characters. Finally, producers may ask for a polish, which cannot be substantial. Conscientious writers sometimes contribute more than the WGA contract specifies because they don't want to be rewritten and they want their material to be as exciting as possible.

Once a screenplay has been approved, the television producer sends it to a duplicating service. After copies are made, the producer distributes them to the various departments concerned with its production. In television, thirty or forty copies go to the casting office. Perhaps sixty copies go to the network and advertising agencies. Other copies go to the executive producer, writing staff, the director, cinematographer, art director, set dresser, makeup department, special effects department, editor, hairdresser, costumer, property master, transportation chief, and construction boss.

Each of these people forms opinions about the characters, their appearance, the style of their homes or offices, their hair or clothing styles, and the types of cars they drive based on what they read in the script. Accordingly, writers need to communicate their vision as clearly as they can.

Action must be so vivid in writers' minds that it will be communicated on paper to all of the artists and technicians responsible for translating it to film or videotape. The art director, for example, has to know what kind of sets to build that will reflect the tastes and life-styles of the scripted characters. The costumer has to understand the style and sophistication of the characters to outfit them appropriately. The transportation boss has to determine what kinds of cars they drive. The director has to understand not just obvious plot developments but also subtleties of characterizations or relationships to extract those subtleties from actors during rehearsal and performance. Communicating such a broad spectrum of information is a major screenwriting responsibility.

Novelist and screenwriter William Goldman (*Misery*) prepares two different versions of a screenplay. The first is designed as a sales piece.

> There is the selling version and the shooting version. When I'm hired to do a movie, I feel I have completed my job successfully if the movie goes. And I have failed if the movie does not go.
>
> For a movie to go, a studio executive must say yes. I want to make my selling version as exciting a reading experience as I can and I'll

throw in anything I can to make it fun, to make it exciting. I'll throw in asides to the reader; I'll do anything I can so the guy will say, "Hey, this can be a good movie! Why don't we do this one?"*

Once Goldman has received a "go" on his project, he then reexamines and reworks his screenplay's structure, aware that now it must conform to solid narrative principles.

Selling versions of scripts also go to **bankable** stars or directors, that is, those stars or directors whose names attached to a project will virtually guarantee its financing.

LEARNING THE SCREENPLAY FORMAT

Read ten movie scripts and you'll find ten formats that differ slightly in style and language. Read ten television scripts and you'll find the same is true. Some writers like to direct from behind their typewriters by putting lots of camera angles into their scripts. Others prefer simplicity: no angles at all. Some pepper their scripts with capital letters to indicate character names, significant props, special effects, or camera directions. Others use almost no capitalized words.

Over the past ten or fifteen years, the format of movie and TV scripts generally has become simpler and simpler. Simplification works to the writer's advantage. What he or she wants most is for the agents or producers who read their scripts to submerge themselves in its world and become emotionally involved with its characters, to forget the truck rumbling by outside the window or the secretaries giggling in the next office. Camera angles become stumbling blocks, hurdles the reader has to leap over, thereby interfering with total absorption.

In eliminating camera angles from your script, you needn't worry that the director will eliminate camera coverage from your scenes. It is the director's responsibility to supply the editor and producer with all the camera angles necessary for dramatizing a scene effectively. It doesn't matter that you have dispensed with close-ups and high angles and fancy trucking shots; the director will supply them. That's his or her job.

The following guidelines are not inflexible rules. They are correct most of the time.

*William Goldman speaking in "Word into Image — Portraits of American Screenwriters," a PBS series.

Every scene begins with a **banner headline** written in capital letters. For example,

EXT. HAUNTED HOUSE - NIGHT

Banner headlines always describe where and when the scene is taking place. The "where" is described by one of two words, either **EXTERIOR** (always abbreviated EXT.) or **INTERIOR** (abbreviated INT.). Note that it's incorrect and insufficient to write INT. or EXT. all by itself. You must include the exact location. Is it the exterior of a mansion or of a country road? Is it the interior of a circus tent or a college classroom? In our sample banner headline, the EXT. is of a haunted house.

Happily, only two words are needed to describe the "when": DAY or NIGHT. (Occasionally, you see DUSK or DAWN in screenplays but usually DAY or NIGHT will suffice.) Notice that in our sample banner headline, a dash separates the "where" and "when."

Banner headlines provide the setting ("where" and "when") for each scene. When the scene changes — that is, when the *locale* or *time frame* changes — a new banner headline must describe the setting for the new scene.

When writers turn in their screenplays to producers, their banner headlines have no numbers. Once the script has been polished and is ready for production, a final shooting script is mimeographed. On this final version, the banner headlines are always numbered (these are scene numbers).

Banner headlines provide a quick orientation for the reader. But they also give essential information to production personnel and the unit manager who will prepare your script for production. He or she will **break down the script**, describing each numbered scene on a narrow cardboard strip and placing it on a **production board**, organizing all the screenplay's scenes by locale for efficiency and economy of shooting.

STAGE DIRECTIONS

Under each banner headline (and separated by a space) are **stage directions** that describe what happens in that locale: what the camera sees and the microphone hears. Let's put some stage directions under our banner headline. Notice that they are single spaced.

EXT. HAUNTED HOUSE - NIGHT

A battered Volkswagen pulls up in front of the house and lurches to a stop. After a moment, a young woman gets out and closes the door gingerly as if afraid of making a noise.

When new characters appear in a script, their names are capitalized and they are described briefly. Names are typed in all-capital letters only once in stage directions, when the characters first appear. (But names are also capitalized above dialog, as we'll see in a moment.) Descriptions usually are brief: two or three words, enough to provide a quick mental picture rather than a detailed character analysis. Good writers prefer to let the characters' dialog and actions provide more substantial clues to their nature.

EXT. HAUNTED HOUSE - NIGHT

A battered Volkswagen pulls up in front of the house and lurches to a stop. After a moment, a young woman gets out and closes the door gingerly as if afraid of making a noise. This is CINDY, seventeen, pretty, painfully thin.

Writers usually keep stage directions brief, avoiding clutter and fancy "literary" verbiage.

DIALOG

When characters speak, their single-spaced dialog appears in a column three and a half inches wide down the center of the page. **Dialog cues** (indications of how a line should be read) always appear centered below the character's name, in parentheses, and lowercased. They appear on a line by themselves, even when appearing within the body of a speech.

EXT. HAUNTED HOUSE - NIGHT

A battered Volkswagen pulls up in front of the house and lurches to a stop. After a moment, a young woman gets out, closes the door gingerly as if afraid of making a noise. This is CINDY, seventeen, pretty, painfully thin. As she starts toward the door, a hollow VOICE calls from within the house.

>   VOICE
>   We've been expecting you, Cindy.
>
>   CINDY
>   (nervously)
>   Who—who are you?
>
>   VOICE
>   You'll see.
>   (laughter)
>   You'll see.

Cindy edges slowly toward the front door. Trembling, she turns the knob and the huge door swings open, CREAKING on its hinges.

Dialog cues should be kept to a minimum because actors resent being told how to read lines. Usually the dramatic context will provide insights into their interpretation. Use cues only when there is a possibility that an actor or director may misunderstand your intention.

On rare occasions words relating to sound or special effects are capitalized in stage directions. Note the word *creaking* in the preceding example.

A DEMONSTRATION OF SCRIPT FORMAT

FADE IN:

EXT. BEACH - DAY

Adorable TRICIA TRACY, twenty, jogs along the sandy beach. A small VOICE makes her stop and look around, puzzled.

> SMALL VOICE
>
> Hey!

She looks toward some moss-covered rocks and discovers a gray, scaly LIZARD looking up at her.

> TRICIA
>
> Did you say that?

> LIZARD
>
> Yes. An evil witch turned me into
> a lizard. Won't you help me?

Tricia hunkers down beside the lizard. She nods.

> LIZARD
> (continuing)
> Put me on your pillow tonight.
> At midnight I'll change back into
> a handsome network executive.

> TRICIA
>
> On my pillow? But you're so ugly!

> LIZARD
>
> I'll make you a star, with your
> very own TV series!

She frowns, considering this intriguing suggestion.

DISSOLVE TO:

EXT. BEACH CABIN - NIGHT

A small, one-story dwelling, windows lighted. In the distance a dog HOWLS mournfully.

INT. BEACH CABIN - NIGHT

A clock above the mantel reads 12:05. After a moment the front door opens and Tricia's muscular HUSBAND enters. Hearing GIGGLING from the bedroom, the husband's face hardens. He crosses to a desk, takes a gun from the drawer, and starts toward the bedroom.

INT. BEDROOM - NIGHT

The door crashes open. The husband stares into the bedroom, gun in hand. Tricia and a handsome NETWORK EXECUTIVE are seated on the bed examining a script. At the sight of her husband, Tricia gasps.

> HUSBAND
>
> Outside, buddy.

> TRICIA
>
> It's not like you think. When I found him, he was just a lizard on the beach!

> HUSBAND
>
> Sure he was.
>> (gestures with gun)
>
> Come on, "lizard." Outside.

> TRICIA
>
> And now he's an important network executive!

Suddenly the Exec's tongue darts out and catches a fly. The husband stares at him, stunned.

> HUSBAND
>
> Well, I'll be damned. He is a network executive after all...

FADE OUT

TRANSITIONS

A film or videotape editor will splice every scene described in your script to the one immediately before it. On screen, the transition from angle 1 to angle 2 will be instantaneous, unless otherwise specified. This instantaneous transition from scene to scene (or angle to angle) is called a **cut**. Usually, in screenplays it isn't necessary to write the word *cut*, since cuts are the normal, unstated way of moving from scene to scene.

Sometimes, however, a writer will use a phrase such as "cut to" or "**match cut** to" (a cut to identical or similar subject matter), or "**shock cut** to" (a cut to jarring subject matter) to separate one scene (or sequence) from another on the script page. Such transition words usually appear at the right side of a page and are followed by a colon (:). For example, "DISSOLVE TO:" in the script sample separates the first scene from the second.

A **dissolve** is a more gradual transition than a cut, one image fading out as the other fades in. It's an optical effect: a blending or melting of images with one briefly overlapping the other. For that reason, early film scripts referred to it as a **lap dissolve**.

Dissolves usually suggest a passage of time or mark a change of locale. They vary in length depending on narrative needs. Most dissolves are three feet in film length, two seconds in playing time. But writers or directors sometimes use longer dissolves for dramatic effect so that the two superimposed images comment on each other.

Let's suppose that a western hero has saved the ranchers from the heavies and won the heart of the beautiful schoolteacher. He kisses her good-bye in front of the schoolhouse, mounts his horse, and rides off — and she stares after him, a tear sliding down her cheek. Now we DISSOLVE slowly (perhaps six or eight seconds) to the hero riding off across the vast expanse of desert. For a moment or two, the images are superimposed, the schoolteacher's face lingering, ghostlike, over the hero on horseback, suggesting perhaps that he carries her face with him in memory or that she holds him in her thoughts, a statement achieved through the superimposition of images.

Dissolves sometimes are used for purposes other than transitions between scenes. For example, in ballet sequences directors sometimes dissolve from one angle to another simply because the dissolve has fluidity, a lyric quality; it is more graceful than a straight cut. Moreover, a slow dissolve presents a superimposition of images that, in ballet, becomes almost poetic.

A fade-in is an optical effect marking a transition from total blackness to full picture. It is the only transition written at the left side of the script page. (See the beginning of our demonstration scene.) A fade-in is the traditional rising curtain at the start of motion picture and TV shows. Like other optical effects, fades (either in or out) may vary in length, depending on narrative needs. Usually, they last two seconds.

A fade-out either signals the end of a motion picture or television show or in TV denotes an act curtain, usually for a commercial or station break. As with other optical effects, a fade-out appears at the right side of a script page.

Sometimes in screenplays we see a fade-out immediately followed by a fade-in. Such a transition suggests a long passage of time, usually far longer than that connoted by a dissolve. For example, a fade-out might follow a shot of a prisoner being conducted into a federal penitentiary as the gates clang shut behind him. An immediate fade-in on the prisoner emerging from the penitentiary would suggest that the term of his imprisonment has passed, perhaps a year or more.

Many writers avoid fades whenever possible, feeling that they stop a story's forward motion cold. They prefer dissolves or straight cuts, thereby maintaining a feeling of movement.

Wipes occur most frequently in comedy or sports programs. A **wipe** is a visual effect in which the incoming scene moves in front of the outgoing scene, replacing it (see Figure 10.1). The movement can be horizontal, vertical, diagonal, or whatever pattern the imagination can devise. Optical laboratories can produce literally dozens of variations. In football games, a commercial sometimes emerges from the center of the screen in the shape of a football, zooming out to fill the screen, replacing the old picture. Television channels sometimes use wipes in the shape of their channel numbers. Because wipes tend to call attention to themselves, they are used rarely in serious screenplays. A writer might use a wipe, for example, to recall Saturday afternoon serials or Mack Sennett comedies.

SCRIPT WORDS

The following words or letters appear occasionally in stage directions or dialog cues:

beat — A momentary pause in dialog or action, like the beat of a metronome

b.g. — Background

f.g. — Foreground

filter — The tinny or mechanical quality of sound reproduced over a telephone or through a loudspeaker

INTERCUT — Sometimes used where two simultaneous (but dramatically connected) actions are taking place. For example, in a phone conversation

montage — Usually a succession of visual images or short scenes for the purpose of making a single plot point

o.s. — Off screen or offstage

P.O.V. (point of view) — A camera angle that reveals what a character sees; his or her perspective

SEGUE — An audio dissolve — that is, a blending of sound elements (for example, a woman's scream SEGUES into a train whistle)

SFX — Sound effects

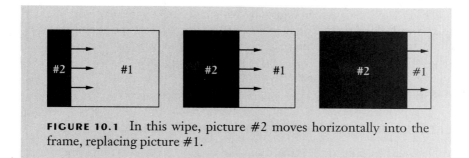

FIGURE 10.1 In this wipe, picture #2 moves horizontally into the frame, replacing picture #1.

SPFX — Special effects

stock — Footage that has been filmed previously, usually purchased from a studio or film library

v.o. — Voice over

Revising the screenplay

To writers who have labored through two or three treatments and multiple drafts of a screenplay, it often appears that their work is never done. In truth, screenplays often continue to be revised until a scene is actually photographed. And sometimes, if the scene doesn't work, it's rewritten and photographed again!

Two types of revisions are performed on almost every script: creative and noncreative. Creative revisions, obviously, are those intended to enrich characters and relationships, to close story holes, to add twists or excitement or honesty to a plot, and to provide more spectacular production values (such elements as lavish scenery or colorful locations). Noncreative revisions are usually performed for reasons of accuracy, legal protection, budget, casting, or censorship.

ACCURACY

Many television series purport to use certain cities as the backgrounds for their stories. In practice, however, much (or all) action usually is photographed in Hollywood, using exteriors in and around southern California. The writers of these series frequently know little about their script's background city. When those scripts are researched, street names and locations frequently must be changed to conform to reality.

In medical series, writers usually confer during the preparation of their stories with doctors who serve as medical advisers. Once the script has been completed, it is sent to the medical adviser, who corrects inaccuracies and supplies appropriately esoteric language. In the same pattern, series dramatizing law, military, or historical stories require consultation with experts to guarantee accuracy.

LEGAL PROTECTION

Whenever a specific locale is mentioned in a script, producers must be cautious in their use of character names. Were an unscrupulous, sadistic doctor in a Cape Cod episode of "Murder, She Wrote" to be named (say) George Frobisher, the producer must make certain that no actual doctor named George Frobisher is practicing medicine in Cape Cod. Such a doctor might (with justification) sue the show, its writer, producer, and network, claiming that his good name and professional reputation had been irreparably damaged.

Even the names of businesses are usually researched, and research organizations provide fictitious names to guarantee that no one might find cause for litigation.

BUDGET

Every motion picture or TV show has a production office whose job (among others) is to protect the budget. Before any screenplay is filmed, the unit production manager draws up an estimated budget. These skilled production veterans are incredibly accurate in predicting costs. They examine the script, break it down scene by scene, investigate the director's track record for staying within budget, and obtain estimates from each of the departments involved, both above the line and below the line. The phrase **above the line** refers to so-called artistic elements such as writer, director, cast, and producer. **Below the line** refers to such production and postproduction elements as camera, set construction and dressing, travel, location costs, properties, crew, and editing.

After assembling estimates of all costs, production managers allow a small percentage for emergencies and arrive at a total that they then pass along to the producer. Such early budget estimates are often high, and the producer must find some way to cut costs before the project can be filmed.

The producer and writer then reexamine the script. Can the cast be reduced? (Perhaps two roles can be combined into one.) Can distant locations be filmed locally? Can the number of location days be reduced? Can the number (and scope) of the sets be reduced? Can the amount of **night-for-night** shooting be diminished? (Night shooting consumes more time than day shooting.) Can the script be shortened? Once possible areas of savings have been identified, the producer discusses revisions with the unit production manager. If the proposed revisions solve the budget problems, they are mimeographed on colored paper and promptly distributed.

Motion picture budgets, of course, are vastly higher than those of TV shows. Shooting schedules for movies are longer; the scope of the action frequently is greater; stars usually demand more money. Yet despite the budgetary differences, both TV and movie production companies exercise diligence in controlling costs.

CASTING

Sometimes, for good reasons, a part in a script is written one way but cast another. A seventeen-year-old student is played by a thirty-year-old. A businessman is played by a female. An Englishman is cast as an American gangster.

The reason for such changes is not that the producer and casting director have lost their road maps. On the contrary, they may be exercising extraordinarily good sense. Often such changes result from a casting opportunity. A superb actress is in town. She'll be here for two weeks. No, she doesn't usually do television, but if the part is right. . . . The producer makes a deal, promising to rewrite the part just for her. No matter that the character's age is different.

Such major casting changes require more than a line-by-line examination of the script. They demand study of the entire character concept. Would, for example, a thirty-year-old woman perform some of the actions scripted for a teenager? If not, whole scenes may need to be reconceived and rewritten. Would other characters be affected by a major casting change? If so, the producer and writer may spend a few sleepless nights revising what both had regarded as a completed script.

CENSORSHIP

Television scripts must be approved by the network's department of **program practices**: the censor. CBS, NBC, and ABC each have their own guidelines for the behavior and language of characters appearing in their shows.

After scripts have been duplicated, the producer routinely sends copies to the censor. The censor reads the material and speeds detailed notes back to the producer. Certain words or lines simply are not acceptable; they must be changed. Certain actions threaten to be too brutal. A bedroom sequence is too overtly sexual. Two lines must be changed and the person may not disrobe as indicated in the script. The scenes can only be approved after the film has been edited.

If producers feel the network censor is unfair, they may debate the disputed area; often compromises are possible. Sometimes, if producers feel they need to protect valuable script material, they may seek help from a higher network authority.

In feature films a similar pattern occurs. After the rating board reads the screenplay, it advises the producer that the film will probably receive a rating of G, PG-13, NC-17, R, or X. Such a rating can only be confirmed after viewing the final cut. If the producer is unhappy with the projected rating, he or she may ask the writer to revise certain sections of the screenplay to obtain a different rating. Similarly, when the rating board assigns a tentative rating after viewing the completed film, the producer may reedit the picture to remove certain offensive actions or language.

Because television programs are viewed in the home where there are often children, the standards for language and behavior — particularly as concerns sex and violence — are considerably more stringent than those for motion pictures. However, current TV and motion picture standards are more lenient than they were a few years ago.

REVISED PAGES

Original script pages are white. To make certain that revised pages are not confused with original pages, revisions usually are copied on colored paper and include the date of their addition.

The first set of revised pages is usually blue. When additional script changes become necessary, pink pages are circulated to cast and crew. When pink pages are revised, the revisions are done on yellow paper. When yellow pages are changed, revisions are green. When green pages are changed, revisions are goldenrod (a deep yellow). When goldenrod pages are changed, revisions are café (gray). In television, where producers sometimes must scramble to get scripts together for a shooting date that is uncomfortably close, scripts occasionally appear as a rainbow of colored pages.

If changes are required beyond the café stage, scripts sometimes are totally reduplicated, and a second draft, or final draft, emerges, printed again on white paper, usually with a colored cover different from the original draft.

*C*HAPTER HIGHLIGHTS

➢ Screenplays have developed from scribbled notes in the movies' early years to today's detailed shooting scripts. Correct screenplay format is secondary to the story and its characters.

➢ Movie scripts average 110 to 120 pages in length. Hour-long TV shows average 60 pages. A script page generally covers between forty-five seconds and a minute. Most scripts are written in three phases: treatment, first draft, and final draft. Both treatments and first drafts usually require revisions.

➤ Once screenplays are duplicated, they are distributed to various departments. Department heads will translate script concepts to film or videotape, so writers must communicate their vision accurately.

➤ Screenplays describe the settings for scenes in banner headlines that describe where and when the action takes place.

➤ Under each banner headline are stage directions that reveal what the camera sees and the microphone hears. Certain words in stage directions are typed in all-capital letters: a character's name the first time he or she appears and sound or special effects.

➤ Dialog appears in a column down the center of each script page. The speaker's name is capitalized. Dialog cues appear in parentheses on a line by themselves.

➤ The most common transitions include *fade-in* (from black to full picture), *fade-out* (the reverse), *dissolve* (a merging of outgoing and incoming pictures), and *cut* (an instantaneous change of picture). A dissolve usually connotes a transition in time or place. A fade-in begins most movies or TV shows. A fade-out usually signifies a curtain.

➤ Script revisions occur for creative reasons or for reasons of accuracy, legal protection, budget, casting, or censorship. Revised pages are distributed in the following color order: blue, pink, yellow, green, goldenrod, and café.

SCRIPTWRITING PROJECTS

EXERCISES DESIGNED TO SHARPEN YOUR NARRATIVE SKILLS

SCRIPT FORMAT

The following self-contained scene is written in totally incorrect format. Rewrite it correctly, according to the guidelines established in this chapter. The corrected version appears in the Appendix.

Dissolve up from total blackness:

Inside a haunted house at midnight. A sudden flash of lightning illuminates the room as teen-aged Debbie Logan trembles in fear. A loud "moan" startles her. She picks up the phone and dials.

Debbie: Brad, Brad, I'm so scared!

In his den, Brad Bascom sips brandy and gently soothes her.

Brad: Don't be such a goddamned coward! Just
get the money and leave.

Debbie: Where is it?

Brad: (IMPATIENT) In the suit of armor, where
else?

Debbie looks around and spots it.

Her perspective: the suit of armor across the room. The moans seem
louder. The suit of armor walks toward Debbie, its rusted metal joints
creaking.

Debbie: It . . . it's coming toward me!

Brad: Just lift off the helmet, Chicken Little.
The money's inside.

Nervously she lifts the visor from the faceplate. Sure enough, there's
money inside. Debbie grabs it and exits fast.

The Suit of Armor picks up phone.

Suit: Brad?

Brad: Yeah?

Suit of Armor moans chillingly into the phone. Brad gasps, screams,
wets his pants, and runs off.

Picture dissolves to blackness.

CHAPTER 11

Comedy

*Through humor we see in what seems rational,
the irrational; in what seems important, the unimportant.
It also heightens our sense of survival and preserves our sanity.*
— *Charles Chaplin* [*]

*P*eople love to laugh. Writers who infuse their screenplays with humor make their material more fun to read, more fun to watch, often more dramatic, and ultimately more salable. In thrillers, humor gives audiences a chance to release nervous energy before beginning the next roller coaster ride to terror. In tragedy, scenes of lightness or humor provide a welcome counterpoint to moments of sadness, enriching those moments and somehow making them more poignant. And in all of the drama between those two extremes, humor offers audiences a ration of good old-fashioned fun.

We all know something funny when we see it. But when authors try to analyze exactly what comedy is, breaking it down into its component

*Quoted in Leonard Maltin, *The Great Movie Comedians* (New York: Crown, 1978), p. vii.

elements, they inevitably get into trouble. Writer E. B. White once described it this way:

> Humor can be dissected as a frog can, but the thing dies in the process and the innards are discouraging to any but the pure scientific mind.*

In this chapter we won't attempt to dissect the frog. Instead we will provide a few solid guidelines for writing screenplay comedy based on personal interviews with successful professionals. The guidelines apply to stage plays, movies, or television. The chapter will not discuss writing for stand-up comedy routines or for the zany humor of farce.

The term *situation comedy* (**sitcom**) has acquired a bad connotation in recent years, but comedy of situation is what most great comedies are. All of Neil Simon's plays and feature films, for example, are comedies of situation. The same is true of Woody Allen, Bernard Slade, James Brooks, and others. Comedy of situation combines comedy with drama in varying proportions; some writers lean more heavily on comedy; others emphasize dramatic values. The following pages will focus primarily on the comedy of situation.

➤ **THE COMEDY OF SITUATION:** the ludicrous, the incongruous, the unexpected

➤ **COMEDY PATTERNS:** humor arising from character; from the situation

*As quoted in Roy Paul Madsen, *Working Cinema — Learning from the Masters* (Belmont, Calif.: Wadsworth, 1990), p. 183.

➤ **WRITING TECHNIQUES**: tested comedy patterns and techniques; the need for identification and goal orientation

➤ **PREPARING YOURSELF**: building awareness; acting as a background; difficulties in beginning

$\mathcal{T}$HE COMEDY OF SITUATION

After a disastrous automobile accident, a man discovers that he is a paraplegic, condemned to bed for the rest of his life, able to speak but that's about all. His fiancée walks out on him. This man wants only to die but his doctors and the hospital won't allow it. Funny material? The basis for a comedy stageplay and motion picture? No way.

Another man wants to cement relations with his son; the two are opposites; they've never liked each other much. A shocking discovery makes this man's need critical: He learns he's dying of cancer. Is this the subject matter of comedy? Could it be the basis for a humorous stage play or feature film? Forget it.

Still grieving after the death of his wife, a third man falls in love again and, in time, remarries. But memories of his first wife continue to haunt him and almost destroy his second marriage. Are you laughing at this hysterically funny situation?

Yet a fourth man is starving. Facing death, he finds an old shoe, which he boils in a pot to tenderize it, and then, to save his life, he eats the disgusting thing.

All of the above characters, of course, have been protagonists in successful comedies. The first, *Whose Life Is It, Anyway?* was a successful play on Broadway and then a feature motion picture starring Richard Dreyfuss. Yes, it contained genuinely funny material. It was a comedy that mixed humor and pathos — as did all of the examples cited here. Most of the comedy grew out of the protagonist's wry sense of humor (more about a character motivating comedy in a few pages).

The second comedy, *Tribute*, starred Jack Lemmon both in the stageplay and feature film. What turned tragedy into comedy was the off-center characterization of the father who faced life lightly — or tried to avoid facing it, always making jokes when disaster threatened. *Tribute*'s author, Bernard Slade, said, "I think that people die the way they live. Scotty Templeton's approach to his predicament is comedic because his approach to life is comedic. What makes comedy different from tragedy is in how the writer views the world: it's like those prisms that you hold up to the light. When you turn them slightly you get another, refracted view."

Another veteran writer, Richard Baer, describes the writing of comedy as coming into a dramatic situation curvingly. You can view the world grimly if you're writing a tragedy or you can view it curvingly, obliquely, from a slightly different perspective, when you're writing comedy. It's finding the absurd in everyday life.

The third comedy was Neil Simon's *Chapter Two*, which he based on a chapter in his own life. Simon bases almost all of his plays on experiences, relationships, or characters from his own life. The pain of losing his beloved first wife motivated him to write about his courtship of and marriage to actress Marsha Mason, his second wife. Simon believes that the most honest comedy (or drama) springs from personal experience. When asked about the difficulty of separating himself from life's painful emotions, he answered, "The more painful the better, because I know I'm getting closer to the truth." When asked if he could find humor in anything, if he could make *anything* funny, he replied, "You can make some part of it funny. There is humor in almost everything."*

The fourth protagonist, the man who ate a shoe, was Charlie Chaplin in *The Gold Rush*. There's nothing funny in a man being so hungry that he's forced to eat a shoe. What made it funny was his eating it with a gourmet's gusto and meticulousness, as if he were dining in a fine restaurant, licking the shoe nails as though they were chicken bones.

We return here to a principle discussed in our dialog chapters, the concept of playing against subject matter. When writers create tragic situations, they *play against* the tragedy, often by creating humor. In real life there's little humor in painful situations, so writers are forced to invent characters whose personality and wit will spark a lighter mood. A paraplegic who wants to die is far from happy subject matter; audiences would run in the other direction unless the writer can find a way to redeem such downbeat material.

In the following scene from *Chapter Two*,[†] Neil Simon helped to create humor in a painful situation by making one of his characters a bit inebriated. Newlyweds George and Jennie have just returned from a disastrous honeymoon. They enter George's apartment carrying suitcases and drop them near the door; George immediately begins looking through his accumulated mail. There is tension between them.

JENNIE

That was fun! Three days of rain and two
days of diarrhea. We should have taken out
honeymoon insurance.

GEORGE

(Without looking up)
Don't forget to put your watch back an hour.

---

*In the PBS *American Masters* series, the program titled "Neil Simon: Not Just for Laughs," first broadcast in July 1991.

[†]From *Chapter Two* by Neil Simon. Copyright © 1978, 1979 by Neil Simon. Reprinted by permission of Random House, Inc. This play or excerpts thereof cannot be performed, recited, recorded, or broadcast in any media without a license from the author. Requests should be addressed to Samuel French, Inc., 45 W. 25th Street, New York, NY 10010.

JENNIE

I don't want the hour. Let 'em keep it! . . . Any
mail for me?

GEORGE

(Reading a letter)
You've only been <u>living</u> here thirty-eight
seconds.

JENNIE

Are you going to read your mail <u>now</u>?

GEORGE

It's from my publisher. He wants some
revisions.

JENNIE

Again? You "revised" in Barbados. . . . Is there
anything soft to drink?

GEORGE

(Testy)
I think there's some beer. I could strain it if
you like.

JENNIE

No, thanks. We have all the "strain" we can
handle.
    (She crosses to the
    fridge)
I read somewhere you can tell everything about
a person by looking inside his refrigerator.
    (She opens it)
Oh, God! Is this the man I married? Cold and
empty, with a little yogurt?

GEORGE

I'll call the grocer in the morning and have
him fill up my personality.

JENNIE

(Takes out a half-empty
bottle of Coke with no
cap on it)
You want to share half a bottle of opened Coke?
None of that annoying fizz to worry about.
    (She takes a swig)

                              GEORGE
                        (Not amused)
How many glasses of wine did you have on the
plane?

                              JENNIE
Two.

                              GEORGE
How many?

                              JENNIE
Four.

                              GEORGE
You had seven.

                              JENNIE
I had six.

                              GEORGE
And two at the airport. That's <u>eight</u>.

                              JENNIE
All right, it was eight. But it wasn't seven.
Don't accuse me of having seven.

                              GEORGE
You're tight, Jennie.
                        (Picks up suitcases and
                        coats)

                              JENNIE
Ohhh, is that what's been bothering you all day,
George? That I drank too much? I can't help it:
I don't like flying. I asked you to hold my hand
but you wouldn't do it. So I drank wine instead.

                              GEORGE
                        (Starts for the bedroom
                        with the bags)
I <u>did</u> hold your hand. And while I was holding
it, you drank my wine.
                        (He goes into the
                        bedroom)

    We promised at the chapter's beginning not to dissect the frog — that is,
not to do an exhaustive (and exhausting) scientific study of the psychology of

comedy and in the process lose sight of what humor is all about. However, a brief overview of the various comedy elements might provide some writing insights.

Scholars have broken comedy into as many as eight basic plots. Media expert Roy Paul Madsen simplified things for us. He narrowed the elements that make people laugh to three: the ludicrous, the incongruous, and the unexpected.

THE LUDICROUS

This comedy category refers to anything that is exaggerated, overstated, or out of proportion. The exaggeration may be *physical* or it may apply to the *dramatic situation*.

As examples of physical exaggeration, we sometimes smile at people who are excessively fat or thin, who speak with a funny accent, who have bizarre hairdos, who are cross-eyed, who wear bizarre clothing, whose noses are too big, or who are unbelievably dumb. There's probably an element of cruelty in this form of humor. Perhaps we smile because we feel superior to these off-center characters; we're normal and they are not. (And perhaps they smile at *us*!)

If a character is too fat, comedy tends to put him in situations where fatness becomes a plot point. He becomes stuck climbing through a small fence opening and other characters have to tug and pull to get him free. But consider: If the character is embarrassed or ashamed of his fatness, then we stop laughing at him. If he laughs at himself, at his difficulties in getting through the fence hole, then we can laugh *with* him — a major difference. Now we sympathize.

The moment we identify with characters, our feelings change. Recall the stereotypical pompous banker who slips on a banana peel and falls. We laugh at him as long as we dislike him or feel no emotional involvement. If we change the pompous banker to a sweet old woman and she slips on the banana peel and breaks her leg, all humor disappears. Once we sympathize, her fall becomes tragic; we can laugh no longer.

Mack Sennett, producer of hundreds of comedy two-reelers in film's early days, many of them screamingly funny, was aware of the dangers in audience identification. I use the word *danger* because identification discourages audiences from laughing at characters who are victims of violent action. Because of this, Sennett impersonalized his characters. They became mechanical toys, falling off roofs, bumping into walls, furniture, or each other; getting hit by custard pies, chairs, streetcars, or falling safes.

His was a comedy of violent motion: human bodies and machines and inanimate objects hurtling across the screen and colliding with each other. In these frantic films, boats sank, automobiles crashed, buildings exploded — but audiences felt no pain. There was never any fear for characters' safety because they were all emotionless machines. Sennett even required operators to under-crank their cameras so that the characters would move too fast, mechanically, like windup toys or automatons. And he never used close-ups because close-ups tended to make audiences relate to a character.

Dumb characters abound in the comedy genre: Lieutenant Frank Grebin in *Naked Gun 2½*, Peter Sellers' Inspector Clouseau, Lou Costello, Judy Holliday in *Born Yesterday*, Jerry Lewis, Gracie Allen, Stan Laurel, Mack Sennett's Keystone Kops, the Three Stooges, even Charlie Chaplin in some of his earliest films. If a character is dumb, comedy writers tend to take his actions beyond the point of believability, to exaggerate the exaggeration. In *Naked Gun 2½*, for example, we find Grebin at a formal government dinner attended by top diplomats and by the president and his wife. At the dinner table Grebin is served an oversized lobster. Trying to crack it, he sends claws and lobster shells flying about the room, into the laps and faces of others seated at the table, totally unmindful of the havoc he is creating. The First Lady gets more than her share.

The element of exaggeration doesn't just cover a character's physical or mental characteristics. It also extends to situations. The Latin phrase *reductio ad absurdum* — reduction to the absurd — aptly describes this comedy gambit. It was a favorite pattern of most of the "I Love Lucy" shows. Each episode began on a fairly normal, totally believable basis and then led us, scene by scene, into greater and greater depths of absurdity. For instance, if Lucy needed money to buy a gift for her husband she might decide to get a job secretly, without telling Ricky. In this situation, she might end up at work she was totally unqualified for (perhaps she lied about her qualifications) and then struggled to fight off the inevitable torrent of preposterous and calamitous problems. As Lucy and Ethel worked on an assembly line for chocolate candies, for example, the conveyor belt began to move more rapidly so that they were forced to move faster and faster and faster as they inserted the chocolates into boxes. Eventually, trying hopelessly to stay in control, they were forced to shove many of the chocolates into their mouths until their cheeks were bulging. Exaggeration: taking a normal, believable situation and reducing it to an absurdity.

THE INCONGRUOUS

Incongruous comedy places together elements that seem wrong for each other, that are mismatched or inappropriate. In *Terminator II*, for example, a ten-year-old boy teaches the hulking cyborg (Arnold Schwarzenegger) from the future to speak in the vernacular of today's youth. Later, when the stony-faced terminator mouths such phrases as "No problemo" or "Hasta la vista, baby," the effect is highly comedic because the words are inappropriate to the character. The terminator is programmed to obey all of the boy's commands, and the idea of a small boy controlling such a powerful, almost indestructible figure also borders on incongruity.

Another film, *City Slickers*, bases most of its comedy on the element of incongruity. Billy Crystal and his pals are city types, unhappy with their jobs and their lives. Searching for personal answers, they sign on as cowhands with a dude ranch, helping to drive cattle from one state to another, a job for which they are physically and emotionally unqualified. They struggle against cattle stampedes, storms, raging rivers, and hostile cowhands, and they mature in the process. Early in the film, Billy Crystal encounters the hard-as-nails trail boss and tries to make a joke: "Killed anybody today?" The trail boss stares malevolently at him and growls: "Not yet."

Incongruity works. When you sit down to write comedy, look for characters or story elements that don't normally fit together. Take a Woody Allen character, for example, and place him in a gym with a lot of broad-shouldered, sweating, muscular guys pumping iron. Because he is totally out of place in this environment, you have the makings of comedy. The Private Benjamin character also was out of her element: a wealthy young society woman who suddenly finds herself in the army, calling for room service, expecting to be waited upon, and having to face a tough army sergeant and demanding physical circumstances.

In the film *The Goodbye Girl*, Marsha Mason's nine-year-old daughter, having been raised in a showbiz environment, casually says words such as "shit," evoking laughter because the words seem inappropriate for a girl of such tender years. Give earthy street vernacular to a grandmotherly woman ("shove it up your ass, buster") and the audience will find belly laughs in the incongruity. Such words also contain the element of surprise and shock. In one of the Monty Python films, a gang of old women travels from town to town in small, innocent-looking packs, and they do nasty pranks to unsuspecting citizens, tripping them, shoving them off sidewalks, or worse. Their actions become hilarious because the actions seem so utterly incongruous for such apparently gentle and innocent characters.

Look around you. You'll find that films are not the only place to find incongruities. The real world is full of them.

THE UNEXPECTED (SURPRISE)

When we expect a story to go in one direction and it unexpectedly veers in another, we are fooled. We laugh, perhaps in embarrassment at having guessed wrong. Charlie Chaplin used that principle repeatedly in his films. For example, *The Immigrant* begins with Charlie leaning over the rail of an ocean liner that tips sickeningly back and forth in a storm. A moment later he appears with a fish flopping on his line. We assumed that he was seasick, but instead he had been fishing — and so we laugh in surprise.

In another Chaplin film, he strides confidently into a business office, crosses to the huge floor safe, and expertly spins the dial of its combination lock. After a moment the large door swings open, and Charlie reaches inside and removes a mop and pail. Instead of his being the executive that we expected, it turns out that he is the janitor. We are fooled again and we laugh.

In *City Slickers*, Billy Crystal helps a sick cow give birth to a calf, and during the film he grows to love the animal, even risking his life to save it from drowning. Later, he returns home to his wife and kids after coming to realize their importance in his life. After hugs and kisses at the New York airport, the family is shocked to discover that he has brought the calf with him. The audience is surprised — and delighted — at the animal's unexpected reappearance, especially in a city environment.

In most jokes, the payoff is usually a twist on what we expect, a surprise. Comedy writer Gene Perrett relates, "In promoting my book last year, I traveled over 50,000 miles . . . which is not really a lot when you consider that my luggage travelled over 100,000."* In addition to the element of surprise, this joke follows the advice of our dialog chapters; it makes the audience think. They have to figure out why the baggage travelled those extra 50,000 miles and because they participate, they become more involved. Recall any joke you heard recently and you will probably find that its payoff line is some sort of surprise, an integral part of all comedy.

One of the first comedy films ever produced[†] featured a gardener watering a lawn. Unseen by the gardener, a small boy wandered by and stepped on the hose, stopping the flow of water. Puzzled, the gardener lifted the nozzle and examined it. The boy released his foot from the hose and — you guessed it — the water sprayed into the gardener's face. Surprise!

But something new has been added here to the comedy equation. When the boy removed his foot from the hose, didn't you know in advance what was going to happen? Even before you saw the water hitting the gardener in the face, didn't you enjoy a delicious sense of expectation, of anticipation?

Anticipation is the opposite of surprise. You know in advance what's going to happen and you're smiling before it does. When possible, screenwriters prolong the moment of anticipation, extending it, before the payoff. Comedy is similar to drama in this respect. Before payoff moments in dramatic scenes, writers (and directors) often invent ways to delay, delay, delay, to build audience anticipation or apprehension, also known as suspense.

Laurel and Hardy are going to push a piano up twelve flights of stairs. We're chuckling before they even begin because we know that something disastrous is bound to happen. Because we're familiar with their characters, their propensity for screwing things up, we know that the piano will inevitably come crashing down the stairs, that Hardy will blame Laurel, that Laurel will cry and scratch his head — and we savor the humor before it even develops.

*In *Comedy Writing Step by Step* (Hollywood: Samuel French, 1990), p. 121.
†Filmed by the Lumière brothers in 1896.

Again, maybe feelings of superiority are part of our pleasure. We anticipate fiasco because we know that the characters attempting to push the piano are inept, incapable of doing the job properly. And maybe we're a little smug. We knew it wasn't going to work. Consider: If experienced workmen were going to take a piano up twelve flights, you'd never anticipate laughter. You might be interested to see how they managed the feat, but that's all. The anticipation and much of the humor grow from knowledge of the characters (more about that later).

COMEDY PATTERNS

In comedy of situation, the humor usually arises from one of two sources (and sometimes both): from the *characters* and from the *situation* itself. In the Laurel and Hardy example just cited, pushing a piano up twelve flights, the humor arose from a situation that was loaded with comedy potential and from our knowledge of the characters' inadequacies.

COMEDY ARISING FROM CHARACTER

In Neil Simon's comedies, you won't find one-liners (for example, "Take my wife — please!"). Even jokes are rare. Most often, the humor originates in the character. Bernard Slade (*Same Time Next Year*) tells us:

> The reason why it is difficult to get laughs at the beginning of a play or movie is that the characters aren't established yet. The biggest laughs in the theater if I repeated them to you out of context wouldn't be funny at all. Essentially, laughs come out of a character saying something that only he could say. If you gave that line to someone else, it wouldn't be funny.*

Slade describes one performance of his *Same Time Next Year* in which the director gave the actors certain business (actions) that evoked tremendous laughter from the audience. But because the actions were dishonest, added to the play just to get a cheap laugh, it took from eight to ten minutes to get the audience back. By "getting the audience back," Slade meant getting them again emotionally involved with the characters, *believing* the characters and their dramatic situation, accepting them as real. He summed up the concept: "You can't bend a character out of shape just to make a joke."

---

*Bernard Slade, personal interview, October 1991.

Lucille Ball was smart enough to realize that what is funny about most people is their foibles. Foibles are also what makes them lovable. Accordingly, she and the show's brilliant writers built a variety of shortcomings into the character's personality, and she has become one of the funniest and best-loved characters in the history of television. Foibles, weaknesses, shortcomings, and character flaws make almost all comedians funny, from Laurel and Hardy to Frank Grebin.

Dialog must be honest. You have to think: Would this person really say this or do this? If you want somebody to speak a certain comedy line, then you must create a character who would honestly say it. In the following scene from *The Graduate*,* there are no jokes. There are no "funny" lines. But the scene itself is hilarious. The humor grows entirely out of contrasting characters: Benjamin, a naive and confused young man fresh out of college, and Mrs. Robinson, a rather worldly friend of his parents. Ever since she seduced him, they have been meeting almost nightly. This is a portion of one of their scenes together.

INT. TAFT HOTEL ROOM - NIGHT

Mrs. Robinson is undoing Ben's necktie.

> BEN
>
> Wait a minute.
>> (pushes her hand
>> away)
> Sit down a minute.

Mrs. Robinson looks at him and raises her eyebrows.

> BEN
>
> Will you please sit down a minute?

Mrs. Robinson walks to the bed and sits. She starts to take off a shoe.

> BEN
>
> Will you leave that shoe on for a minute?
> Please.

She straightens up.

> BEN
>
> Now—do you think we could say a few words
> to each other first this time?

*Reprinted by permission of Buck Henry and Calder Willingham.

MRS. ROBINSON

If you want.

BEN

Good. I mean, are we dead or something?

MRS. ROBINSON

Well, I just don't think we have much to say to each other.

BEN

All we ever do is come up here and throw off our clothes and leap into bed together.

MRS. ROBINSON

Are you tired of it?

BEN

I'm not. No. But do you think we could liven it up with a few words now and then?

MRS. ROBINSON

What do you want to talk about?

BEN

Anything. Anything at all.

MRS. ROBINSON

Do you want to tell me about some of your college experiences?

BEN

Oh my God.

MRS. ROBINSON

Well?

BEN

Mrs. Robinson, if that's the best we can do, let's just get the goddamn clothes off and . . .

She reaches for her shoe.

BEN

Leave it on! Now we are going to do this thing. We are going to have a conversation. Think of another topic.

MRS. ROBINSON

How about art?

> BEN
>
> That's a good subject. You start it off.

> MRS. ROBINSON
>
> You start it off. I don't know anything about it.

> BEN
>
> Art. Well—what do you want to know?

She shrugs.

> BEN
>
> Are you interested more in modern art or more in classical art?

> MRS. ROBINSON
>
> Neither.

> BEN
>
> You're not interested in art?

> MRS. ROBINSON
>
> No.

> BEN
>
> Then why do you want to talk about it?

> MRS. ROBINSON
>
> I don't.

Ben nods and looks at the rug.

> MRS. ROBINSON
>
> Can I take off my clothes now?

> BEN
>
> No. Think of another topic. Tell me what you did today.

> MRS. ROBINSON
>
> Do you really want me to?

> BEN
>
> Yes I do.

> MRS. ROBINSON
>
> I got up.

Ben starts shaking his head.

> MRS. ROBINSON
>
> Do you want to hear it or not?

                      BEN

Yes. But you might try to spice it up with a
little originality.

                    MRS. ROBINSON

I got up. I ate breakfast and went shopping.
During the afternoon I read a novel.

                      BEN

Which one?

                    MRS. ROBINSON

I don't remember.

Ben nods.

                    MRS. ROBINSON

Then I fixed supper for my husband and waited
until —

                      BEN

There!

                    MRS. ROBINSON

What?

                      BEN

Your husband! Mrs. Robinson, there's something
we could have a conversation about.

                    MRS. ROBINSON

Him?

                      BEN

I mean everything. I don't know anything about
how you — how you work this. I don't know how
you get out of the house at night. I don't know
the risk involved.

                    MRS. ROBINSON

There isn't any.

                      BEN

There's no risk?

She shakes her head.

                      BEN

How do you get out of the house?

                    MRS. ROBINSON

I walk out.

> BEN
>
> You walk right out the door?

She nods.

> BEN
>
> What do you say to him?

> MRS. ROBINSON
>
> He's asleep.

> BEN
>
> Always?

> MRS. ROBINSON
>
> Benjamin, this isn't a very interesting topic.

> BEN
>
> Please. Now tell me. How do you know he won't
> wake up and follow you?

> MRS. ROBINSON
>
> Because he takes sleeping pills. He takes
> sleeping pills every night at ten o'clock.

> BEN
>
> But what about the noise from the car?
> What if—

> MRS. ROBINSON
>
> The driveway's on my side of the house.

> BEN
> (smiling)
>
> We're talking.

> MRS. ROBINSON
>
> What?

> BEN
>
> We're talking, Mrs. Robinson. We're talking!

Most good comedy writers — as well as writers of drama — look for contrasting characters such as Benjamin and Mrs. Robinson. Out of the incongruity or the friction between them often comes humor. Neil Simon's *The Odd Couple* is the prototypical example. The playwright once told a class of student writers: "What I try to do is set up a conflict — a confrontation between two people that has the possibility of humor in it."*

*From the PBS *American Masters* series, "Neil Simon: Not Just for Laughs," July 1991.

COMEDY ARISING
FROM SITUATION

The best situation comedies often are based on fundamental audience wants or needs. Probably the most common example: We want to see bad guys get their comeuppance. Countless comedy sketches and motion picture screenplays have been based on this extremely obvious concept.

Let's return to our swaggering, pompous banker. We itch to see him deflated, and when he slips on the you-know-what, we laugh in appreciation. In the nerd comedies of the late 1980s, the cool, socially accepted teenage studs ridiculed and sometimes played cruel tricks on the unloved, unappreciated misfits. As audience, we sympathized with these decent but less than dashing characters, perhaps because we recognized something of ourselves in them. We hated their tormenters and yearned to see the nerds avenged. There was always delight and humor when, finally, the misfits triumphed.

The character Woody Allen so often plays is also a misfit. In many of his early films, he competed against studs to win the woman of his heart. All of us nonstuds in the audience identified with him and rooted for him and felt that if this awkward, spectacled, balding character could triumph, maybe there was hope for us. If Woody Allen could do it, we could, too!

Fundamental audience wants or needs: In *Ferris Buehler's Day Off*, as in so many teen comedies, youth rebelled against authority. Significantly, the writers always made sure it was a harsh and unfair authority that the youths rebelled against so that the audience could root for them wholeheartedly, even when, as in *Ferris Buehler*, the teenage protagonist broke the rules. As I remember, the high school principal in that film was a caricature: a spiteful, mean-minded despot who actively disliked Ferris and was determined to see him punished.

Fundamental wants or needs: Another comedy, *The Sting*, was about cheating cheaters, the good con men finding devious ways to outwit the bad con men. If the good con men had cheated widows and orphans, all humor would have disappeared and so would our rooting interest. In the early days of television, James Garner starred in a comedy western series called "Maverick," playing the role of a shrewd gambler whose good instincts invariably won out over his larcenous ones. In each episode, there was always someone a little more larcenous than Garner, a cruel and deceitful scoundrel whom we yearned to see punished, so that when Garner used larcenous methods against him, we cheered and tuned in again the following week. Incidentally, the character played by Garner in Maverick and Paul Newman in *The Sting* is archetypal — that is, it's part of the cultural heritage of many races and nations, found in their legends, myths, and folk ballads. Psychiatrist Carl Jung calls the character "Trickster." You'll find him in Saturday morning kids' cartoons and in the legends of Apache Indians.

I once wrote an article for the *Hollywood Reporter Yearbook* in which I demonstrated that most successful television series are based on games that children play: cops 'n' robbers, cowboys 'n' Indians, playing doctor, playing house. We're back to fundamental wants or needs, aren't we? All of those childhood games are based on role playing, pretending to be someone we're not, usually someone whose life is more glamorous or exciting than ours. Such games allow us to escape from our humdrum daily lives and from the domination of sometimes unfair authority figures. Bottom line: Such childhood games and dreams are really what entertainment is all about. When we identify with characters on the screen, we enter their world; we experience their problems; we become someone we're not. Comedy is often based on that same concept carried to an extreme: role playing, becoming someone we're not.

In *Same Time Next Year*, the characters played new roles once each year, escaping from their routine lives and living a chapter from a romance novel. In *Pretty Woman* (romantic comedy), Julia Roberts escaped from her gritty life on the streets and for a short time became a princess, leading a life of glamor and excitement as the consort of one of America's richest men. Whoopi Goldberg in *Ghost* assumed the role of a hoity-toity society matron to great comedic effect, and citified Billy Crystal in *City Slickers* assumed the role of a cowhand. In other comedy films of the recent past, characters have changed sexes, bodies, jobs, and life-styles to reach their story goals and along the way have brought laughter to delighted audiences.

In Academy Award–winning *Some Like It Hot*,* Tony Curtis and Jack Lemmon took jobs masquerading as women in an all-female dance band. It was a way of hiding from mobsters who were out to kill them. But the inventive writers gave Tony Curtis still another role to play. Because the woman he loved (Marilyn Monroe) dreamed of marrying the owner of an expensive yacht, Curtis sneaked aboard and pretended to be the yacht's owner in this delightful scene — a prime example of comedy arising from situation.

INT. SALON OF YACHT - NIGHT

Joe and Sugar are drinking champagne in this mahogany-paneled salon.

SUGAR

You know, I've never been completely alone with
a man before — in the middle of the night — in
the middle of the ocean.

*Reprinted by permission of United Artists Pictures, Mrs. I. A. L. Diamond, and Billy Wilder.

                    JOE

Oh, it's perfectly safe. We're well-anchored—the
ship is in shipshape shape—and the Coast
Guard promised to call me if they see any
icebergs.

                  SUGAR

It's not the icebergs. But there are certain men
who would try to take advantage of a situation
like this.

                    JOE

You're flattering me.

                  SUGAR

Well, of course, I'm sure you're a gentleman.

                    JOE

Oh, it's not that. It's just that I'm—harmless.

                  SUGAR

Harmless how?

                    JOE

Well, I don't know how to put this—but I have
this thing about girls.

                  SUGAR

What thing?

                    JOE

They just sort of leave me cold.

                  SUGAR

You mean—like frigid?

                    JOE

It's more like a mental block. When I'm with a
girl, it does nothing to me.

                  SUGAR

Have you tried?

                    JOE

Have I? I'm trying all the time.

He casually puts his arms around her, kisses her on the lips.

                    JOE

See? Nothing.

> SUGAR

Nothing at all?

> JOE

Complete washout.

> SUGAR

That makes me feel just awful.

> JOE

Oh, it's not your fault. It's just that every now
and then Mother Nature throws somebody a
dirty curve. Something goes wrong inside.

> SUGAR

You mean you can't fall in love?

> JOE

Not any more. I <u>was</u> in love once—but I'd
rather not talk about it.

He takes the glass bell off the cold cuts.

> JOE

How about a little cold pheasant?

> SUGAR

What happened?

> JOE

I don't want to bore you.

> SUGAR

Oh, you couldn't possibly.

> JOE

Well, it was in my freshman year at Princeton.
There was this girl—her name was Nellie—her
father was vice president of Hupmobile. She
wore glasses too. That summer we spent
our vacation at the Grand Canyon. We were
standing on the highest ledge watching the
sunset. Suddenly we had an impulse to kiss. I
took off my glasses, she took off her glasses.
I took a step toward her—she took a step
toward me—

> SUGAR

Oh, no!

                              JOE
Yes. Eight hours later they brought her up on
my mule. I gave her three transfusions — we
had the same blood type — type O — it was
too late.

                            SUGAR
Talk about sad.

                              JOE
Ever since then —
                    (indicating heart)
numb — no feeling. Like my heart was shot full
of novocaine.

                            SUGAR
You poor, poor boy.

                              JOE
Yes, all the money in the world and what good
is it?
                    (holding out plate)
Mint sauce or cranberries?

                            SUGAR
How can you think about food at a time like
this?

                              JOE
What else is there for me?

He tears off a leg of pheasant.

                            SUGAR
Is it that hopeless?

                              JOE
                    (eating)
My family did everything they could. Hired the
most beautiful French upstairs maid — got a
special tutor to read me all the books that
were banned in Boston — imported a whole
troupe of Balinese dancers with bells on their
ankles and those long fingernails — what a
waste of money!

                    SUGAR
        Have you ever tried American girls?

                    JOE
        Why?

She kisses him—pretty good, but nothing spectacular.

                    SUGAR
        Is _that_ anything?

                    JOE
            (shaking head)
        Thanks just the same.

He resumes nibbling on the pheasant leg, sits on couch.

                    SUGAR
        Maybe if you saw a good doctor...

                    JOE
        I have. Spent six months in Vienna with
        Professor Freud flat on my back—

He stretches out on the couch, still eating.

                    JOE
        Then there were the Mayo brothers—and
        injections and hypnosis and mineral baths.
        If I weren't such a coward, I'd kill myself.

                    SUGAR
        Don't talk like that. I'm sure there must be
        some girl _some_ place that could—

                    JOE
        If I ever found a girl that could—I'd marry her
        like that.

He snaps his fingers. The word "marry" makes something snap inside
Sugar, too.

                    SUGAR
        Would you do me a favor?

                    JOE
        What is it?

                    SUGAR
        I may not be Dr. Freud or a Mayo brother or
        one of those French upstairs girls but could I
        take another crack at it?

> JOE
>> (blasé)
>
> All right—if you insist.

She bends over him and gives him a kiss of slightly higher voltage.

> SUGAR
>
> Anything this time?

> JOE
>
> I'm afraid not. Terribly sorry.

> SUGAR
>> (undaunted)
>
> Would you like a little more champagne?
>> (refills glasses)
>
> And maybe if we had some music—
>> (indicating lights)
>
> How do you dim these lights?

> JOE
>
> Look, it's terribly sweet of you to want to help
> out—but it's no use.
>> (pointing)
>
> The light switch is over there.
>> (she dims lights)
>
> And that's the radio—
>> (she turns it on)
>
> It's like taking somebody to a concert when he's
> tone deaf.

By this time there is only candlelight in the salon and from the radio comes soft music. Sugar crosses to the couch with two champagne glasses, hands one to Joe and sits beside him. He drinks the champagne and she hands him the second glass. He drains that, too.

> SUGAR
>
> You're not giving yourself a chance. Don't fight
> it. Relax.

She kisses him again.

> JOE
>> (shaking head)
>
> It's like smoking without inhaling.

> SUGAR
>
> So inhale!

This kiss is the real McCoy and they stay locked in each other's arms.

Some Like It Hot is a prime example of a writer finding comedy in role playing: pretending to be what you're not.

Comedy arising from a situation takes many forms. In parody, the plot situation often pokes fun at other well-known entertainments. Woody Allen parodied *Casablanca* and actually re-created Humphrey Bogart in *Play It Again, Sam*. Mel Brooks' *Young Frankenstein* was a spoof of Frankenstein films and his *Blazing Saddles* parodied the entire western genre. *Naked Gun 2½* parodied police detective films, reducing the genre to an absurdity. It also poked fun at the popular *Ghost*, "stealing" that film's highly sensual sequence in which the lovers shaped clay on a potter's wheel.

Satire is a more sophisticated form of parody. Rather than burlesquing a film or TV series, satire frequently pokes fun at the hypocrisies of society or mismanagement in government or big business, exposing or discrediting those institutions with its irony and wit. Because satire tends to be more intellectual than emotional, it does not often find its way onto motion picture or TV screens.

𝒲RITING TECHNIQUES

"The funny part always goes at the end." Those were comedy writer Dick Baer's first words to his writing classes. In a joke or comedy situation you save the payoff until the last line or, when possible, the last word, especially when you're going for an explosive laugh.

> "Inflation is getting terrible. I went to the supermarket today and put a down payment on a leg of lamb."

If you change the order of words, the comedy disappears. If you say, "I put a down payment on a leg of lamb at the supermarket today," you have killed most of the line's effectiveness. Save the payoff for the end.

> "I have a friend who's so lazy he won't even go to a ballgame until the second inning. That's so he won't have to stand for the National Anthem. He's never done anything for himself. He even married a woman who was pregnant."*

---

*From Gene Perrett, *Comedy Writing Step by Step* (Hollywood: Samuel French, 1990), pp. 111 and 131.

Again, in both of these jokes from a stand-up comedy routine, the punch line comes with the final words. The element of surprise (discussed earlier) may be a factor here.

When writing dialog in a comedy of situation, the funny line occasionally pops up in the middle of a speech. Bernard Slade advises that writers should invent some business (actions) for the character to perform before continuing with the balance of the speech, to give audiences a chance to laugh. If actors continue their speeches without pausing, they will kill the laugh by talking over it. In motion pictures and TV, as opposed to the stage, actors cannot hear audience reactions and cannot time their speeches to accommodate the laughs. So anticipating audiences' reactions by providing suitable business seems especially necessary for the screen.

If you have a good sense of humor, trust your instincts.

> Write what makes you laugh. Don't try to outguess an audience. Don't say "Well, I don't think this is funny but they will." You can't write down to an audience. If it makes you laugh, it probably will make an audience laugh. If you tell an anecdote around a dinner table and they laugh, generally that will make an audience laugh. I used to think that something that was funny in a living room wasn't funny in a theater. It's not true.*

Some writers feel it's wise to prepare your audience for comedy by establishing the ground rules up front, telling them early that they shouldn't worry too much, that it's all right to laugh. In the theater, musical overtures help to establish a mood. In feature films or television, title sequences and title music help to build audience expectancy. (Realistically, newspaper ads have done some of this preparatory work for you; the audience comes to the theater expecting to see a comedy film.) The earliest moments of your screenplay (or, occasionally, the action behind titles) will tell the audience how to react to the scenes that follow, whether to laugh or cry.

Most writers of situation comedy begin their creative thinking by searching for a dramatic situation that has (a) elements of humor in it (for example, male musicians masquerading as females) or (b) a character or characters who will inject humor into an otherwise serious situation (for example, the wise-cracking father in *Tribute*). Begin with drama; the comedy comes later. Neil Simon was never a student of comedy. The playwrights who influenced him the most were dramatic playwrights. He wanted to write like them. But he wanted to write *comedy* like they did.

The dramatic principles discussed in this text's early chapters work as well for situation comedy as they do for drama. Let's reprise those elements quickly.

---

*From a personal interview with Bernard Slade.

IDENTIFICATION

Audiences became emotionally involved with Charlie Chaplin's Little Tramp character because he was a sweet, gentle, good-hearted innocent, always on the outside of the world of luxury and gentility, wistfully looking in. We cared about him. We rooted for him. We recognized something of ourselves in him. We sympathize with Woody Allen because we see something of ourselves in him. Like Chaplin, he's a misfit, fighting battles against more socially acceptable characters. We sympathize with Archie Bunker's wife, Edith, because she too is an innocent. Again and again her domineering husband tramples on her feelings — and our hearts go out to her. We identify with her and so we care.

Only in the comedy of violent action (farce) is the need for identification missing. When custard pies fly into faces and pompous bankers slip on banana peels, identification actually gets in the way. But in the more realistic comedy of situation, identification with one or more characters is crucial.

ORIENTATION TO A GOAL

Quoting from a conversation between brothers in his *Broadway Bound*, Neil Simon said, "I know what writing is. It's all about wanting something. It works all the time. In every movie, *he* wants something. *She* wants something. You just can't write about somebody without them wanting something. Otherwise, it's just not interesting."

In *Chapter Two*, the new wife wants a successful marriage. Her husband wants to exorcise his guilt at marrying again. In *Whose Life Is It, Anyway?* the protagonist wants to die. In many of Woody Allen's films, his goal is simply to get the girl. In all dramatic comedies, the protagonists have a want or need (a goal), and someone or something stands in the way of their reaching it. And don't forget: The antagonist has a goal, too. It's diametrically opposed to the protagonist's goal, and he or she will fight like crazy to prevent the protagonist from succeeding. The battles that ensue are what your screenplay is all about.

PREPARING YOURSELF

You have already learned the fundamentals of writing drama. Now you must find a curving approach to the material you create, a way of looking at your dramatic situation obliquely, through a comedy prism. What remains for you, finally, is to write.

To write. And to observe. Become aware of the drama and comedy that are taking place all around you, every day, no matter where you are. Open your eyes to the subtleties in relationships, the frowning look that she gives him, his attempt to cover a conversational gaffe, their self-satisfied awareness of secrets they've concealed from family and friends. Watch who goes through a door first. Speculate why the host was absent from his party for half the evening.

Don't create carbon copies of television shows or movies, life two or three times removed. Instead, go to the source: Begin with life experiences. Find your own voice.

Read newspapers and magazines. They will keep you tuned in not only on news of the day but also on the smaller, personal stories that sometimes become beginning points for comedy or drama. Read good books. See good stageplays and movies. They will stimulate your imagination and keep you aware of what other talented writers are creating.

If you get the chance, act. Yes, *act*. Many professional comedy writers acted before they graduated to their ultimate careers. Bernard Slade acted in about three hundred plays before he turned to writing. He learned that there was a rhythm with which characters speak; he learned comedy timing; he learned what makes a scene work; he learned that a very specific placement of words in a speech gains maximum comedic effect. So put aside your timidity. Take the plunge. Join a little theater group. Act.

Don't be discouraged if your first writing effort doesn't knock their sox off. It took Neil Simon three years to write his first play. Because it took him so long, working nights and weekends, he was convinced he'd never write more than one other play in his lifetime. Each time he began a new project, he felt he didn't understand how to write it. He called professional friends in panic, saying, "How do you start? Where do you begin?" He got "stage fright" with each of his first ten plays. And yet, in spite of initial insecurities, Neil Simon has become the most prolific writer of comedy stage and screenplays ever — and the most financially successful. If you panic somewhere along the way, don't give up. You're in good company.

Early in this text I claimed that the words "Be dissatisfied" were the key to successful writing. If that's true for drama, it is doubly true for comedy. Why do you suppose it took Neil Simon three years to write his first play?

What about a sense of humor? Obviously, you can't write comedy without one. You certainly can't acquire one from a textbook. And your family doctor can't give you an injection of comedy hormones. If you don't have a sense of humor, better stick to writing more serious stuff: drama or melodrama. But I'm guessing that you do have a well-developed comedy sense or you wouldn't have read this chapter.

> Writing comedy can be a joyful thing. When you stand in the back of a theater or movie house watching something you've written and you hear an entire audience laughing their heads off — it's a very heady experience.*

*Bernard Slade, personal interview, October 1991.

CHAPTER HIGHLIGHTS

➤ The comedy of situation combines comedy with often serious, sometimes tragic drama. Humor makes the tragedy palatable. Three categories of humor are the ludicrous, the incongruous, and the unexpected.

➤ Ludicrous comedy exaggerates. The exaggeration may be physical, or it may apply to the situation itself as in many "I Love Lucy" shows.

➤ Incongruous comedy combines elements that seem mismatched or inappropriate. An example is citified Billy Crystal and friends working as cowhands in *City Slickers*.

➤ When we expect a story (or a scene or a speech) to go in one direction and it veers in another, we are delighted at the surprise. This is the unexpected element of comedy.

➤ In the comedy of situation, humor arises from characters and from the nature of the situation. Comedy arising from character must be honest, what the character would actually say, not contrived to make a joke. Foibles are often the basis of character comedy.

➤ Comedy arising from situation is often based on fundamental audience wants or needs such as seeing cheaters cheated. Reversal of normal roles is also a prime comedy situation.

➤ The comedy line or payoff always comes last in dialog. The elements of drama also apply to comedy situations: identification with protagonists and their want or need to achieve a positive goal.

➤ Preparation begins with knowing the rules of dramatic construction and staying aware of the human condition. Acting is valuable. So is being dissatisfied with your work.

SCRIPTWRITING PROJECTS

EXERCISES DESIGNED TO SHARPEN YOUR NARRATIVE SKILLS

COMEDY THROUGH CHARACTER

1. Find a screenplay situation that is essentially downbeat or tragic. Describe it in not more than a page.

2. Create a character to integrate into the above situation who will provide the sparks of comedy, thereby making your screenplay more palatable to audiences.

3. Write a key scene (two or three pages) from this screenplay, one that gives you the opportunity to demonstrate the effectiveness of your comedy character.

COMEDY THROUGH SITUATION

1. Create a comedy plot based on the principle of (a) reversal of roles or (b) mistaken identity.

2. Write a three- to five-page scene that crystallizes your comedy concept. Put it aside for three days and then polish the scene, adding humor in dialog or business wherever possible.

COMEDY THROUGH CONTRASTING CHARACTERS

Find two characters who by their very natures are in conflict. Write a scene (three to five pages) that demonstrates their differences with humor.

CHAPTER 12

Adaptation

How many times have you heard people complain that a certain feature film or TV movie wasn't as good as the book? Their protests usually damn the producer, director, or writer for changes in the plot: "Why couldn't they leave a good thing alone?"

The answers to such a question form the basis for much of this chapter's discussion. First, literature is not drama; drama is not literature. Accordingly, writers frequently must make changes to give a movie dramatic form and structure. Second, much of a novel's richness exists because the written word forces readers to use their imaginations. The representational nature of movie images often contradicts those imagined by readers. Finally, audiences tend to remember the failures and forget the successful adaptations in which the movie was superior to (or certainly as good as) the novel or short story from which it was adapted.

Most professional writers recognize the substantial differences between novels and screenplays. William Goldman, who has written both successful novels and successful screenplays (and has adapted his own novels into screenplays), notes:

> They are entirely different forms. The only similarity is that very often they both use dialog. Otherwise, the way that one handles a scene in a movie and the way one handles a scene in a book have nothing to do with each other.*

Some writers mistakenly believe that adapting someone else's story is not creative; it even seems vaguely plagiaristic. Screenwriters who adapt novels or short stories usually possess a solid understanding of dramatic form and structure. They determine a visual approach to written material. They find new plot directions to replace unworkable literary ones. In short, they often demonstrate as much creativity as is found in most original screenplays.

If most novels and short stories aren't dramatic in form, why do producers spend vast sums buying legal rights and suffer the rigors of adapting them to film? For several reasons. Best-selling novels often achieve a small measure of publicity, which thereby presells them to movie audiences. The fact that they have sold tens (or hundreds) of thousands of copies tells the producer that audiences find the subject matter appealing. Such reasoning is not always logical, since readers represent only a tiny fraction of a potential motion picture or TV audience. Nevertheless, this reasoning often becomes a security blanket for insecure producers or for the financial institution that bankrolls the project. Another appeal of adaptation is that

*John Brady, ed., *Craft of the Screenwriter* (New York: Simon & Schuster, 1981), p. 88.

244

novels represent a vast supply of fresh and often innovative story material in a market where fresh material is surprisingly scarce.

This chapter will discuss:

➤ **LITERATURE VERSUS DRAMA**: an examination of two elements often missing in literature — *economy* (of time, content, and characters) and *structure* (its pyramidal form, logic, orientation to a goal, and progression) — plus the one element that must be retained in adaptation, the novel's essence

➤ **DEMONSTRATING THE ADAPTATION PROCESS**: an investigation of the changes necessary to adapt a short story to screenplay form

LITERATURE VERSUS DRAMA

We have all seen dozens of motion pictures successfully adapted from novels. The two do not appear to be vastly different. Yet because screenplays are usually dramatic in form and structure, the following key areas separate them from novels:

- Novels often cover vast time spans. Screenplays usually don't.
- Novels frequently include dozens and dozens of characters. Screenplays usually don't.
- Novels tend to be episodic in form. Screenplays usually aren't.
- Novels seldom introduce all major characters in their "first act." Screenplays usually do.
- Novels rarely build in progression, from crisis to crisis. Screenplays usually do.
- Novels often describe their characters' thoughts and emotions in explicit detail. Screenplay form does not permit this. Accordingly, novels usually are more internal than films.
- The dialog in many novels does not translate directly to film; it often won't stand the test of being spoken aloud.

At California State University, Northridge, a professor initiated a course in adaptation. He spent the early weeks in class carefully pinpointing the differences between novels and screenplays. When the students later turned in their treatments, the professor was astonished to discover that most had clung tenaciously to the novel's structure, even though it totally violated the dramatic principles discussed in class. Eventually, most of the students threw out their treatments and started over.

When the professor taught the course a second time, he described this tendency to the new students, and the class discussed reasons why the earlier students failed to recognize the differences in form. Many felt that insecurity had caused a reluctance to discard or change a pattern that clearly worked in novel form, pointing out that it requires courage to throw out a successful author's work. It also takes hours or days to come up with new and original story patterns to replace unworkable material. And, let's face it, most of us are overburdened; we'll take the easy road rather than a difficult one.

After much discussion and another examination of dramatic principles, the students went off to write their treatments. This time the professor felt certain that the stories would be closer to the mark. He was shocked to find that he was mistaken. Again, despite a class-long discussion of the folly of clinging to an unworkable structure, students had done exactly that.

Apparently, emotional factors were at work that ruled out any dispassionate, objective approach. Students rejected simple logic in spite of themselves, dazzled by the magical world that the novel's author had created. The professor then changed the approach of the course, assigning short, adaptive projects at the outset, allowing students to fail on these and learn the bitter lesson early in the semester before beginning the larger work of writing a treatment. Happily, the new approach was successful.

This example is intended to demonstrate the psychological booby traps inherent in adaptation and to help you avoid weeks of wasted effort writing and rewriting a treatment that does not work.

In defining the differences between novel and screenplay, the dramatic principles discussed in early chapters apply.

ECONOMY

Some writers believe that the ideal story for a two-hour movie is one in which dramatic events transpire during an actual time period of two hours. Such a pattern is seldom attempted in motion pictures or television because it is restricting to writers. The need in drama is to condense time rather than allow it to span months, years, or centuries. This approach is sometimes called the unity of time.

The first of our dramatic economies, therefore, is *economy of time*. Economy of time occurs in most successful TV plays and motion pictures but not often in novels. Consider, for instance, novelistic sagas, which sometimes cover two or three generations. When novelists extend events over a long period of time, they diffuse (and defuse) dramatic tension. By compressing time, screenwriters place pressure on their characters, forcing them to act and thereby maintaining dramatic tension.

Many writers, especially those of the so-called suspense genre, use a limited time frame to build audience anxiety, locking dramatic action into a specified number of minutes or hours. For example, Nicole desperately needs $25,000 to pay off a blackmailer, and she only has twelve minutes to get to the bank before it closes. Robin Hood must infiltrate the castle and rescue Maid Marian before the evil Sheriff of Nottingham can wed her, apparently only minutes away from now. "Bomb" stories are the classic example: the good guys must locate and defuse the bomb before it blows up and destroys the planet Earth. Repeated cuts to the superbomb ticking relentlessly away show the time span diminishing. The audience agonizes in suspense.

Such patterns demonstrate how tension can be increased through time pressure. When stories cover extended periods of time, they frequently lose unity; tension dissipates; air goes out of the balloon.

Television miniseries frequently ignore economy of time. They resemble novels in that their stories sometimes span months or years. Miniseries are usually adapted from best-selling novels and often parallel the novel's story patterns. Their length, sometimes four to six hours, permits this luxury.

Because novels usually contain far more material than can be presented in a normal feature film, the writer may condense time—and simultaneously eliminate much of the novel's excess material—simply by jumping into the story at (say) the halfway point, just as pressures begin to build. The deleted material necessary to understand the plot may be presented in exposition. Describing great chunks of background material can present a formidable challenge for the adapter.

The second method of achieving dramatic economy is by *reducing content*. Although some novels are slender, describing a simple story in infinite detail, the majority contain enough plot material to fill two or three motion pictures. Such novels usually present a major story pattern plus several subplots. An effective adaptive technique is to thin out a story, deleting one or two of the subplots without disrupting the primary plot. Such deletions usually require the screenwriter to rework the novel's structure, pasting together story elements that were connected by deleted incidents. Frequently, the writer will find it necessary to explain some aspects of the deleted material if they are essential to understanding the primary plotline.

Subplots weave intricately in and out of the primary story line in heavily plotted novels, making it difficult for the screenwriter to disentangle them. Writers sometimes diagram the story structure on paper, making the relationship between the various story threads more graphic. Before attempting such diagrams, they first must gain a razor-sharp understanding of their material; this comes only from repeated readings.

Eliminating one or more subplots also helps with the third of our economies: *characters*.

Paddy Chayefsky commented earlier that there shouldn't be a character in the script who doesn't have to be there to answer the demands of the main character's story. No matter how delightfully a character is written, he is a bore if he serves no definite plot purpose.

Novels often contain dozens of characters, many of whom are relatively unnecessary. Such characters do more than clutter a script; they take attention away from principal characters. If characters in a novel do not contribute to the protagonist's struggle to reach a goal—or to the antagonist's efforts to prevent it—they should be ruthlessly eliminated.

If two characters share the same backgrounds, attitudes, or points of view, they are, in effect, the same character. If a character in a novel duplicates the viewpoint of another, one of the characters probably should be deleted or changed. When brother and sister agree that their parents should get a divorce, for example, they have little to say to each other; they present the writer with few opportunities for exciting scenes. By changing the brother's attitude, making him passionate in his belief that the parents must remain together, the writer creates sparks in encounters between the two.

STRUCTURE

Some novels tend to be **episodic** in form. Their stories consist of a series of incidents occurring one after another, like articles of clothing strung on a clothesline.

Some novels are internal in form, dwelling on the thought processes and emotions of their characters. At times, whole chapters take place within a character's mind as he or she recalls past incidents, mulls over the present, or speculates about the future.

Because some novels use characters' thoughts as a major narrative device, their stories tend to move backward and forward in time. Early chapters of John LeCarré's best-seller *A Perfect Spy*, for example, devote about 80 percent of their content to antecedent action that characters recall, continually hop-scotching from present to past.

Screenplays use a more rigid pattern. What happens in act two must grow out of the incidents in act one. What happens in act three must grow out of material established in acts one and two. Thus, screenplays are pyramidal in structure, the antithesis of the novel's often-episodic pattern.

Because act one constitutes the base of the pyramid, all of a screenplay's major characters usually are established in this act. The major story conflict — protagonist versus antagonist — is also established in the first act. The conflict develops throughout acts two and three as the protagonist struggles to achieve a goal.

Orientation to a goal gives dramatic stories a sense of purpose. It also provides structure; the story has a specific, defined direction. Orientation to a goal implies one additional factor: movement. If the goal is to reach the top of a mountain, the hero climbs higher and higher while the antagonistic force (the weather, wild animals, a mad scientist, the hero's fears) fights to prevent it. Thus, the story becomes a series of battles as the hero reaches the mountain's first plateau and then the second and then the third.

Movement holds our interest, but not movement for its own sake. The hero has to make progress or receive setbacks in relation to the goal. When the dramatic progression stops cold, especially for any extended time, audiences lose interest.

Movement toward a goal represents plot progression. Progression may also occur in terms of character. Protagonists may undergo changes in behavior, morality, or psychology as a result of story pressures. Such changes may be for the better or for the worse, as, for example, when a coward achieves courage or a mother loses respect for her daughter.

The motion picture *Kramer vs. Kramer* demonstrates vividly how a writer can add progression during adaptation. *Kramer vs. Kramer* is the story of a husband, Ted Kramer, whose wife abandons him, forcing him to cope with raising their five-year-old son. A year or two later, Joanna Kramer returns and demands custody of their son, Billy. She takes Ted to court and wins custody, but later relents and disappears from the scene.

After Joanna's initial disappearance in the novel, Ted has many problems: how to get his life together socially and professionally, how to repair his shattered ego, how to cope with being adrift again in the singles scene. His son, Billy, misses his mommy for a while, but with the help of grandparents and friends recovers nicely.

Robert Benton's brilliant adaptation places the diffuse story in a tight dramatic frame through a series of character progressions. He focuses sharply on the Ted-Billy relationship. At the outset, father and son do not know each other. Their relationship is awkward, their words to each other tentative, distrusting. When Ted tries to play homemaker, he fumbles badly, adding to his son's sense of insecurity. Ted's failures as a father/mother make him insecure. Fights erupt between the two.

Such an adversarial relationship does not exist in the novel. Why did Benton add it? So that the father-son relationship could change and grow.

Then Joanna reappears to claim her son. By the time the film reaches that second-act crisis, the Ted-Billy relationship has blossomed. The two have developed mutual trust and love — a rare, beautiful, and very moving relationship. When Joanna reappears and claims her son, she becomes a major threat to our protagonist. If the scriptwriter had begun the Ted-Billy relationship with preexisting love and trust, he would have had nowhere to go. By beginning with awkwardness and misunderstanding, he created a dramatic progression.

Benton added another major progression in the transition from novel to screenplay. In the latter, Ted first appears as an ambitious workaholic. By the third act, because of the relationship that has developed between himself and Billy, he will take any job in order to retain custody of his son. Joanna also progresses in the screenplay, changing from an unhappy, insecure wife seeking a new direction for her life to a mature, responsible woman who respects the love that has grown between son and father and who is therefore able to selflessly withdraw.

The *Kramer vs. Kramer* screenplay displays almost every adaptive principle we have described. It economizes in characters, reducing the cast from thirty or forty to only six. It economizes in time frame. It economizes in story content. If you get the opportunity, read both the novel and the screenplay for a vivid demonstration of the adaptive process.

ESSENCE

When adapting a novel, the screenwriter often revises structure, eliminates characters, or reduces the passage of time to make the screenplay dramatic. In most cases, audiences will accept such changes without question, provided the writer has maintained the theme and spirit of the book.

It is easy to get so wrapped up in fixing a difficult novel that screenwriters sometimes forget the qualities that made it successful. One way to avoid such a trap is by pinpointing the book's special attributes. Why did readers buy it?

What special qualities, characters, style, or atmosphere made it unique? So important is the book's theme or spirit that the screenwriter sometimes has to adjust or modify structural changes to preserve it. If the writer succeeds in dramatizing a book's plot but fails to preserve its raison d'être, he or she has failed as an adapter.

$\mathcal{A}$DAPTATION:
A PRACTICAL DEMONSTRATION

The following short story by Alexander Woollcott provides an excellent opportunity to examine the adaptive process.* "Entrance Fee" is literary in form and requires changes to transform it into screenplay drama.

This delightful story has been anthologized many times, but even if you've read it before, read it again now with adaptation in mind. Don't allow the French phrases to get in your way. After you have finished, take a few minutes to consider: What would you do if a producer hired you to adapt this extremely short story into a feature motion picture?

This, then, is the story of Cosette and the Saint-Cyrien, much as they tell it (and these many years have been telling it) in the smoky popotes of the French Army.

In the nineties, when one heard less ugly babel of alien tongues in the sidewalk cafés, the talk at the aperitif hour was sure to turn sooner or later on Cosette — Mlle. Cosette of the Varietes, who was regarded by common consent as the most desirable woman in France. She was no hedged-in royal courtesan, as her possessive fellow citizens would point out, but a distributed Du Barry, the chere amie of a republic.

Her origins were misty. Some said she had been born of fisherfolk at Plonbazlanec on the Brittany coast. Others preferred the tale that she was the love child of a famous actress by a very well-known king. In any case, she was now a national legend, and in her pre-eminence the still bruised French people found in some curious way a balm for their wounded self-esteem. Her photographs, which usually showed her sitting piquantly on a café table, were cut from *L'illustration* and pinned up in every barracks. Every French lad dreamed of her, and every right-minded French girl quite understood that her sweetheart was saying in effect, "Since I cannot hope to have Cosette, will you come to the river's edge at sundown?" Quite understood, and did not blame him.

*Alexander Woollcott, *The Portable Woollcott* (New York: Viking, 1946). From *While Rome Burns* by Alexander Woollcott. Copyright 1934 by Alexander Woollcott, renewed Copyright 1962 by Joseph P. Hennessey. Reprinted by permission of Viking Penguin, Inc.

Everyone had seen pictures of Cosette's tiny, vine-hung villa at Saint-Cloud, with its high garden wall and its twittering aviary. And even those for whom that wall was hopelessly high took morbid pride in a persistent detail of the legend which said that no man was ever a guest there for the night who could not bring five thousand francs with him. This was in the nineties, mind you, when francs were francs, and men — by a coincidence then more dependable — were men.

The pleasant blend of charm and thrift in Cosette filled the cadets at Saint-Cyr with a gentle melancholy. In their twilight hours of relaxation they talked it over, and all thought it a sorrowful thing that, so wretched is the soldier's pittance, not one of those who must someday direct the great Revanche would ever carry into battle a memory of the fairest woman in France. For what cadet could hope to raise five thousand francs? It was very sad. But, cried one of their number, his voice shaking, his eyes alight, there were a thousand students at Saint-Cyr and not one of them so lacking in resource that he could not, if given time, manage to raise at least five francs.

That was how the Cosette Sweepstakes were started. There followed then all the anxious distraction of ways and means, with such Spartan exploits in self-denial, such Damon-and-Pythias borrowings, such flagrant letters of perjured appeal to unsuspecting aunts and grandmothers, as Saint-Cyr had never known. But by the appointed time, the last man had his, or somebody's, five francs.

The drawing of numbers was well underway when a perplexed instructor stumbled on the proceedings and reported his discovery to the commandant. When the old general heard the story he was so profoundly moved that it was some time before he spoke.

"The lad who wins this lottery," he said at last, "will be the envy of his generation. But the lad who conceived the idea — ah, he, my friend, will someday be a marshal of France!"

Then he fell to laughing at the thought of the starry-eyed youngster arriving at the stage door of the Varietes with nothing but his youth and his entrance fee. The innocent budget had made no provision for the trip to Paris, none for a carriage, a bouquet, perhaps a supper party. The commandant said that he would wish to meet this margin of contingency from his own fatherly pocket.

"There will be extras," he said. "Let the young rascal who wins be sent to me before he leaves for Paris."

It was a cadet from the Vendee who reported to the commandant next afternoon — very trim in his red breeches and blue tunic, his white gloves spotless, his white cockade jaunty, his heart in his mouth. The commandant said no word to him, but put a little purse of gold louis in his hand, kissed him on both cheeks in benediction, and stood at the window, moist-eyed and chuckling, to watch until the white cockade disappeared down the avenue of trees.

The sunlight, latticed by the jalousies, was making a gay pattern on Cosette's carpet the next morning when she sat up and meditated on the day which stretched ahead of her. The little cadet was cradled in a sweet, dreamless sleep, and it touched her rather to see how preposterously young he was. Indeed, it quite set her thinking of her early days, and how she had come up in the world. Then she began speculating on his early days, realized with a pang that he was still in the midst of them, and suddenly grew puzzled. Being a woman of action, she prodded him.

"Listen, my old one," she said, "how did a cadet at Saint-Cyr ever get hold of five thousand francs?"

Thus abruptly questioned, he lost his head and blurted out the tale of the sweepstakes. Perhaps he felt it could do no harm now, and anyway she listened so avidly, with such flattering little gasps of surprise and such sunny ripples of laughter, that he quite warmed to his story. When he came to the part about the commandant she rose and strode up and down, the lace of her peignoir fluttering behind her, tears in her violet eyes.

"Saint-Cyr has paid me the prettiest compliment I have ever known," she said, "and I am the proudest woman in France this day. But surely I must do my part. You shall go back and tell them all that Cosette is a woman of sentiment. When you are an old, old man in the Vendee you shall tell your grandchildren that once in your youth you knew the dearest favors in France, and they cost you not a sou. Not a sou."

At that she hauled open the little drawer where he had seen her lock up the lottery receipts the night before.

"Here," she said with a lovely gesture. "I give you back your money."

And she handed him his five francs.

Before we discuss possible directions for the adaptation of "Entrance Fee," why don't you try to find some answers on your own? You'll learn a great deal more by struggling with the problem than if you read the answers in a book.

Although there is no single, correct way to adapt any story, you might begin the process by asking questions. Who will be the protagonist in this story? What will be the protagonist's goal? Who or what will fight to keep the protagonist from reaching that goal, thereby creating your central story problem? Remember that conflict is the essence of drama. If a protagonist reaches a goal easily or conveniently, the story may become boring.

Take a few minutes to think about "Entrance Fee." After you've found some answers to the above questions, answers that you would hand to a producer as an example of your creative skill, continue reading this chapter.

Have you done your homework? Give the story some additional creative thought before continuing. Remember the two most important words in a writer's life: Be dissatisfied. When you're ready, continue on.

What makes "Entrance Fee" special? Well, the payoff is delightful — funny and unexpected. But all it is, really, is a fillip, a curtain line that works well in a short story. In drama, we can't depend on a single line of dialog. We need more substantial elements to sustain us.

The fun of the story and a large part of its charm is the concept of the sweepstakes, the selection of one cadet who will spend a night with the fabled, unattainable Cosette. By focusing on the sweepstakes, we automatically exclude Cosette as a choice for the protagonist. It appears that the young cadet must be our protagonist. Was that your decision? Good for you.

Let's give him a name. We can change it later if it doesn't wear well. It's always easier to discuss a story if we have handles for our characters. Let's call him Jean-Claude.

If Jean-Claude's goal is to win the sweepstakes — and he does — we face two roadblocks: (1) since he achieves his goal quickly and easily, our story lacks a problem; there is little or no conflict; (2) with a thousand cadets at Saint-Cyr, it seems an incredible coincidence that our hero would win. His selection seems to be at the writer's convenience rather than a logical outgrowth of story elements. Coincidences that solve a hero's problem are always forbidden.

How can we create problems for Jean-Claude? What was that? You suggest that the general might be opposed to the sweepstakes? Good idea! He might be an old-line, blood-and-guts soldier, all military efficiency, no time for foolishness. When he learns of the sweepstakes, he forbids it. Perhaps he has had occasion to discipline Jean-Claude in the past. Perhaps there's real antagonism between them.

The cadets go ahead and hold the drawing in spite of the general. Now we have pressure on our story. Now, by winning, our cadet gets into trouble; he (and perhaps others) will be punished for disobeying the general's edict. I worry that Jean-Claude's winning the sweepstakes still seems convenient, but it is certainly less so than in the original circumstances, since his winning now gets him into trouble with the general.

Part of the short story's charm is the consummation of the Jean-Claude–Cosette relationship: an innocent enjoying the favors of a famous courtesan. We cannot lose that. Perhaps the cadets are confined to quarters as punishment for defying the general's orders. Now we must develop a conspiracy in which the cadets arrange to smuggle Jean-Claude out of his quarters and into town. Such clandestine undertakings would be highly entertaining and would create enormous suspense. Jean-Claude's buddies must outwit the general's military police who patrol the grounds. We will need to solve the problem of sneaking Jean-Claude back into his quarters the following morning without the general's knowledge — or, perhaps, the general finds out and punishes Jean-Claude. But our hero doesn't care for he has glimpsed paradise. We have an additional factor going for us now, an antiestablishment flavor that is often popular with teenage moviegoers.

How do you feel about our adaptation so far? No question, it works; it's scriptable in traditional dramatic terms, but it smacks a little of formula, doesn't it? We almost expect the general or some authority figure to oppose the scheme. Part of the story's charm is the general's unexpected and warmhearted endorsement of the lottery. The best drama defies expectations, providing surprising twists and turns. Sometimes it's healthy not to grab the first idea that occurs to us. Let's dig a little deeper. Remember those two magic words: Be dissatisfied!

Is there any other possible way in which Jean-Claude's winning of the sweepstakes could become not an answer but a problem? Well, many times when plot elements don't provide the answer to a story dilemma, we must examine and perhaps change the nature of our characters. How could we change Jean-Claude's character to make our story work? Suppose he were a shy, good-hearted country boy who has never been with a woman. Perhaps he has lied about his background (as young soldiers often do), pretending to be an experienced man of the world. But his more sophisticated comrades see through him, aware that he is making up stories, encouraging his fabrications for their personal amusement.

When the idea of the sweepstakes emerges, Jean-Claude becomes nervous. He's timid, uncomfortable with the opposite sex, actually afraid that by some fluke he might win. He wouldn't know how to behave with a sophisticated woman like Cosette. Perhaps a couple of his buddies become aware of his fear and engineer circumstances so that he wins the sweepstakes. Would they really do that, when each wants to win the lottery himself? It seems unlikely.

Perhaps we could find a compromise in which they start to rig proceedings, throwing out most of the lottery tickets. But then a heated battle ensues between cadets, and they abandon their plan. Back in the barracks, meanwhile, Jean-Claude is praying that he doesn't win. But fate moves its huge hand and he does win! Now his victory may be acceptable to audiences because it represents a problem for him; it's just what he didn't want to happen. Such a gambit would wipe out much of the coincidence and would give audiences the fun of seeing a nice, likable kid thrust into a difficult situation.

This pattern gives us a less melodramatic story and a more human one. Now the third act of our story would concern the magic night itself in which Jean-Claude meets Cosette. He is embarrassed and ill at ease. She's disbelieving at first and then is charmed by him, enjoying his lack of sophistication, a welcome relief from the wealthy businessmen she has known. The next morning, aware that Jean-Claude's comrades are covertly watching, she's highly demonstrative, lavishing affection on him ("the most magnificent night of my life, Jean-Claude!"), making him look good in the eyes of his buddies. The short story's final line can still be included, but only as the payoff to a scene, not as the reason for telling the story.

Early in the chapter we mentioned that well-constructed drama presents all its major characters in the first act. But in our preliminary adaptation, Cosette would not appear until the third act or perhaps the second-act curtain. We face a small problem: How do we introduce her early in the show? Well, perhaps the sight of her sets the wheels of our story in motion. Perhaps the cadets glimpse her getting into a carriage after a performance at Les Varietes and lose their hearts. Perhaps Jean-Claude makes a fool of himself trying to help her or fetching something she has dropped. (Perhaps she gives him five francs for his trouble!) Perhaps her gentleman friend demeans Jean-Claude, making us feel sorry for him. Now that Cosette has appeared and has spoken dialog, she becomes a real character and not a faceless shadow.

Let's examine the new structure and see if it conforms to our basic principles of drama. Do we have a character we can care about and root for? Certainly, in our protagonist Jean-Claude. Does he have a specific goal in the show? Yes, to avoid winning the sweepstakes. Winning would plunge him into a sexual encounter that he feels incapable of handling. Does he achieve his goal? No, but he emerges happy that he did not.

Who or what is Jean-Claude's antagonist in this story? His comrades are his antagonists, stacking the deck against him, pushing him toward Cosette. Also, realistically, Jean-Claude is his own antagonist, at war with himself; his instincts as a man and his social fears are on opposite sides. Is the general an antagonist? Perhaps, if we need added pressure on the story. But the general's attitude in the original story is delightful and warming. Whether he remains friend or foe is an option we can examine when we write the treatment.

Our attempt to adapt "Entrance Fee" has demonstrated several dramatic principles: (1) When a story has no protagonist, create one; (2) when a story has no problem, create one; (3) when a story has no antagonist, create one; (4) when coincidence exists, find a way to make it appear logical; (5) introduce all main characters in the first act; (6) preserve the essence of a story, the characters, or incidents that made it successful.

*C*HAPTER HIGHLIGHTS

➤ Readers of short stories or novels enrich written material by using their imaginations to create vivid scenery and characters. Screenwriters find it difficult to compete with the scope of the reader's imagination.

➤ Successful adapters understand that drama is fundamentally different from literature. Primary differences are economy, structure, and progression.

➤ Drama uses economy of time. Novels sometimes cover decades, even centuries. Successful screenplays condense the time frame. In suspense patterns, writers often inflict time pressures on their characters to heighten tension.

➤ Drama uses economy of content. Novels often contain multiple plots, too much material for a two-hour film. Some adapters begin their screenplays deep in the story, eliminating early material. Others delete one or more of the subplots.

➤ Drama uses economy of characters. Novels often have dozens of characters. Successful screenplays eliminate all but the most necessary. To create conflict, good writers look for contrast in their characters.

➤ Although the structure of novels is often elastic, moving backward and forward in time and changing point of view, the structure of screenplays is pyramidal. Act one provides the foundation, establishing major characters and the central problem. Act two grows from material established in act one. Act three builds on material established in the first two acts.

➤ Drama usually is oriented toward a goal. The protagonist seeks to achieve the goal; the antagonist fights to keep him or her from achieving it. Ultimately, the protagonist achieves the goal or fails.

➤ Well-structured screenplay drama grows, develops, climbs, progresses in tension. When stories fail to grow in tension, audiences become restless. Because of story pressures, characters and relationships also must develop and grow.

➤ When adapting, writers may exercise dramatic economy and change a novel's structure, but they must retain the qualities that made the novel unique, usually its theme or spirit. Failure to retain this narrative essence often defeats an adaptation.

$\mathcal{S}$CRIPTWRITING PROJECTS

EXERCISES DESIGNED TO SHARPEN YOUR NARRATIVE SKILLS

ADAPTING NOVELS

Select a novel you have enjoyed reading and prepare an adaptive analysis in two parts. The first part should synopsize the novel as written (not more than a page, please). The second part should outline your ideas for adapting it into screenplay form, based on the principles discussed in this chapter. By outlining, I mean a terse, point-by-point enumeration.

ADAPTING SHORT STORIES

Go to the library, find a copy of O. Henry's "Gift of the Magi" (or another O. Henry twist-ending story), and prepare a five-page treatment describing how you would dramatize the story in a screenplay. You will probably have to add developments to create sufficient content. A treatment simply tells the story in narrative form, as you would develop it chronologically. Add some dialog if you like; it's not essential.

If necessary, read again this chapter's discussion of "Entrance Fee," which is similar structurally to many O. Henry stories. Warning: This is a tough assignment, so take your time. Give your ideas a day or two to simmer. Be dissatisfied.

CHAPTER 13

Launching Your Writing Career

PRACTICAL REALITIES OF THE MARKETPLACE

*W*hich is more difficult: writing a magnificent screenplay or selling it? Both are difficult. Each requires different skills. Each, in its own way, is creative.

One type of writer feels comfortable and secure while writing a script. Even though the work is frustrating and time consuming, the writer is in control. The writer makes all creative decisions — altering or deleting characters, changing locales, moving scenes about, rewriting, and polishing — with no one to interfere. The creative process generates excitement and a sense of real joy.

But once the writing is finished, everything changes. Now the writer has to knock on strange doors and seek help from uncaring executives. The comfortable security disappears and uneasiness sets in. The entertainment world seems wrapped up in its own urgent affairs, disinterested in screenplays from newcomers. Far worse, it seems disinterested in you. Secretaries coldly protect their bosses, rejecting you with polite disdain. When new writers somehow manage to see agents, their stomachs tighten, their voices rise, their palms moisten. If they are lucky enough to meet with a producer, they develop a form of office aphasia, forgetting 75 percent of the English language.

A totally different breed is the second type of writer, who suffers endlessly putting words on paper, agonizing over each scene, hating every word and every character. When the tortuous process is finally over, this writer is thrilled to leave the cramped office and be out in the real world, breathing fresh air, talking to flesh-and-blood people instead of a humorless word processor.

The second writer jokes with secretaries, flatters agents, is glib and resourceful with producers. The second writer is a salesman; the first is not. Although these two types are extreme, their characteristics exist in varying degrees in almost every writer.

When I produced TV series, I learned a big lesson: You cannot judge writers from their behavior in an office. Some writers create an aura of confidence, winning you instantly with their friendliness, their intelligence, their sense of humor, and their obvious command of the English language. They sell their ideas with confidence and consummate skill. You can't wait to give them an assignment. Others limply shake your hand, and you try to dry it unobtrusively on your trousers. These writers promptly retreat into their chairs, sinking deep into the cushions as if for protection. They fumble through their stories almost apologetically, seemingly unsure of their characters and the direction of their plots. If you give these writers an assignment, you do so with misgivings and trepidation.

Which writer turns in the better script? No one can predict. Sometimes writers who tell a story badly also write badly. Sometimes writers who tell a story well, also write well.

Of the two skills, writing and selling, writing is by far the more important. If you're a magnificent writer, a dozen agents will fight to represent you (once they're aware of your talent), hoping to sell your material, saving you that chore. If you're a magnificent salesperson, you will probably sell a screenplay or two. But ultimately, it is the written word that will sell you (or undo you) rather than any fancy footwork you may perform in a producer's office.

This chapter will examine the entertainment industry from the viewpoint of the emerging writer. Discussions will focus on these areas:

➢ **THE PROFESSIONAL WRITER:** training and background, habits (good and bad), ways of growing as a writer, how to appear professional in script and attitude

➢ **PROTECTING YOUR WORK:** the need for protection against plagiarism, WGA registration, copyrighting, signing release forms

➢ **LITERARY AGENTS:** getting them to read your material, finding the right agent, problems with agents

➢ **SELLING TO TELEVISION:** TV series versus TV movies, submitting material, making contact, following through, problems with new series

➢ **SELLING TO MOTION PICTURES:** advantages and disadvantages, subject matter, pay scales, adaptations

➢ **METAPHYSICS OF SUCCESS:** the good news and the bad, winning attitudes, the need for perseverance

➢ **WRITER REVELATIONS:** million-dollar screenwriter Kathy McWhorter describes her amazing odyssey from student to professional

*T*HE PROFESSIONAL WRITER

This section is based on a working or personal relationship with seventy or eighty writers in the development of approximately 350 screenplays. From this background we will sketch a composite picture of professional writers, their backgrounds, attitudes toward work, most significant characteristics, and the qualities that make their scripts salable.

Most television and motion picture writers graduated from college with a B.A. degree in liberal arts. A few never attended college. A few went on to earn M.A.s or Ph.D.s. No one asks to see their diplomas. No one cares. The important factor in achieving success is not that they graduated but that they learned something.

Many television and cinema students try to cram into their program all the courses in their major field they possibly can, feeling that such courses will best prepare them for a professional career. This is not necessarily so; such a pattern can be restricting. Top writers know their own field, to be sure. But they also have knowledge of theater and its history, of literature, political science, sports, world history, religion, and art. In addition, they can cite fashion trends, economic predictions, and the latest wrinkle in Middle East politics.

The point is, most good writers are educated. (Those who didn't graduate from college usually read incessantly.) They have learned about the world from school and from books and newspapers. They have learned about people and human relationships from personal observation. Such extensive knowledge allows them to develop scripts dealing with widely varied subject matter.

Another factor is common to the backgrounds of most writers: They have written. That is, they worked on school newspapers, wrote short stories, or dabbled in scripts, some as early as junior high school. Some wrote professionally in other fields before transferring to the entertainment industry.

Ask any group of writers what is the best way to learn to write and they will usually tell you: by writing! Their recommendation in no way undercuts university writing courses. Most professionals feel these classes are an excellent preparation; they teach you the fundamentals of structure, character, and dialog. But once you have learned the basics, the next step is to develop facility. And the best way to do that is by writing.

The ability to write correlates with muscular exercise. When we first learn any new physical activity such as aerobics, we tire quickly. Our muscles simply aren't used to the strain; they need development. By the end of the second week, the exercises seem easier. By the end of two months, our muscles have strengthened considerably and we move to the head of the class. Our verbal skills (muscles of the brain) respond in a similar way.

When we first write, the words come slowly and laboriously. We read them over the next morning and they seem awkward, amateurish — and so we rewrite them. Later, we may rewrite them again. After a week or two, the muscles of our mind develop facility. The words come more freely; so do ideas. Because we are always dissatisfied, we throw aside inferior ideas, searching for fresher, more creative ones. We discover with pleasure that not only are we writing faster and more fluently but also the words seem crisper and more professional.

Writing teachers recommend that anyone seriously interested in writing develop the discipline of writing every day, five (or more) days a week. Read biographical material by professional writers, and you'll discover that they structure their lives. They're at their desks every morning at the same time. First, they polish the work of the previous day, and then they tackle new material. If ideas don't come, they don't shrug their shoulders and walk away. They continue to write, jumping into new projects, blasting their way through mental blocks. They have maintained a discipline that keeps their mental gears turning.

Don't condemn yourself if you tend to put off writing. You're experiencing a normal human reaction. Good writing is hard work. (Bad writing is easy.) We all tend to avoid work when we can. An old industry joke defines a writer as a person who sits down at the word processor and hopes the telephone will ring! Most writers begin the day by sharpening pencils, rearranging their desks, and making telephone calls. When they run out of delaying tactics, they go to work.

STAYING SHARP

Do you remember motion pictures that you saw many years ago, films that thrilled and excited you? Have you seen them recently, rerun on a cable channel? Chances are, they seemed old fashioned, subtly different from the tastes and styles of today's world. To be sure, a few classic films are so timeless in theme and execution that they never appear dated. But they are the exceptions. Most films reflect their period.

One way of staying in touch with today's entertainment world—and simultaneously stimulating your imagination—is to see quality motion pictures as often as possible, whether on television or in the movie theater. Exposure to such films works on two levels. We consciously absorb the subject matter as expressed through form and content. And we subconsciously absorb the film's style, the writer's and director's approach to material, the characteristics and techniques that make the film subtly different from those made five years earlier.

One writer I know sees films two or three nights a week, every week: new films, old films, documentaries, avant-garde films. He even watches bad movies, probably to learn what *not* to do. He goes to museum screenings of classic films, including oldies made in the teens and twenties to rediscover writing and directorial techniques, forgotten film styles, and unusual approaches to stories. He is among Hollywood's most successful writers. Does that tell you something?

Another way to fine-tune writing skills is through reading screenplays by good writers. In addition to learning techniques, the practice has a delightful fringe benefit: It creates excitement; it makes you want to write! Many universities maintain collections of motion picture screenplays even though they are copyrighted and sometimes difficult to obtain. A few successful scripts have been anthologized and are available in the film departments of major bookstores.

In the beginning, many writers "steal" from screenwriters they admire. They don't steal ideas; they steal writing techniques. Such a practice is normal. Out of these borrowings eventually comes a synthesis of style and technique that is truly yours.

Good writers also read books, magazines, and newspapers as a way of discovering stories or characters. I promise you: The pages of tomorrow morning's newspaper will contain the seeds of a marvelous screenplay. It remains only for you to discover it. Dozens of successful motion pictures have derived from newspaper stories.

APPEARING PROFESSIONAL

Most studios or production companies employ readers to assess the screenplays that are submitted almost daily. These readers then synopsize each screenplay, including an appraisal of the project's overall quality and potential for success. From time to time, readers talk to my scriptwriting classes. Their words are remarkably consistent. If submitted material is sloppy, if it contains misspellings or is written in awkward script format, they are predisposed from the outset to consider it the work of an amateur.

The message is clear. Even if you aren't a professional, you certainly can look like one. Keep a dictionary handy. If you aren't sure of a word's spelling, look it up. If a page contains erasures or typing overstrikes, throw it away and start over. If you haven't mastered script format, take a few minutes and study it. It's not difficult. A reasonably intelligent ninth grader can learn it in an hour. We can't all be geniuses, superbly gifted in scriptwriting, but there's no excuse for scripts to appear unprofessional.

Professional readers advise against expensive or fancy leather bindings. The quality of the cover won't sell your work. Only the words inside can do that. Put it in a simple cardboard folder or binder. Place the title of the screenplay and your name on it. That's all. Inside, on the title page, again give the screenplay title and your name. That's all. No set and cast list. No date.

Most readers feel they can evaluate a script from its first ten pages. So give those early pages special attention. Be sure that you can hook your reader in those pages either with an unexpected plot twist, an offbeat character, or a compelling scene.

A final "don't" passed along by readers: If you have your script registered by the Writers Guild of America to protect it from plagiarism, the guild will take one copy, microfilm it, and keep the film in its files for five years. (The cost is $20.00 for nonmembers. You don't have to belong to WGA.) They will also stamp your copy, the imprint indicating that the script has been duly registered, protecting you in some degree from theft.

When writers submit scripts to producing companies, they sometimes submit a copy bearing the Writers Guild imprint. In the back of their minds, I suppose, they're trying to appear experienced and professional, demonstrating by the imprint that they're wise enough to protect themselves.

Unfortunately, the WGA imprint makes a totally different statement to producers. It seems to say "I've had this script registered because I don't trust you, you thieving rascal!" If you register your screenplay, keep the imprinted copy in a file drawer. Never, never, never submit it to a producer.

PROTECTING YOUR WORK

Registering your script provides only a limited degree of protection. It establishes for the record the date you wrote your screenplay. If, subsequently, someone writes or produces an identical or similar project, you can prove in a court of law that you came up with the idea (and script) first. Some writers send a copy of their script to themselves by registered mail, hoping that this procedure also will establish the date of the writing. According to some lawyers, this practice is far from foolproof. Can the writer prove, for example, that the envelope has not been steamed open and the material inside tampered with? Other writers go to the trouble of copyrighting their material.

There's certainly nothing wrong with protecting yourself. But many beginning writers tend to be paranoid. (Forgive me, beginning writers!) They think that everyone is out to steal their material. If your idea is truly unique, a totally new direction in filmmaking, then maybe, just maybe someone will rip you off. In the twenty-plus years I was in television, I saw only one example of a producer stealing a writer's idea. Most producers are far more interested in finding good writers than they are in good ideas. Surprisingly, good ideas are fairly common; good writers simply aren't.

When you submit material to networks, advertising agencies, or production companies, they usually will refuse to read your material until you have signed a standard release form. They generally will provide such a form when they return your material. They will be able to return your screenplay because you provided them with a stamped, self-addressed envelope.

Most production companies refuse to read free-lance material unless it is either submitted through a licensed literary agency or accompanied by a release form. The reason is obvious: to avoid lawsuits. In the early days of motion pictures, a number of people managed to win large sums of money by submitting material to studios and later suing for plagiarism. They won in many cases because juries sided with the little guy facing the wealthy, monolithic corporation. Because of such judicial tendencies, motion picture studios developed the habit of settling these nuisance suits out of court. It became a convenient way for litigious souls to pick up large chunks of money. Eventually, the studios wised up and demanded release forms before they would read unsolicited material.

What is a release form? It's a legal paper promising to pay the writer equitably for the story, provided it is actually produced. However, the release form asks the writer to recognize that, because of the volume of story ideas submitted, some similarities will inevitably exist between stories received and those actually produced. By signing, the writer agrees not to sue in the event of such unintentional similarity.

Many beginning writers worry about signing such a form. Don't. It may be the only way you'll get your material read. Most producers are honest. If they read your material — and like it — they will pay you for it. I cannot promise that no one will ever steal your material. If you lock your material in a vault, it's true that no one will steal it from you, but neither will anyone buy it. My advice is to show your material to anyone and everyone in the industry who will read it — with a release form or without, with a copyright or without, with a WGA registration or without. If the material is good, someone will buy it. If it isn't, all the release forms, copyrights, and WGA registrations in the world won't make a particle of difference!

Some production companies refuse to read unsolicited material even with a release form. Such practices are rough on new writers. But take heart from the knowledge that good writers are rare; they are in constant demand. You have to believe that or find another line of work.

If you submit your material through a licensed literary agent, you will have some measure of protection.

ℱINDING AN AGENT

Every industry has a favorite whipping boy. In the entertainment field, that whipping boy is the agent. According to the unsuccessful, agents lie, cheat, and steal — but not all the time. Only when they're awake. They will sell their sisters to the highest bidder. They will use their grandmothers' crutches for kindling when the weather gets cold. All of the above will seem true until that magic moment when an agent sells your screenplay. At that point he or she becomes godlike, your best friend in the entire world!

What exactly do agents do? They advise, critique, pound on doors, plead, sell, demand, negotiate, package, counsel, comfort, and commiserate. An agent is the go-between for the writer and producer. The good ones more than earn their 10 percent commission.

A beginning writer's second-most-difficult task is getting someone in authority to read his or her material. (The first, of course, is writing the breakthrough script.) A literary agent can help. If agents believe in their clients and like their material — and have some clout — they can help. They can get past the producer's secretary. They can insist that the producer read your material and read it quickly, because another producer appears to be interested.

The writer's beginning problem is finding such an agent. There are a hundred times as many writers as there are agents. And most of those writers are less than competent. That's a crushing statement, I realize, but it's categorically true. Agents are reluctant to read new material because it probably will be bad.

In addition, most agents are overworked: too many phone calls, too many bases to cover, too little time. Each weekend, agents take home armloads of material written by their clients to read. To undertake the reading of still more material submitted over the transom by nonclients is asking a great deal. And yet agents occasionally do read material from new writers, at least some agents do. The Writers Guild of America, West, has prepared a list of licensed literary agencies, indicating those that read material from new writers.*

All agents are not the same. Large agencies represent many, many writers, most of whom are successful, with long lists of credits. Ask yourself: Would such an agency want me? The answer is obvious. Agencies are in business to make money. If they represent two clients, one of whom is easy to sell and the other, a newcomer, extremely difficult, which are they going to favor? A new writer inevitably gets short shrift in a large agency, unless his or her talent (or screenplay) is truly extraordinary.

Small agencies, on the other hand, are more willing to represent unknown writers. If they believe in you (and that's important), they will fight your battles, trying to build their client list. As you become successful, earning more and more money, they, in turn, will earn more money.

I've read advertisements of agents who charge a fee for reading material. Most deal with literary rather than dramatic material. I've never met an agent

---

*Send $2 and a stamped self-addressed envelope to Writers Guild of America, 8955 Beverly Boulevard, Los Angeles, CA 90048.

in the entertainment industry who exacts fees from potential clients. Be wary of such individuals.

When sending material to agencies or producing companies, always enclose a self-addressed envelope with stamps sufficient to cover mailing costs.

SELLING TO TELEVISION

The television industry gobbles up hundreds of screenplays daily: drama, comedy, variety, documentaries, soaps. Because its appetite is huge, television represents an attractive market for writers. It includes commercial networks, PBS, cable outlets, local stations, and production companies. Within the framework of those markets are two major writing areas: TV series and TV movies.

TV SERIES

Episodes of a series usually feature the same cast each week. In each story, the permanent cast deals with problems that arise among its members or problems created by new characters.

Each TV series promises its audience a specific, sometimes unique, style of comedy, drama, or melodrama; when audiences tune in, they know what to expect. Audience expectancy also applies to story patterns. Each series has its own approach to storytelling that helps define its flavor and personality.

Almost all TV series have their own stable of writers: five or six (sometimes more) permanent staff members who work on scripts produced for that series. In addition to handsome salaries, they are given an assortment of prestigious but ultimately confusing titles: coproducers, consulting producers, supervising producers, associate producers, coexecutive producers, and so on. Are they really producers? No. What do they do? They write. (The exception is the *line producer* who probably is production oriented.) Producing companies give writers these seemingly prestigious titles instead of paying them additional money. These staff writers create original scripts for the series and they rewrite submitted material that isn't good enough. In addition to staff writers, the story editor (sometimes called story consultant) also lends a hand with writing chores. With all of these writers on staff, are there any opportunities for free-lancers to sell scripts to TV series?

Yes. The door is open, but only a little. According to a provision of the Writers Guild contract, all producing companies must provide some access to the open market. So TV series do occasionally accept scripts from free-lancers. Just a few per season. Fact of life: TV series do not constitute a major market for beginning writers.

Before writers move into staff positions, most begin as free-lancers, submitting story ideas or scripts to TV series. Typically, a successful free-lance writer in time becomes a story editor or staff writer; a few eventually become producers. As I've indicated, good writers are rare; to a producer they are golden. When production companies discover them, they are quick to snap them up and put them on staff. Because solid scripts are so essential to the success of any series, almost all television producers have backgrounds as writers.

The Market.   If you are interested in writing for a television series, the first step is an obvious one: Study the series. That doesn't mean just watching weekly episodes. It means analyzing the characters, the special habits, speech patterns, and backgrounds of each. It means studying the kinds of stories the series presents as well as its patterns of storytelling. For example, does the series always feature the same star, or does it alternate story patterns, giving the focus to a different star each week? Does it follow the star from one incident to another, or does it cut back and forth between the star's story and a secondary story? Do the episodes deal primarily with the series' stars, or do they feature guests who plunge the stars into the guests' problems? Do the episodes play solely in permanent sets, or do they feature colorful locations, such as city streets, beaches, or mountain resorts?

Select a series that you like, that you feel comfortable with. It's always easier to write from positive inner feelings than from negative ones. Moreover, if you like a series, your feelings inevitably will be reflected in the words you put on paper.

Once familiar with the style and character of the series, you are ready to attempt a story. In building your story, try to involve the series' star or stars as centrally as you can. Why? Because audiences identify with the stars. Many writers tend to focus on characters they have created, allowing the series' stars to become almost peripheral. Such a story pattern can be self-defeating. Perhaps you can introduce a character from the permanent cast's background, thereby illuminating that background (producers will love you for this!) and involving the permanent cast deeply and emotionally in a story problem that concerns them.

Assuming that you have selected a series you like and have dreamed up a fresh and appropriate story, the next step is to put the story on paper. Sometimes writers submit treatments (the story described in prose-narrative form); more often they submit scripts. But even when they submit scripts, they must first write a treatment for themselves. Writers who attempt a screenplay without writing a detailed story outline or treatment doom themselves to mediocrity.

If your script gets read, it probably will be the story editor who reads it. The desks of most story editors groan from the weight of scripts submitted by agents or writers. Your job is to make it easy for a story editor to read your material. One hint: Clip a dazzling half-page summary of your story to the script's cover. Now the story editor can get a thumbnail description without having to wade through dozens of pages. If intrigued, he or she will open the cover and read the contents. If you've done your work well, you'll get a phone call, either from the producer or his or her business office or from your agent, if you've signed with one. The grim alternative, of course, is that the script will be returned.

If you receive a phone call, you may be asked to sell your story idea or you may be invited to meet with the producer. (Producers almost never produce a script as submitted. Every script goes through a series of rewrites and polishes.) Even though you live a thousand miles away, you should try, if at all possible, to meet with the producer. If you're going to work as a writer, you have to be where the action is. And most of the television action is in Los Angeles.

The producer will probably be bright, friendly, interested in your ideas. He or she will applaud the elements that work in your script and will tactfully describe the elements that need fixing. Remember, the producer is far more familiar with the series than you are. He or she knows the stars' pet peeves, the budget problems, the sponsors' taboos, and the content of scripts in the works. So listen attentively and look for answers to the producer's problems rather than clinging defensively to favorite plot gambits.

Sometimes a series asks to buy your idea with the intention of giving the project to a staff member for the rewrite. Use all of your persuasive powers to avoid this. The sale of a script will look far more impressive on your résumé than will a simple story credit. Promise to do the rewrite for nothing, if necessary. If the series refuses to allow you that privilege, then you must agree to sell your idea.

After you have submitted your script and a signed release form, you wait apprehensively for an answer. How long should you wait? If you have an agent, he or she will nag the producer. If you don't have an agent, you should wait a month or two and then write, telegraph, or telephone the story editor. You may have trouble getting your phone call through. Secretaries are fiercely protective of their bosses. Sometimes, surprisingly, it's easier to reach the producer than the story editor.

Once you get through, you have only a few seconds to convince the story editor or producer that you have something they need, an innovative idea, a surprising new story direction, whatever. Let them feel that you're a professional, that you've written before: for newspapers, advertising agencies, New York publishers, or Canadian feature films. Most producers have been burned by incompetent writers. They don't want to waste time on amateurs. They need to feel that if they read your script, it will pay off.

New TV Series.   Avoid them. New series frequently have trouble finding their way. Here's the disquieting pattern: A production company makes a **pilot** (a sample program, filmed for sales purposes). The pilot sells. Perhaps it sells with the proviso that one of the stars be replaced or a character concept changed. As the producer begins the preparation of scripts, the network may suggest other changes, alarmed by treatments that go in unexpected directions. Reexamination by the network during this preproduction period may even fundamentally change the series.

Early scripts may be far from perfect. At the outset on any new series, the producers and writers are finding their way, exploring new directions, determining what works and what doesn't. The network or production executives may be unnerved by early scripts and suggest other changes in the series concept.

Once the show airs, ratings may not be optimum. Networks become apprehensive, suggesting further changes, some of them drastic. Writers who began scripts with the initial concept must now stop and revise their scripts to accommodate the changes. Sometimes, if a series is in trouble (which is normal for most new series), concepts change three or four times. Writers who work for such series are caught in a meat grinder. They good-humoredly agree to revise their stories, but before they can turn in a first draft, the series concept has changed. When they rewrite it, which may represent an enormous amount of effort and time, they discover in shock that the concept has changed again.

Don't wander into that chamber of horrors. Don't waste your valuable creative efforts on new TV series. After a show has been on television for a season or two, the network and producer understand it. They know where the pitfalls lie. They know what to look for in scripts. And writers can watch the series on television and determine with some accuracy what the producer really wants.

TV MOVIES

TV movies apparently represent a smaller market than TV series, and yet they offer far more opportunities for new writers. First, when you write for a series, you're writing for a specific format and specific characters. Yes, there are many series, but you're writing for just one. If your script is rejected, you're stuck with it. There's no place else to market it. True, you can change the story and characters, adapting them to another series. But that usually involves a major reworking; you're almost starting over. To be sure, you (or your agent) can exhibit the script as an example of your work. But that's not a sale.

Secondly, writing for a series is something of a crap shoot. You're writing in limbo. You cannot know what other stories are in work. The producer may already have assigned someone to write a story identical to yours. You don't know what taboos the network or advertisers have imposed or the likes and dislikes of the producer. You're gambling a couple of months of your creative time (and a lot of damned hard work) that you can come up with all the right creative elements. If you want to gamble, fine. But you should realize that it's a long shot.

Writing for TV movies has many advantages over writing for series. First, you're dealing with your own characters rather than someone else's. Chances are, you will understand them better, feel closer to them, be more capable of bringing them to life on paper.

Second, multiple markets now open up to you. If one production company turns you down, you can submit your script to another. If several production companies reject your script, you still have access to the three commercial networks. (Production companies often determine network interest in a project before they commit themselves to it.) Beyond the commercial networks, you have potential markets in Public Broadcasting and cable companies such as Home Box Office (HBO), Showtime, USA, Turner, and Lifetime. If no one in television wants to tackle your script, you still can turn to the motion picture industry, which has dozens of production companies and independent producers.

Finally, if a movie script doesn't sell at once, perhaps it will sell next year or five years from now. Tuck it away in a file drawer for a year or two. Then dust it off, polish it, and market it again. Such timelessness doesn't exist for a TV series, which may be off the air a year from now.

That's the good news about writing for TV movies; there's also bad news. Commercial networks usually prefer to be a part of the development of a movie project from the beginning. If they like your screenplay, it's unlikely that they will produce it as written. If they are impressed by your writing and your concept, they will probably invite you to a meeting to discuss the concept with you and, most importantly, *how they would like to see it developed*. The network may offer you (directly or through your agent) a developmental deal. That is, a sum of money for a new treatment, additional money for the screenplay, and a final sum if the screenplay is actually produced. Yes, you are beginning over but at least you have sold yourself and the quality of your writing. You have a deal. And that counts for a lot.

Sometimes it is difficult to disengage yourself from a screenplay on which you've spent months conceiving a story, constructing a screenplay, massaging its scenes, refining its dialog, agonizing over every comma. Often you feel that your version was the better one. But part of becoming a professional is letting go, accepting new ideas and new directions, especially when those new directions represent a new source of income.

SELLING TO MOTION PICTURES

For writers, the sale of a motion picture screenplay represents the top rung of the ladder, particularly if the screenplay is actually filmed and especially if it emerges as a prestigious, class A production. As with other markets, writing for feature films has both advantages and disadvantages.

ADVANTAGES

Motion pictures can make you look good. Because their budgets usually are larger than those of TV shows, feature films can afford better stars, a finer director, and more spectacular production values (lavish sets, costumes, locations). Because of their larger budgets, movies can schedule more production time than television, allowing months rather than weeks to film a project. The additional time permits greater refinement in almost every production area and most notably in staging and performance.

You also have greater story freedom in motion pictures. Producers will accept almost any subject matter, the more adventurous or outrageous the better. Television tends to stick to familiar, tested areas and to story material that will offend no one.

A survey several years ago revealed that motion picture audiences were largely between the ages of fourteen and twenty-four. This information has colored the thinking of many commercially minded producers who tailor their films for that specific age group. They concentrate on material that reflects rebellion against authority, that deals with teen problems, and that is strongly sexually oriented.

Because motion pictures are designed initially for theatrical exhibition, they may be more sexually explicit than television material and more graphically violent. Commercial networks censor all material — especially in areas of sex and violence — because TV shows usually are family oriented and viewed in the home. Now that videocassettes are proliferating, movie producers may eventually place greater emphasis on family-oriented subject matter.

A final advantage of selling to motion pictures rather than television: It usually pays better. Top writers during a "feeding frenzy" (multiple eager competing buyers) have made as much as three million dollars for a single screenplay, although such extravagant figures seem now to be diminishing somewhat. TV series and movies pay handsomely, but they cannot match the salaries in the motion picture industry.

An agent can help writers to merchandise their screenplays by *packaging* them — that is, by finding a star or director or both to be part of the screenplay package. Such a commercially viable package can be most attractive to a studio or production company because some of the difficult preparatory work has been done for them. For packaging, agents receive 10 percent "off the top," that is, for the writer-director-star package, which can represent a sizable sum.

For a writer, packaging can also have negative aspects. As part of an agency package, the writer must serve the needs of the packager, meaning that he or she may have to rewrite the screenplay to make the package more salable or more acceptable creatively for the director or star. There can be a conflict of interests here because an agency may feel it is politically more expedient to serve the demands of a bankable star or director than to serve the needs of the writer, perhaps in the process sacrificing the writer's best interests.

Industry colleagues have told me they feel that writing a feature motion picture screenplay represents a beginning writer's best avenue for getting started. Understand, there is no right way or wrong way to get started. What works for one writer may prove disastrous for another. Luck is always a factor. And the nature and quality of the material is the most important factor of all; is it subject matter that today's producers will respond to positively and is it well written?

If your screenplay doesn't sell as a feature motion picture, other options remain. Perhaps you can sell it as a television movie. Failing that, you will have created an effective writing sample, a "calling card" script with which to entice agents or producers. Over the years, countless screenwriters have been hired by producers who read and liked their material. A writing sample doesn't have to be a movie screenplay. An episodic script would suffice, provided its quality were good enough.

One market that is frequently overlooked by aspiring writers consists of producers of low-budget and nonunion feature films. These small production companies are off the beaten track and usually interested in screenplays they can buy for a few thousand dollars. You won't get rich selling to such companies, but a sale, any kind of sale, will do wonders for your morale and will instantly transform you from an amateur into a professional.

Screenwriter Edward Jay Whetmore brings a bonus to this chapter with a way of tapping into the low budget and nonunion market.* Read his words carefully. They make enormous sense.

"Nobody knows anything."

When screenwriter William Goldman (*Marathon Man, Butch Cassidy and the Sundance Kid*) coined this oft-quoted Hollywood phrase in his book *Adventures in the Screen Trade,* he explained that "not one person in the entire motion picture field knows for a certainty what's going to work." He was talking about the sticky business of predicting the next blockbuster movie — but the same can be said for the sticky business of becoming a successful screenwriter.

"Nobody knows anything."

When I first came to Hollywood I was told that the only way to establish yourself as a screenwriter was to get an agent. So I spent months mailing screenplays to various agents. There were follow-up calls. There were rude secretaries. There were phone calls unreturned. Landing an agent as an unknown screenwriter is reminiscent of Groucho Marx's quip about not wanting to be in any club that would accept him as a member. The agent you want is not the one who spends time going through piles of unsolicited scripts. *The way to get an agent is to get a deal.* No matter how powerful they may be, agents

*Reprinted by permission of Edward Jay Whetmore.

do not make deals. Producers who buy scripts and shoot movies make deals. These are the folks you want to put your efforts into contacting. They are the ones who should be treating you rudely and shunning your phone calls.

"O.K., but how can I get through to MGM or Paramount? Only a super agent with great contacts can do that." The thing is — you *don't want* to reach the seven major studios. You want to reach the other thousand or so independent production companies, all of whom employ legions of readers and executives in search of one thing and one thing only: a great script. Your script.

What's more — you don't want to waste your time pitching your love story to a company that makes a steady stream of action films about Vietnam. But since "nobody knows anything," how do you know?

Here's one sure-fire method employed by many insiders that has yet to appear in print as far as I know. Four times each year *The Hollywood Reporter* and *Daily Variety* publish bulky Special Editions in conjunction with each of the international film marketing events. Whether it's the glitz of Cannes or the chaos of the American Film Market, each is a convention of sorts where producers and distributors get together to attend screenings and cut deals. Reading these special editions will tell you which companies are active in the marketplace and what kinds of films they are making.

Successful low- and medium-budget producers tend to stick with tried and true formulas. Your task is finding the companies that have already done your type of project successfully. Yes, your film is unique, but in almost every case it can be described as a "relationship film," "buddy movie," "teen thriller," "horror movie," "psychological drama," or whatever.

Once you've narrowed the list, get on the phone. Call the company and simply ask who handles incoming scripts. When you reach someone, begin by letting them know you're knowledgeable about their company. "I loved *Killer Bimbos from Outer Space*," you might say, "and I just know you'd want to take a look at my script. It has many of the same elements — but with some great new twists."

Then you pitch your story to them. Try to keep it to a minute or so but don't hesitate to go longer if you're sure you have their attention. Beforehand, practice on anyone who will listen. Use a tape recorder. Eventually the person on the phone will say something like "O.K., we'll take a look at it." Be sure to ask if they would like a release form. [See "Protecting Your Work" earlier in this chapter.]

But maybe they say "No thanks. We have eight pictures just like that in development." Either way, you follow up with a letter thanking them for their time. You want to establish a *relationship*. Hollywood is a place where relationships are everything. Above all, you want them to remember your name and the call. You're on your way to building your own network of contacts with people who are in a position to *buy* what you have to sell.

Selling your own screenplay will put you in a position to land a quality agent and give you the confidence and credentials you need to build a career. Agents love nothing better than "done deals." The hardest part of their job has already been done for them. Nevertheless, they can be useful in negotiating the best possible contract terms for your project. Since their fee is 10 percent of your earnings, you can be sure they will extract the maximum from the producer.

Of course, none of this matters unless you are sure you have a salable screenplay in hand. Even though "nobody knows anything," everyone who reads scripts for a living can spot the work of an amateur a mile away. That's why proper format is a must. Obtaining a copy of a *current* screenplay in your genre will help.

The main thing to remember is that while Hollywood is a town overloaded with scripts, there is always a severe shortage of original, innovative, and interesting stories. If yours is one of them, don't overlook the low-budget market. It has provided a starting place for many of today's best-paid screenwriters.

DISADVANTAGES

Despite the advantages cited above, hundreds of writers turn their backs on the motion picture industry. Why? Because the market size is limited. Since 1946 the number of films produced each year has steadily decreased. Television is one cause; another was a court decision forcing studios to divest themselves of their theaters.* Also, inflated costs have made the bankrolling of feature films more difficult. Inexpensive films that once were made for under a hundred thousand dollars now cost as much as five million, and more prestigious features today soar closer and closer to the hundred million figure.

Television, on the other hand, seems to be growing in scope. While audiences for commercial networks have dwindled slightly, the growth of PBS and the proliferation of cable channels have expanded an already large market, creating a growing programming void. The syndication of old series and old TV and theatrical movies fills part of this void, but the need for new programming is still enormous. And almost all programming begins with the script.

Therefore, despite the writer's difficulties in making initial sales (true of any writing market), television seems to offer a greater potential for beginning writers than most other media because of its continuing hunger for material.

---

*The so-called Paramount decision of 1949, a result of lawsuits filed by independent theater owners.

In addition, motion pictures sometimes are two and three years in preparation. In that same time frame, a successful writer can sell three or four TV screenplays. The faster turnover makes for greater emotional security.

ADAPTING A NOVEL

Selling an original screenplay represents the optimum in dollars and prestige for many writers. Adapting a novel represents a different, but certainly attractive, avenue for sales. Some years ago, director Norman Jewison planned a trip to Los Angeles to discuss a feature project with the Mirisch Company. At the New York airport, he bought a paperback to read on the plane. It was called *In the Heat of the Night*.

When he arrived in Los Angeles, Jewison took the novel to Walter Mirisch, excited at the possibility of converting his discovery into a film. Mirisch called the publisher, discovered that rights to the novel were available, and optioned it. Two years later the film was celebrated for its suspenseful story values as well as it pungent social commentary; it won multiple Academy Awards.

Producers generally are insecure. With millions of dollars as well as their reputations at stake, they look for screenplays that cannot fail. (Such a screenplay, of course, doesn't exist.) When a writer submits a script adapted from a successful novel or submits the novel itself, the producer can find security in the fact that someone liked the story well enough to publish it and thousands of people were sufficiently interested in the subject to buy it. Thus, adapting a novel can act as a security blanket for a writer's submission.

But don't submit a novel or a screenplay adaptation until you have taken an option on the motion picture rights. Without those rights, the producer doesn't need you. He or she can call the publisher, make a deal, and hire a favorite writer, leaving you with a pat on the head and out in the cold.

Realistically, it's not always easy to find a novel like *In the Heat of the Night*. The difficulty is compounded by the fact that studios and major independents, alerted by publishers, often read galley proofs of likely new novels. They also subscribe to services (such as the Virginia Kirkus Service) that describe and evaluate forthcoming novels. But the volume of novels published each year is enormous; studios cannot read them all. And unproduced novels from last year and the year before are still on store shelves.

If a novel grabs your interest, don't write an adaptation until you find out if the screen rights are available. Spending months writing an adaptation and then discovering that screenplay rights are already owned by a studio is a tragic waste of time. Write the publisher. You'll find publishers' addresses and names of department heads in a book called *Literary Market Place* published yearly by

Bowker and available at most public libraries. The publisher will either give you an answer or will provide the name of the author's agent.

Warning: Rights to successful novels can be expensive. You probably need only an option. But be smart; hire a lawyer—if possible, an entertainment lawyer—to represent you in negotiating for any property. Contracts for published material can be complicated and require expertise in motion picture practices.

METAPHYSICS OF SUCCESS

G worked as a casting assistant for a TV series, spending each day on the telephone contacting agents. During one winter hiatus, he wrote a script on **spec** (speculating with his time). When the series again began production, he submitted it to the producer. The producer read it and found that it duplicated other scripts in work, but he was sufficiently impressed with G's writing ability that he gave him a commitment to develop another script.

Altogether that year, G wrote six scripts for the series. He quit his job with the casting company after the first three, devoting himself to writing full time. In the years since, he has become one of television's most sought-after writer-producers. You've seen his name on many series and some of TV's most prestigious movies.

B worked as an assistant editor for Universal. He submitted an idea to a TV series; it was only a treatment, but it demonstrated such an understanding of the nature and problems of the series that the producer was impressed. He decided to let the writer do a rewrite on a script in trouble. The writer did a workmanlike job, but problems still remained. The producer and writer locked themselves in a room, going through the script act by act, scene by scene, page by page. The writer went home. With only days before preproduction, he worked around the clock, missing meals and sleep, to accomplish everything that he and the producer had discussed. Bleary eyed but triumphant, he brought the script in forty-eight hours later. The producer changed two words (the title) and filmed it as written. Five years later, on another series, B won a Writers Guild Award for best script of the year. He works now as a successful writer-director.

A third writer, T, was a student in one of my classes. She did excellent work during the semester, but when the final project was due (an original thirty-page script), T was nowhere to be found. I was disappointed; she had shown considerable promise. At the end of Christmas vacation T knocked on my office door, sheepish and yet proud. She had gotten so excited by her story that she had allowed it to develop, mushrooming in size. At the end of the semester it was only partially finished. Rather than turn in a half-finished screenplay, she had continued to write all through Christmas vacation. She handed me a fat envelope. I gulped. It contained over a hundred pages!

The screenplay was uneven, occasionally brilliant, occasionally lacking in logic. But T had demonstrated professional ability and come up with some genuinely creative ideas. Six months later when I was producing a miniseries for ABC, I called her in and assigned her a rewrite. A year later, she had a staff position on a police series, happily writing full time.

These three stories demonstrate that there is no single correct way to break into the profession; writers can emerge from anywhere. Although these three writers were laboring in different fields, they knew where they were going; they had selected a goal and worked to get there. They believed in themselves.

A very corny, old-fashioned word applies: perseverance. Because the entertainment field is competitive, success usually is not quickly achieved. Aspiring writers need to write and keep writing, to submit and keep submitting, to use whatever industry contacts they have, to keep knocking on doors. They have to believe that someone — sometime, somewhere, somehow — will read their material and give them a break.

The scripts for many successful feature films and TV series were rejected the first time around. Sometimes those scripts were rejected by every studio in town — and more than once. *One Flew over the Cuckoo's Nest* is a typical example. "Too downbeat," all of the studios exclaimed. "Audiences will never pay to see it." Finally, when Jack Nicholson committed himself to the project, someone took a chance. As you know, *Cuckoo's Nest* ultimately won Academy Awards in every creative category — seven in all! The moral: Keep knocking on doors. Persevere.

One of the first TV series I ever produced, "The Untouchables," was adapted from a published biography. It was offered to every studio in town. Every studio turned it down until, finally, Desilu took a chance. It became ABC's first hit series. The moral: Keep knocking on doors. Persevere.

Every month of every year new writers break into the entertainment industry. They have to come from somewhere. If you have ability, there's no reason why one of them can't be you.

Keep knocking on doors. Persevere.

CHAPTER HIGHLIGHTS

➢ Most professional writers are bright, possess strong liberal arts backgrounds, and have a keen awareness of world happenings. They stimulate their imaginations by reading novels and seeing fine motion pictures and plays.

➤ Successful screenwriters discipline themselves. They write daily to maintain fluency. They demonstrate professionalism in their scripts through proper spelling and format.

➤ Many writers protect their work from plagiarism by registering it with the Writers Guild or through copyright. Production companies and networks protect themselves from plagiarism lawsuits by having writers sign release forms. New writers are needlessly wary of such forms. Writers need to show their material as often as possible.

➤ Literary agents provide protection for both writers and producers and can be helpful in marketing material. New writers often get shortchanged in large agencies. They receive more attention in small ones, provided the agent believes in them.

➤ Television series provide a limited market for new writers because many employ writing staffs and generally ignore outside material. Because they repeatedly change format, new series present frustrating problems for writers.

➤ When submitting to series, writers should send material to story editors and then follow through with letters, telegrams, or phone calls. Appending an intriguing synopsis sometimes helps get material read. Speculative writing for a series is precarious.

➤ TV movies provide multiple opportunities for writers. Markets include production companies, networks, PBS, and cable companies, as well as feature film producers. Writers may feature their own characters.

➤ Motion pictures present the optimum in prestige and remuneration. They also offer greater quality and more latitude in subject matter. Because the movie market is small, few screenplays are filmed. Adaptations of novels sometimes present opportunities if writers first secure options on movie rights.

➤ Successful writers are goal oriented. They come from many different worlds but all have a single-minded sense of purpose. In spite of competition, they persevere.

SCRIPTWRITING PROJECTS

EXERCISES DESIGNED TO SHARPEN YOUR NARRATIVE SKILLS

TV SERIES

Select a favorite TV series and then study it as if you were going to write for it. Based on no fewer than three viewings, write a detailed description of the following areas:

1. *The characters.* The full name of each and as much background history as you can determine. Relationships between characters, habits, clothing styles, personality, type of car, profession, and so forth.

2. *Script patterns.* The kinds of stories usually presented, for example, action-adventure or situation comedy. Is the story pattern dramatized from a star's point of view? How are other continuing characters used? If more than one plot is used, how are multiple plots interconnected?

3. *Production patterns.* Does the series use the same interior set(s) every week or use colorful locations? Does the series use guest stars or rely solely on its permanent cast? Size of cast? Stunts? Extras?

Devise an original story for this series (a paragraph or two) that reflects items 1, 2, and 3 above. The story should capture the style and character of recent episodes and should feature one of the series' stars.

NEWSPAPERS AS A STORY SOURCE

Select a recent newspaper story that provides the springboard for a theatrical or TV movie. Paste the newspaper story to page one of your presentation. Write a brief dramatic adaptation of this news story on page two. Describe the primary characters, including protagonist and antagonist, and suggest a beginning, middle, and end.

WRITER REVELATIONS

ODYSSEY OF A NEW WRITER

One of my former screenwriting students telephoned me one day and asked a question. "Can you tell me who earned the most money for a script of any female writer in history?" I hazarded a few guesses and she said, "You're wrong. It's me!"

Kathy McWhorter had sold a screenplay to Paramount Pictures for a cool one million dollars, more money than anyone, anywhere had ever paid a woman writer. She was suddenly the subject of articles in newspapers and national magazines. Virtually overnight her name was recognized by writers, directors, and producers throughout the entertainment industry. Kathy's saga is an amazing one. It may help you find the appropriate career path or to avoid missteps.

Read her words. They will restore your faith in fairy tales. Cinderella is alive and well.

$\mathcal{I}$ always believed that if stardom could happen to Joe Schmoe, it could happen to me. Ten months ago, it did.

I went back to college when I was twenty-three. I was tired of being a day-care teacher's aide. Tired of making five dollars and twenty-five cents an hour. Tired of having to live with my mom and grandma. I wanted a career in pictures. I wanted to write movies that would win Academy Awards and maybe even change people's lives. But how do you scale those heights with only a high school degree and a job that leaves crayon marks on your clothing? I remember sitting on a park bench one afternoon. My life was going nowhere and I was so depressed that I started to cry. And I thought, what is it that successful people have that I don't? They have a plan.

I decided I would start all over. Work my way through junior college, transfer to the least expensive four-year college that offered a screenwriting department, and while I was there I would write the best four screenplays I was capable of. I would write constantly. I would stockpile the little suckers. And I'd produce as many different genres as possible so that I'd have a variety of styles to represent my ability.

In the four and a half years that followed, I took as many classes as I could. I paid close attention to them all because I figured the more subjects I knew about, the more plot ideas I'd be able to hatch.

It took me two years to finish my first screenplay, "The Boy Who Eats Rocks." With one completed script, I was ready to find an agent. But how? When you're starting out, everywhere you look you face a Catch-22. You can't get an agent unless you have an agent or you've already sold something. And if you've already sold something, what do you need an agent for? You gotta know somebody, right?

But I figured, "Hell, if Joe Schmoe can get an agent, why not me?" So I formulated another plan. The first thing I did was buy a copy of *The Writer's Market* (published by Writer's Digest), which lists about 40,000 places to sell your writing. The best thing about the book is that it tells you step by step how to write letters designed to get agents interested in your work and how to make charming follow-up calls.

After reading this book I wrote a short query letter describing myself and a few of my ideas. Then I got a copy of the Writers Guild list of literary agents (which the WGA will send you for $2). On that list I found about ten agencies that expressed an interest in seeing work from new writers. I sent my letter to six of them. In three weeks I had my first agent. He wasn't a great agent. He wasn't even a good agent. But he got my work out there. It got noticed by a few development executives and one of these people helped me to find another agent.

Development people, by the way, can be enormously helpful in setting up a writer with an agent. After all, they talk to literary agents all day. Say you don't have an agent and you don't know anyone in development. Get a studio list. Call development offices. Find out the names of the development people. Just ask. Send them a letter. Tell them you're a big fan of the company's work and that you're a young writer; ask if they would be willing to read your work and tell you if you have talent. Tell them you're not looking to sell them anything, you just want their opinion. Most of them will say no. A few will say yes. If the ones who say yes like your material, ask them if they would recommend an agent who is looking for new clients, and would it be okay to drop their names. It's worth a try.

By the time I landed my second agent, I had finished my second screenplay. We were sending them both out about the same time and I was having meetings with a lot of producers around town. I was young and goofy and incredibly naive. I spilled my guts about my whole life and I made a lot of friends that way. Lots of people were interested in my work. No one wanted to buy it.

Then, one week before graduation, my second script, "Bats," was optioned by an independent producer. A month or so later, "The Boy Who Eats Rocks" (which will be produced in spring 1993) was optioned by Tri Star. Three months after that, I sold my third script, "The Cheese Stands Alone," for one million dollars. In one afternoon I went from being a relative unknown to the highest paid female screenwriter in history. I had finally walked through Hollywood's golden gates. My little park bench plan had worked.

Less than a week later, my story was in all the trade papers. TV shows were calling for interviews and I was being whisked off to New York to meet the people who had purchased my script. Did my problems end? Hardly. Am I a happier person for it? I feel about the same as always. Do I feel that I've finally made it? That's the strangest part of all. I know now that there's no such thing as "making it." Success is a journey, not a destination.

People have asked me: What is it like to be an overnight success, a millionaire, a name in Hollywood? I'll tell you the truth, it ain't half bad. It means sometimes getting chauffeured around in limousines, staying in the finest hotels, and meeting a lot of creative geniuses. It means getting tickets to premieres and having enough money to buy decent clothes to wear to them. It means having the power to communicate your ideas to audiences. It means doing what you want to do and being well compensated for it.

But — it also means taking meetings at night and on weekends. Cancelling long-awaited vacations because a project that's been lying around doing nothing suddenly demands immediate attention. It means having to fight for your work and in some cases having to step away from your project so that another writer can come in and rewrite you. It's knowing that if your next script isn't as good as your last, the whole town will be talking about it. It's having everyone you know ask to borrow huge sums of money. It means having to hire three or four people to handle your business affairs because, truly, your own life is no longer something you can govern alone. Is it fun? Yeah, it's fun. Is it a pain in the ass? Absolutely. Is it worth going for?

Well, I'll tell ya. If what you want most of all is a soft, noncombative life, you've probably chosen a disappointing path. On the other hand, if all you really want to do is write — if your greatest pleasure is in the simple act of putting words and ideas on paper — if you know in your heart that you were born to write, with or without success — then you're destined to walk this path, no matter what. For those of you who know what I'm talking about, just keep this in mind: If Joe Schmoe can make it, maybe you can too.

TWENTY QUESTIONS

What follows is a checklist that may help you spot (and correct) trouble areas in your concept, treatment, and screenplay.

1. Did you select a concept that excites you, that you can feel passionate about?

2. Does your concept have sufficient color, freshness, or human appeal to intrigue audiences?

3. Can audiences become emotionally involved with your protagonist? Deeply involved?

4. Does your protagonist have a worthwhile goal in your story?

5. Does a strong antagonist fight to keep your protagonist from reaching that goal?

6. Do you introduce all or most of your major characters in the first act?

7. Do you introduce your major story problem in the first act?

8. Do you hook your audience early? If you cannot introduce your major problem until late in the act, have you created another, smaller problem — or scenes with sufficient entertainment — so that the audience won't lose interest?

9. Does the tension build from scene to scene? From act to act? (Does your protagonist's problem worsen?)

10. Does every scene either move your story forward or reveal some significant new fact about a major character?

11. Does every scene contain the seeds of conflict?

12. Did you create characters who contrast with each other?

13. Does every character contribute to your main story line?

14. Have you managed to avoid clichés in plot, characters, and dialog?

15. Is your dialog economical? (Have you pruned it for redundancy? Eliminated meaningless detail?)

16. Is each character's dialog appropriate to that character and no other?

17. Is your dialog generally simple? Does it have the sound of everyday speech?

18. Did you try to visualize the setting and action as you wrote your scenes? Did you include appropriate character business?

19. Now that you have completed your screenplay, you can ascertain if it has a theme. What is that theme? Are all of your scenes and narrative actions consistent in expressing that theme?

20. Does your screenplay form look crisp and professional? Are you guilty of telling your story in stage directions?

Good luck with your writing. Remember that the only way to improve is by being dissatisfied!

CHAPTER 10 SCRIPTWRITING PROJECT

What follows is the corrected version of the haunted house scene at the conclusion of Chapter 10.

FADE IN:

INT. HAUNTED HOUSE - NIGHT

A sudden FLASH of LIGHTNING illuminates the room as teenaged DEBBIE LOGAN trembles in fear. A loud MOAN startles her. She picks up the phone and dials.

                      DEBBIE
             Brad, Brad, I'm so scared!

INT. DEN - NIGHT

BRAD BASCOM, a supercilious young man, sips his brandy and tries to soothe her.

                      BRAD
             Don't be such a goddamned coward. Just get the
             money and leave.

                                    INTERCUT:

                      DEBBIE
             (trembling)
       Where?

                      BRAD
             In the suit of armor, dummy.

Debbie looks around and spots it.

HER POV

The Suit of Armor across the room. The MOANS seem LOUDER. The Suit of Armor walks toward Debbie, its rusted metal joints CREAKING.

ANGLE ON DEBBIE

Gripping the phone, knuckles white.

DEBBIE
It—it's coming toward me!

BRAD
Just lift off the helmet, chicken little. The
money's inside.

Nervously she lifts the visor from the faceplate. Sure enough, there's
money inside. Debbie grabs it and exits fast. The Suit of Armor picks up
the phone.

SUIT
Brad?

BRAD
Yeah?

The Suit of Armor MOANS CHILLINGLY into the phone. Brad gasps,
screams, wets his pants, and runs off.

FADE OUT

*T*HE MARK: A TREATMENT FOR A TELEVISION MOVIE

It's a year and a half since the incident in the Honolulu PX, and DAVE CAR-LIN has almost managed to erase it from his mind. He's a civilian now. That helps. He's had some therapy. That also helps. And he's fallen in love with a spectacularly beautiful girl. That helps most of all.

Now, returning to his drafting table at a San Francisco construction company, he glances idly out the window and almost blacks out from a sudden spasm of terror. Below in the yard, walking along the line of parked trucks, searching, stalking a prey, is (impossibly) THE MAN! The man from the Honolulu PX—and from a thousand forgotten childhood nightmares!

How do you know when someone threatens your life? Is it animal instinct, some inner awareness that nature has implanted for self-preservation? Dave Carlin knows. He knows with unmistakable certainty that this tall, grotesquely handsome stranger is his enemy. An enemy on the elemental level of life and death.

He races across the room, down the stairs, and into the corridor, and bursts out the door and into the yard, just in time to glimpse the man disappearing through the front gate. Dave streaks after him, knowing he must stop him and find out what it all means. Why is he being pursued? There's no other possible conclusion. First the encounter in Honolulu. Now here, half a world away — the man appears again, apparently searching for him. A man he has never met except in the innermost corners of his mind.

Dave races to the gate and looks down the street. The man is getting into a white Corvette. It pulls away from the curb and disappears in the late afternoon traffic.

Thus begins a bizarre series of events in which Dave Carlin discovers the nightmare world of his own past.

He recounts part of it for JILL ATHERTON, the stunning twenty-four-year-old he has understandably fallen in love with. Three years ago Dave had been wounded in Vietnam. The Army sent him to a hospital in Honolulu. His wounds healed slowly.

One afternoon he went to the main PX to pick up some beer and blew his mind. The reason: He encountered a tall, grotesquely handsome man he had never actually met but whose face haunted Dave all through childhood, a face that had repeatedly awakened him in the night and sent him sobbing to his parents' bed for comfort.

In that Honolulu PX, Dave Carlin's war-weary mind exploded in sudden rage. Convinced that this man (for whatever reason) was determined to kill him, Dave grabbed a knife from a counter and hurled himself at the stranger, slashing at him. M.P.s finally dragged him away; Dave was incoherent, screaming threats.

Army doctors blamed the incident on battle fatigue and sent Dave back to the States, where he was given a medical discharge. Subsequently, he'd gotten psychiatric help, but the V.A. doctor had been unable to diagnose the strange series of circumstances.

Now, today, incredibly, Dave saw that same man again. He describes to Jill the chase through the construction yard and the stranger's escape in the white Corvette. He doesn't notice Jill's sudden reaction to his mention of the white Corvette.

There's fog. The cobblestone street echoes with the horse's metallic clip-clop as it pulls the carriage past a lone man standing in front of an apothecary shop. The carriage disappears into the fog. The man, dressed in handsome nineteenth-century clothing, checks his pocket watch in the lamplight. It is Carlin. Clearly he's waiting to keep an appointment.

A woman comes by and murmurs something to him. He waves her away. Then another carriage emerges from the fog and stops at the curb. The door opens and a gaunt man appears. A man with a grotesquely handsome face. The background music is the theme heard earlier in the construction yard: eerie, melodic, played on a theremin.

The stranger carries a horsewhip. He raises it and lashes out savagely at Carlin. Again. And again. And again.

We're in Dave Carlin's bedroom. He screams hoarsely and sits up in bed, face glistening with sweat. He turns on the light.

ED MEISTER appears more hippie than psychiatrist, with his long hair, full down-swept mustache, and youthful face. He's thirty-one but looks a lot younger. Ed's a very "today" kind of guy: into metaphysics, parapsychology, chemotherapy, and whatever other new wrinkles may happen along to shake up the psychiatric establishment.

At the moment, he's fascinated with what Dave Carlin has told him. In the course of their psychiatric sessions, their doctor-patient relationship ripened and they became friends. So Ed's fascination is colored with genuine concern.

He pours Dave a cup of coffee and tries out a nutty idea on him. During the course of the last year, Ed has been reading the works of Dr. Ian Stevenson from the University of Virginia as well as those of Dr. Alexander Cannon. They and others have been researching an area of parapsychology scoffed at by most so-called intellectuals: reincarnation.

Dave almost spills his coffee. But Ed continues, grinning, acknowledging his friend's disbelief. He picks a volume from the bookshelf, and as he leafs through the pages, he tells Dave that Dr. Cannon has degrees from nine European universities and was knighted by the queen. And then he reads the following:

> For years, the theory of reincarnation was a nightmare to me, and I did my best to disprove it and even argued with my trance subjects to the effect that they were talking nonsense. And yet as the years went by, one subject after another told me the same story in spite of different and varied conscious beliefs. Now well over a thousand cases have been investigated, and I have to admit that there is such a thing as reincarnation!

Dave Carlin nods tiredly. He's read some of that stuff where you're a dog in one life and a monkey in another.

The psychiatrist shakes his head. That's not what he's talking about. He's talking about a person being reborn in another human body. A lot of very bright people have believed it can happen.

Such as?

Such as Plato, Pythagoras, Virgil, Ovid, Schopenhauer, Emerson, Walt Whitman, Carlyle, Thomas Edison, Luther Burbank. . . .

Dave whistles softly, impressed. Ed picks another volume from his bookshelf and reads a poem from English poet laureate John Masefield.

> I hold that when a person dies
> His soul returns again to earth
> Arrayed in some new flesh disguise,
> And another mother gives him birth.
> With sturdier limbs and brighter brain
> The old soul takes the roads again.

Psychiatrist Ed Meister believes that Dave Carlin conceivably has lived before, that Carlin's déjà vu relationship with the man from the Honolulu PX is a carryover from a previous existence. He believes the dream is a confirmation of this. He prevails on his stunned friend to allow him to try an experiment in hypnosis.

The psychiatrist puts Dave under and then slowly regresses him back through his teens, into his childhood, and then to infancy. Meister directs his subconscious mind to go back through the years, to remember a time before his birth. Then he asks Dave to describe what he sees.

The psychiatrist waits. But Dave is silent. His face twists as if in pain. Meister repeats his instructions. He repeats them again. And then the words come — slowly, laboriously, and in German. Meister's knowledge of German is sketchy, but he is able to converse haltingly with his hypnotized patient, asking questions.

The answers, in German, come from the tape recording that Meister has made. It is some time later. He has brought Dave out of hypnosis and the two are listening to the conversation. Dave, who understands no German at all, cannot believe the voice is his. Ed translates for him.

The time is the eighteenth century. The place: München (Munich), Germany. The speaker is a man named Karl Schoendienst, and he is desperately unhappy. His wife asks him what is wrong, and he will not tell her. In grief and pain he runs out of his home.

Now Meister takes us further back into Schoendienst's life. The German is in a marketplace. Another man comes up to him, a strange, evil man who stares at the small scar on Schoendienst's wrist. It is shaped like a half moon. The stranger grins and says something mocking, and Schoendienst hurls himself at the man, beating at him with his fists. He picks up a wooden mallet and. . . .

"No! Stop it!" Dave Carlin shrieks. Meister turns off the tape machine and gazes at his friend soberly. But Dave is staring at his wrist — at the small birthmark shaped like a half moon.

At her apartment, Jill Atherton pleads with Dave to take her away from San Francisco. She's afraid for him, afraid for herself, afraid that his "mysterious stranger" will destroy their plans for a future together.

Dave wants to stay. He's determined to find answers. He tells her about the sessions he has had with Meister and how significant he feels they are. He describes the experiment in regression and, with some embarrassment, the concept of reincarnation.

Jill sees the glint of fear in Dave's eyes and hugs him. She accuses him of being naive, a dreamer, a wide-eyed mystic. She adores him; she'd like to believe everything he believes but she cannot. She's just too damned practical. Please, why can't he forget all of Meister's mumbo jumbo and go away with her now? They had talked of living in Europe one day. Why can't they go now? Today?

Dave's a little puzzled at the desperation in her voice. He kisses her and says he'll think about it.

The driver of the white Corvette watches Dave drive away. He gets out of his car and goes to Jill's apartment.

When Jill hears the knock, she assumes it's Dave returning, that he has forgotten something. When she opens the door, her smile turns to ice.

The man, BEAL, slaps her. Hard. He throws her onto the couch. His face reflects his fury. She's like a bitch in heat. Every time he leaves the country, she's off in the bushes with another man.

Jill shakes her head in despair. It's not her fault. This man, this Carlin, made her come with him. He's crazy. She's afraid of him, afraid for her life!

She gets up from the couch and goes to Beal. She puts an arm around him, begging for forgiveness. It's Beal she loves. Only Beal. She kisses him on the neck. She has been miserable without him.

Beal stares at her. He says nothing, disbelieving.

Jill touches his face. "Would you like a drink, love?"

A long moment and then Beal nods slowly, old hungers returning. Yeah, he'd like a drink.

In Meister's office, Dave and the psychiatrist listen to a tape recording of their latest regression experiment. Dave's voice is speaking in the person of a fifth-century Roman soldier in Constantinople, in the hire of the emperor Justinian. The Fifth Ecumenical Congress has assembled, and the soldier (Dave) has spied among its members an old enemy whom he has just slain in a fight.

Meister turns off the tape recorder and gulps down the last of his coffee. He offers his friend a theory, for what it's worth. There can be no doubt in Meister's mind that Dave's psyche has appeared again and again through the centuries — in different bodies, in different countries. The psychiatrist believes that Dave, in each of his incarnations, has lived a predestined pattern. He and one specific other person, like actors whose moves on a stage have been carefully charted by the author, have inexorably searched for and found each other, with the same fateful result. Each time they met, Dave has emerged a killer.

But why? It's almost like a curse!

Meister shrugs. He doesn't like what it seems to suggest. He gets up and starts to pace. It's like saying that human volition has no meaning. "Unless someone — meaning you, of course — breaks the chain, makes friends with the enemy, refuses to do battle."

Dave shakes his head and then grins. He doesn't believe any of it. The whole concept is wild, impossible. But what the hell, if there is such a chain, he's going to break it!

Jill comes to Dave's apartment trembling, in a state of shock. She knows who his stranger is. She just left him. His name's Beal. He's her former husband, a psychotic, jealous man intent on Dave's destruction. She shows him the bruise on her face where Beal slapped her.

Dave wonders why, if Beal's no longer married to her, he should display such proprietary interest.

All right, Dave might as well know the truth. Jill takes a breath. She's still married to Beal. She has tried again and again to get a divorce, to escape him. But the man's a monster, fiercely possessive. She has run from him and always, always he finds her.

Jill holds Dave tightly, her eyes moist now. She's afraid — partly for herself but mostly for him. She loves Dave. He has become her life. She can't face the possibility of losing him.

Dave stares at her, concerned at the depth of her feeling, still acutely aware of his pledge to Meister. Is she certain that Beal means to kill him?

She nods. She has seen it happen before.

She ran off with a man before?

Jill shakes her head, shocked at the accusation. No, no, Beal merely thought she had. He almost shot an innocent man. Thank God the police prevented it. But this time he forced her to admit her love for Dave. This time he'll certainly carry it through.

She produces a small, pearl-handled pistol, presses it into his hand, and urges him to take it and to use it if Beal threatens him.

Dave hands it back to her. He has no intention of using a gun against anybody. Then a sudden thought strikes him. It would be convenient for her if he killed Beal, wouldn't it? She'd be out of an inescapable marriage, free to marry again.

Immediately contrite, Dave goes to her and takes her in his arms, ashamed of his accusation. He only wants the same thing she wants, for both of them to be free of the yokes they wear, to be together in a fulfilling new life.

He has to go to the construction site now to deliver some blueprints. He'll meet her afterward for dinner, okay?

She nods, holding him close. O.K. She slips the pearl-handled pistol into his pocket.

Beal takes his time in answering the telephone. The filtered voice tells him, "He's going to a construction site. It's at the corner of Geary and Polk."

Beal hangs up without bothering to thank Jill. He slips into his coat and leaves the motel room.

Dusk. The hard-hat crew has finished its work, crawling down from steel girders and heading for beer at Anselmo's.

Dave Carlin is on the building's second level. He watches the unit contractor make notes on his blueprints, ride the skeletal elevator down to ground level, and take off. Dave lights a cigarette and looks around at the silhouetted city, its windows great splashes of orange reflecting the sunset sky. It's very quiet. . . .

And then a voice from below. Beal. The gun in his hand is directed upward. Beal grins. He's lucky. He has a chance to get rid of Dave with no risk of being convicted. Dave's a psycho (Army records prove it) who forced Beal's wife to come away with him. She'll testify to that.

With quiet logic, Dave explains that Jill came with him willingly, that he never knew of their marriage. But Beal comes closer, unhearing, uncaring.

Suddenly Dave's hand finds the pearl-handled pistol in his pocket. He starts to withdraw it, then stops. He explains carefully to Beal that he has a gun but he will not use it. He has his reasons; he will not use the gun! Beal mutters an obscenity and fires at him. Dave ducks back behind a girder and withdraws the gun from his pocket. Then, with some effort, he forces himself to re-place it.

Beal fires again at Dave, wounding him in the side. Dave grimaces in pain, then scurries back, away from Beal. He climbs the ladder to the third level, taking cover by a pile of scrap metal debris, determined that he will not kill.

Relentlessly, Beal follows, climbing to the second level, again sighting his gun on Dave.

Frightened now, convinced that Beal will certainly kill him, Dave again takes the gun from his pocket, aims it, starts to squeeze the trigger, hand shaking, and then abruptly throws the gun from him. It lands on the second level. "It's over, Beal. The killing is over!"

Beal picks up the pistol and stares at it for a long moment, recognizing it, trying to understand why his wife's gun is in Dave's possession. Then he hurls it angrily aside, not liking his conclusion.

Beal again aims his gun. Dave darts back behind the pile of scrap metal debris, seeking protection. Beal walks along the steel beam to a position directly beneath Dave, for the first time finding an unobstructed line of sight. He smiles grimly, again taking aim. In a final move of desperation, Dave shoves at the debris and the metal tumbles noisily down between girders, down to the second level, smashing into Beal, knocking him from his precarious perch to the ground below. He lies very still.

Dave Carlin stares down at the body three floors beneath, shock and realization on his face. He closes his eyes, his hand pressing against the bullet wound. His mouth twists in pain.

Jill finds herself attracted to Ed Meister. She doesn't really believe any of that stuff about the endless generations of killing, but the tragedy at the construction site makes her curious.

Ed stares out the window at the San Francisco skyline. His voice is flat, almost bitter, as he recites his theory. He speculates that the killings may very well go all the way back to the Bible. Indeed, to the Old Testament.

Jill is incredulous. She reminds him that he had mentioned something about the birthmark on Dave's wrist. The half moon.

Ed nods. From one angle it looks like a half moon. From another, the mark looks like the letter C.

He walks into his office and closes the door, leaving Jill alone.

GLOSSARY

Note: Words that are traditionally capitalized in screenplays appear capitalized below.

Above the line — Those production elements traditionally placed at the top of a budget breakdown. The so-called artistic elements: writer, producer, executive producer, director, composer.

Act — A dramatic unit consisting of a number of individual scenes. Most hour TV shows divide into four acts, separated by commercials or station breaks. Movies often divide into three acts, usually without separation.

Action — Movement within a scene. Also, the events or developmental happenings of a screenplay, such as a protagonist falling in love.

Adaptation — A stageplay, novel, or short story rewritten as a screenplay.

Adversarial force — Usually the antagonist: a person, the environment, or a facet of the protagonist's character. For example, a fear.

Agent — *See* Literary agent.

All About Eve ending — The conclusion of a movie or TV show that parallels its beginning, creating the feeling that the show has come full circle.

Antagonist — The protagonist's adversary. That person, thing, or force that fights to prevent the protagonist from reaching his or her goal.

Antipathy — Intense dislike or hatred.

Arc — A character's growth, change, or development through the course of a screenplay.

Archetypes — Primordial images; characters, relationships, or events that are the subject matter of many myths, folk ballads, and fairy tales. They often strike deep responsive chords in an audience's subconscious mind.

Art director — The person who designs sets, coordinating visually related production materials.

Art films — Films outside the commercial mainstream purporting to be artistic. Often a psychological study of a character or relationship or a film that accentuates atmosphere.

Backstory — *See* Biography.

298

Bankable — Term applied to stars, directors, or scripts capable of generating financing for (usually) motion pictures.

Banner headline — As used in this text, the capital-letters heading that begins each camera shot, specifically stating the location, whether day or night, and sometimes the camera angle.

Beat — A momentary pause in dialog or action.

Below the line — Those production elements traditionally placed below the line in a budget breakdown, separating so-called artistic from technical components. For example, camera crew, electricians, carpenters, editing, transportation, and overhead.

b.g. — Background.

Biography — A character's history before the start of a screenplay, usually highlighting events of emotional significance. Sometimes called a *backstory*.

Blocking — The manipulation of performers or camera within a scene: their movement, relative positions, business.

Body language — A character's posture, physical attitude, or manner of movement, suggesting his or her emotional state.

Bookends — Script openings and closings that are similar or identical, enclosing the central body of the story. Sometimes used when an entire story is a flashback.

Breaking down a script — Describing the individual scenes, actors, and other production elements on cardboard strips and placing them on a production board.

Business — Literally, "busyness." The actions that characters perform within a scene, such as mixing a drink, applying lipstick, reading a newspaper, washing a car.

Catharsis, emotional — Purging one's self of (usually) painful emotions.

Characters — The fictional people who participate in the action of a screenplay.

Cinema verité — Literally, "truth cinema." Often used in documentary filmmaking. Cinema verité achieves a newsreel quality, avoiding the glossy studio look: life as it is rather than as idealized.

Cinematographer — Also called director of photography and cameraman. The person in charge of photographing screenplay action.

Cliché — A trite, hackneyed phrase or expression that has lost meaning through overuse.

CLOSE-UP (CLOSE SHOT) — A close angle (head and shoulders) to create impact, reveal detail, or to establish rapport between character and audience.

Coincidence — Events that happen by accident, apparently without logical cause or for the writer's convenience. *See* Deus ex Machina.

Conflict — Two forces in opposition. In screenplays, the main conflict occurs between the protagonist and antagonist. Most common dramatic conflicts are with other characters, with the environment (nature, society), and with one's self.

Contrasting characters — Characters with opposing points of view who tend to generate conflict in scenes together. As, for example, in *The Odd Couple*.

Covering the action — Photographing scenes in such a way that character actions can be clearly seen.

Crisis — A screenplay development in which the protagonist's goal appears threatened, often occurring at the end of an act. A plot turning point.

Cut — An instantaneous change of camera angle effected by joining together separate film or videotape segments or by electronically switching between cameras. Used both as a verb and a noun.

Denouement — The descending action following a story's climax, a resolution. The final knitting together of story elements.

Deus ex machina — Literally, "god from a machine." The expression describes events that occur without logical story preparation, apparently at the writer's convenience, often to solve the protagonist's problem.

Dialog — The words spoken by characters in a screenplay.

Dialog cues — Brief scripted suggestions to actors as to how dialog should be spoken.

DISSOLVE — A transition effect in which the picture of a concluding scene blends or melts into a new beginning scene, each briefly overlapping the other. Usually marks a change of scene or time lapse.

Drama — A play presented on stage, film, or videotape in which a protagonist struggles against an antagonist to reach a goal. A story told through the actions and dialog of actors.

Dubbing stage — Where sound effects and music are added to a film's (or videotape's) dialog track, creating a final composite track.

Editing — Splicing together the various "takes" that the director has photographed in order to create an effective narrative continuity.

Empathy — Awareness of a character's background or experiences, which affords a better understanding of that character's actions. An intellectual identification.

Emphasis — The stress that a writer or director places on elements believed to be significant. Close-ups, for example, add emphasis to significant dialog, actions, or reactions.

Ensemble film — A film with multiple protagonists.

Entertainment elements — Script ingredients that please audiences: spectacle (sound, motion, color), sex, conflict, order and symmetry, and humor and surprise.

Episodic — A screenplay or novel structured in a series of episodes, like articles of clothing pinned to a clothesline.

Exposition — Information that the audience needs to know to understand the story, the background and nature of its characters, and their relationships.

EXTERIOR (EXT.) — A script term that, together with a more specific locale, describes the exterior setting for a scene. For example, EXT. MANSION.

External motivations — Those motivations for movement in a scene that arise from sources outside the actor. For example, scripted instructions to answer a telephone.

Externalize — To reveal to an audience what is occurring within a character, usually through facial expression, gestures, actions, dialog, or use of symbols.

FADE IN — An optical effect in which the picture emerges from blackness to full brilliance.

FADE OUT — An optical effect in which the picture dissolves away, usually into blackness.

f.g. — Foreground.

Filter — The tinny or mechanical quality of sound reproduced over a telephone, radio, or loudspeaker. Also, a glass or gelatin element placed before a camera lens to alter the visual image.

First draft — The screenplay version that a writer first turns in to a producer.

Flashback — The dramatization of earlier events, usually from the perspective of a specific character and thus colored by his or her emotions.

Footage — Film or videotape of scenes or other screenplay material.

Foreshadowing — An indication of dramatic developments to come. Often used by writers as a device for building suspense.

Genre — A group of motion pictures or TV programs that reflect similar stylistic, thematic, and structural elements.

Guild — *See* Writers Guild.

Heavy — A slang term for a villain.

Identification — The perception of another as an extension of yourself. Becoming so absorbed in a character that you experience that character's emotions as your own.

Inciting incident — An event that triggers the story, that launches the major story problem.

Incongruous—A comedy category that places together elements that seem wrong for each other, that are mismatched or inappropriate.

INTERCUT—Sometimes used where two simultaneous (but dramatically connected) actions are taking place. This script term replaces numerous cuts from locale to locale, as in telephone conversations.

INTERIOR (INT.)—A script term that, when used with a more specific locale, describes the interior setting for a scene. For example, INT. BEDROOM.

Internal motivations—Those motivations for movement in a scene that arise from thoughts or emotions within an actor.

Leitmotif—A musical theme associated with a character, situation, or idea.

Line producer—Usually a production-oriented person who works directly with writer, director, and post-production personnel.

Literary agent/agency—A person or firm that seeks to market a writer's work for a percentage of the writer's earnings.

Ludicrous—A comedy category referring to anything that is exaggerated, overstated, or out of proportion.

MATCH CUT—A cut to virtually identical subject matter.

MEDIUM SHOT—A camera angle approximately halfway between a close and a full shot. Usually includes a character's waist or hips.

Melodrama—A sensational or highly emotional story designed to thrill audiences. A story or action that intensifies sentiment, often featuring one-dimensional characters, with music liberally underscoring action.

Mind games—Techniques necessary to create a specific mental attitude, such as generating the excitement needed to write a scene or screenplay.

Mise-en-scène—The physical setting for dramatic action. May include the movement of characters, choice of scenery, control of the time frame, and selection of camera angles.

MONTAGE—Usually a succession of visual images or short scenes for the purpose of establishing a single plot point.

Musical score—Music composed to accompany dramatic action, enriching and complementing that action.

Narrative—A story. In screenplays, a story dramatized with involving characters through their actions and dialog. *See* Screenplay.

Narrative action—The events in a screenplay that move the story forward.

Night-for-night shooting—Scenes actually photographed at night. Because of cost, night scenes sometimes are photographed in the daytime, using filters.

Objective camera — In which the camera photographs action as a neutral, dispassionate observer.

On the nose — Phrase used to describe dialog, actions, or casting that is obvious, heavyhanded, or cliched.

o.s. — Off screen or offstage.

Outline (story) — Similar to a treatment; writing the screenplay story in prose form in the present tense.

Packaging — Putting together certain production elements; for instance, a screenplay, director, and star.

Parallel plot — A story or subplot that develops simultaneously with the main story line. Cutting between two developing plots seems to propel a story forward dynamically.

Pathetic fallacy — Nature suggesting the inner state of characters (for example, rain and thunder during a burial scene). Also, *all* external factors that mirror the internal, including costume, lighting, scenery, and makeup.

Peeling layers off an onion — A plotting technique in which revelations during the story progression change or reverse the audience's perception of characters or plot.

Person — As used in this text, a character with whom an audience may become emotionally involved, usually the protagonist.

Pilot — A sample program filmed or videotaped for sales purposes.

Plagiarism — The unauthorized use of someone else's written material and claiming it as your own.

Playbacks — Repetitions of lines of dialog, actions, pieces of business, and, occasionally, costumes or locales to generate emotions triggered by the original moment.

Playing against — Dialog or actions that contradict the essential thrust of a scene. For example, playing humor in a tragic scene or tragedy in a humorous scene.

P.O.V. (or POV) — Point of view. A camera angle that depicts what a character sees.

Premise — The basic idea of a story; its essence. Sometimes described in a sentence or a paragraph.

Preparation — The period prior to the start of principal photography in which the screenplay is polished and all production elements readied.

Producer — The individual who oversees and supervises a project, often hiring writers and working with them in the development of screenplays.

Production board — A hinged, several-panelled board containing the cardboard strips that describe a show's scenes, actor-days, stunts, extras, and other production elements.

Production values — The elements that add color and richness to a movie or TV production. For example, exotic locations, extravagant costumes, expensive sets.

Program practices — A euphemism for censor. The network office that supervises the content of TV programming, primarily its treatment of sex and violence.

Progression — The growing, building, climbing action of most well-written screenplays, scenes, and speeches. An increase in tension. Movement from the least important to the most important.

Property master — The person who secures or provides all props.

Props (Properties) — Objects used by actors in a scene, such as weapons, chess sets, pencils, newspapers.

Protagonist — A character or characters that move a story forward, usually the star or hero. As described herein, a protagonist strives to reach a worthwhile goal while an antagonist struggles to prevent it.

Radio lines — Dialog that describes what the audience can see and is therefore unnecessary. A holdover from radio drama.

Reductio ad absurdem — Taking a normal situation to an absurd extreme.

Release form — A brief legal document that production companies ask writers to sign before reading their material, to prevent lawsuits for plagiarism.

Rhythm — As used in this text, a recurring theme; the repetition of dialog, actions, music, or locales for dramatic effect.

Running gag — A joke or humorous business that is repeated, sometimes with variations, throughout a movie or TV show.

Scene — A single event or interchange between characters with a unity of time or place. Ideally, each scene contributes a new plot development or character revelation.

Screenplay — A story written in a series of scenes, containing characters, and dramatized through their actions and dialog, usually for the purpose of filming or videotaping.

Script — Short for *manuscript*. A screenplay.

Segue — An audio dissolve; that is, a blending of sound elements. For example, a woman's scream SEGUES into a train whistle.

Sequence — A group of scenes tied together by a single story purpose or direction (for example, an escape from prison).

Setting up — Laying the groundwork for events that will occur later in a screenplay; establishing facts or events so that later incidents or revelations will be based on information already known by the audience.

SFX — Sound effects.

SHOCK CUT — A cut that is deliberately jarring or unnerving, sometimes to grotesque subject matter.

Sitcom — A situation comedy. Term usually applies to TV shows.

Sound track — The portion of a film or videotape that contains the sound elements of a movie or TV program.

Source music — Music that originates from a source within a scene such as a radio or rock group, as opposed to a musical score composed to accompany or dramatize the film's action.

Spec (writing on spec) — Speculating with your time to write a screenplay; any writing that is not immediately paid for.

Special effects (SPFX) — Trick photography, optical effects, or those devised on the set (for example, smoke, explosions, bullets striking a target.)

Spectacle — A screenplay element that audiences find sensually pleasing, consisting of sound, motion, and color.

Stage directions — The descriptive material in scripts that defines the dramatic action, usually all that the camera "sees."

Step sheet (step outline) — Describing a plot tersely in a scene-by-scene, act-by-act construction.

Stock — Footage that has been filmed previously, usually purchased from a studio or film library. Also, any situation that has been dramatized often is said to be stock.

Story analyst — A person hired by studios or production companies to read and analyze script submissions.

Story editor/supervisor — A person who assists a producer in reading, analyzing, or rewriting submitted literary material.

Storyboard — A series of hand-drawn sketches of screenplay action as viewed by the camera, angle by angle.

Subjective camera — When the camera seems to become a character, photographing action from his or her point of view (P.O.V.). Suggesting a character's mood or emotions through a more generalized camera treatment.

Subplot — A story line subordinate to the primary plot, usually involving one of the principal characters.

Subtext — Meanings underlying the plot or dialog that audiences must glean from hints or innuendo.

Suspense — Apprehension generated by concern for the safety or well-being of the protagonist. All successful screenplays generate suspense since they cause viewers to worry that the protagonist will fail to reach his or her goal.

Symbol — An object that represents something else. For example, a toy panda bear symbolizing the person who presented it as a gift.

Symmetry — A balance of dramatic elements.

Sympathy — A harmony or agreement in feelings between two persons — or between an audience and a protagonist.

Tag business, tag lines — A final line of dialog or action that punctuates a scene, sometimes for humorous effect.

Tag scene — Usually a scene that occurs after a screenplay's climax. A tying together of plot threads, a final punctuation.

Theme — The underlying meaning of a screenplay: its moral, message, or root idea.

Time frame — A single, continuous passage of time.

Treatment — The screenplay story told in prose, similar to a short story except that it is written in the present tense.

Trucking — A lateral camera movement, usually beside characters as they walk.

Unexpected — A comedy category in which a story element veers in an unexpected direction.

Unit production manager — The person in charge of all technical (below the line) elements of a movie or TV program, also responsible for budget.

Vernacular speech — The language or vocabulary peculiar to a profession, geographic location, or group of people.

v.o. — Voice over.

WGA — Writers Guild of America, the union representing professional screenwriters.

Wipe — An optical effect used for transitions, usually in comedy or sports programming. The incoming scene slides across frame, replacing the outgoing scene. Wipes may be vertical, horizontal, and diagonal.

BOOKS THAT
MAY BE HELPFUL

Beaver, Frank E. *Dictionary of Film Terms.* New York: McGraw-Hill, 1983.

Blum, Richard. *Television Writing: From Concept to Contract.* Boston: Focal Press, 1984.

Bordwell, David. *Narration in the Fiction Film.* Madison: University of Wisconsin Press, 1985.

Brady, John, ed. *The Craft of the Screenwriter.* New York: Simon & Schuster, 1981.

Campbell, Joseph. *The Hero with a Thousand Faces.* Princeton, N.J.: Princeton University Press, 1968.

Egri, Lajos. *The Art of Dramatic Writing.* New York: Simon & Schuster, 1972.

Field, Syd. *Screenplay.* New York: Dell, 1982.

Goldman, William. *Adventures in the Screen Trade.* New York: Warner Books, 1983.

Hauge, Michael. *Writing Screenplays That Sell.* New York: McGraw-Hill, 1988.

Hilliard, Robert L. *Writing for Television and Radio.* Belmont, Calif.: Wadsworth, 1991.

Jung, Carl G. *Man and His Symbols.* New York: Doubleday, 1964.

Lees, David, and Berkowitz, Stan. *The Movie Business.* New York: Vintage, 1981.

Madsen, Roy Paul. *Working Cinema: Learning from the Masters.* Belmont, Calif.: Wadsworth, 1990.

Mehring, Margaret. *The Screenplay: A Blend of Form and Content.* New York: Focal Press, 1990.

Miller, William. *Writing for Narrative Film and Television.* New York: Hastings House, 1980.

Root, Wells. *Writing the Script.* New York: Holt, Rinehart and Winston, 1979.

Saks, Sol. *The Craft of Comedy Writing.* Cincinnati: Writers Digest, 1985.

Seger, Linda. *Making a Good Script Great.* New York: Dodd, Mead, 1987.

Seger, Linda. *Creating Unforgettable Characters*. New York: Henry Holt, 1990.

Strunk, William, Jr., and White, E. B. *The Elements of Style*. New York: Macmillan, 1979.

Thomas, Sam, ed. *Best American Screenplays*. New York: Crown, 1986.

Thomas, Sam, ed. *Best American Screenplays 2*. New York: Crown, 1990.

Vale, Eugene. *The Technique of Screenplay Writing*. New York: Simon & Schuster, 1986.

von Oech, Roger. *A Whack on the Side of the Head*. New York: Warner Books, 1983.

Wald, Malvin, and Werner, Michael, eds. *Three Major Screenplays*. New York: Globe Books, 1972.

Walter, Richard. *Screenwriting: The Art, Craft and Business of Film and Television Writing*. New York: NAL/Penguin, 1988.

INDEX